WITHDRAWN

Governing Buildings and
Building Government

BRYAN D. JONES

Governing Buildings and Building Government

A New Perspective on the Old Party

The University of Alabama Press

Library of Congress Cataloging in Publication Data
Jones, Bryan D.
  Governing buildings and building government.
  Bibliography: p.
  Includes index.
  1. Chicago (Ill.).   Dept. of Buildings.   2. Democratic
Party (Ill.)   3. Corruption (in politics)—Illinois—
Chicago.   4. Building laws—Illinois—Chicago.   I. Title.
JS714.A13B85   1985   320.8′09773′11   84-167
ISBN 0-8173-0227-1

To Diane and Laura
who followed me to Chicago

Contents

Illustrations

Figures

Tables

Preface

The project that has resulted in this book began when the Department of Political Science and the Center for Urban Affairs at Northwestern University invited me to spend the 1978–79 academic year in Evanston. I am indebted to the center and to Louis Masotti, its director at the time, for the generous support afforded this work. While the project (and the visits to Chicago) continued long after I left Evanston, the study could not have been done without the support of the center.

For me, the opportunity to spend a year in Chicago came at a particularly propitious time. I had become intrigued with the role of urban bureaucracies in the production of policy outputs, yet I recognized that the view of urban service agencies I had acquired intensively studying Detroit's thoroughly reformed bureaucracies could be misleading. Moreover, I had become increasingly convinced that two generally uncontested propositions in public administration were, if not simply wrong, at least overly simplistic. The first, the idea that policy and administration were inseparable, seemed not to incorporate the real influence of the policy-making branches and of statutes and ordinances on the behavior of agency administrators. The administrators I have interviewed distinguished situations in which they made policy and those in which they administered it, and they were usually appropriately cautious in policy-making situations. Although occasionally policy making was disguised under the rubric of administration, often the urban administrators I observed did not take action because that action was not permitted by statute or explicitly ordered by supervisors. Furthermore, there seemed to be a lack of clarity in the literature in distinguishing between *political* and *policy-making*. This lack of clarity probably came from earlier public administration literature that referred to the political and the policy-making branches of government interchangeably.

The second questionable proposition in the study of urban bureaucracies came into the literature as a result of several superb studies of face-to-face encounters between citizens and government employees. The proper observation that such street-level bureaucrats had substantial discretion in interpreting statutes, ordinances, and directives was over-generalized into the notion that street-level personnel "make policy." In my view, this approach underemphasizes the role of organizational decision rules that reinforce hierarchy. Furthermore, the focus on "street-level bureaucracy" seemed to cause investigators to overlook other sources of problems of control in service agencies. Central management often must deal with independent divisions, bureaus, and other organizational subunits rather than just organizationally undifferentiated street-level personnel.

The agency serving as the focal organization of this study, the city of Chicago's Department of Buildings, was an ideal setting for the rigorous examination of several of the conventional wisdoms of public administration and urban politics. No claim, of course, can be made that this case is in any way generalizable, at least in the statistical sense of the term. However, if one views the role of the careful, quantitative case study as a method of probing the situations within which certain behavior patterns emerge, then the study is generalizable.

The Department of Buildings suffered extreme problems of organizational control. Its bureau chiefs ran their fiefdoms with undisguised contempt for the attempts of central management to impose more hierarchical control. Several of its bureaus were thoroughly corrupt; one departmental administrator commented to me that he thought that the department was "probably the most corrupt municipal department in the country." Ward politicians often contacted agency administrators directly to request favors for their neighborhoods (usually that enforcement efforts be increased). The department's personnel system was a mixture of civil service and patronage. The building and housing codes that the department enforced were detailed and rigorous, and had the potential of imposing very high costs on owners, builders, architects, and renters. The agency had to interact with a number of other governmental units to accomplish its goals, including the fire department, the corporation council, Cook County Court, the United States Department of Housing and Urban Development, and the city's Planning Department. It thus faced an organizational environment that complicated the task of service delivery.

By studying a case in which central control was weak, organizational boundaries were extremely permeable, and the political party structure was powerful, I hoped to be able to assess the role of politics, policy, and bureaucratic hierarchy in an extreme (to America) situation. By examining such extremes, I hoped to probe the limits of several of our conventional wisdoms: politics does not affect policy outputs; policy and administration are inseparable; political parties count for little in explaining urban outcomes. I came slowly, doubtless much more slowly than would a student of political parties, to the realization that the urban political party was performing a dual function, one contributing to integrated policy making, the other corroding it. Moreover, *both* functions hinged on material benefits, and especially patronage, to an extent I believe generally unrecognized. It is this dual function of urban political parties that serves as the central thesis of this book.

Urban parties have atrophied organizationally, and state and national parties have changed dramatically. Yet political scientists staunchly held to what Leon Epstein has termed "a persistent . . . pro-party commitment."[1] I hope this study will contribute to a more realistic evaluation of what urban political parties did and can contribute, and to an understanding of why they will never do so again.

In the complex organizational setting that was the study site, I found complex human adjustments and behavior patterns. Some of these complexities affected the course of the study. Some people with whom I dealt were both cooperative and generous with their time. Others were hostile and suspicious to an extent that I have not found in other political environments.

Although I am indebted to all of those who were cooperative, several deserve particular thanks. Richard P. Moran and his coworkers in the department's Systems Division spent hours and hours in producing and interpreting data for me and in commenting on Chicago politics. Joseph Fitzgerald, commissioner of the department, gave generously of his time and allowed me to interview members of his department. Three departmental administrators, John Dean, William Browning, and Art Moisan, tolerated numerous visits as I explored both their insights and their data. Finally, Jane Byrne's choice of Lou Masotti as the head of her transition team after her election in 1979 provided surprise benefits. Previously tightlipped administrators suddenly talked freely, assuming (wrongly) that I was investigating the department on behalf of Masotti. Neither repeated denials on my part nor the fact that my presence in the department had preceded Byrne's election dissuaded my informants.

I owe a debt of gratitude to Tony Fowler and Clarence Stone, the reviewers of this book for The University of Alabama Press; their comments were unusually helpful and detailed. Finally, thanks are due to Pearl Carlson, who helped me assemble a large clipping file in my absence from Chicago.

Governing Buildings and
Building Government

1

Party Government and Public Policy

The telephone rang in the Systems Division of the city of Chicago's Department of Buildings. Denny, a muscular young systems analyst of Irish descent, reached for the receiver. "Eleventh Ward Headquarters," he blurted into the 'phone, "er—I mean, Systems Division, Department of Buildings." As the young man blushed at his confusion of his political and governmental roles, his colleagues laughed uproariously.

⊠

Among thoughtful citizens in and out of academics, there seems to be a yearning for the stability, order, and predictability that strong political parties once brought to the confusion of the American governing process. After spending some two hundred pages analyzing America's economic ills in his book *The Zero-Sum Society,* economist Lester Thurow blames politics, commenting:

> Our problems arise because, in a very real sense, we do not have political parties. A political party is a group that can force its elected members to vote for that party's solutions to society's problems. Instead of having two parties, we have a system where each official is his own party and is free to establish his own party platform. Parties are merely vague electoral alliances. But this means a splintering of power that makes it impossible to hold anyone responsible for failure.[1]

American parties, of course, have never been strong as devices for presenting policy alternatives. They have traditionally been instruments for forging consensus on policies through accommodation of diverse interests—interest aggregation, in the language of political science. The American Assembly, in a recent report, has lauded this role of political parties in American society in no uncertain terms: "At their fullest potential, political parties are mediating institutions that provide some measure of continuity, stability, and orderliness in politics. They are instruments of accommodation which enable us to smooth out our rough edges of differences over public policy and by so doing construct policies that endure and a polity that survives."[2]

What concerns the American Assembly is that American political parties no longer perform at their full potential. They have been weakened by changing technologies that have allowed candidates to bypass the party structure in reaching the voter; by declines in patronage positions in government, which have reduced the incentives for political activity; and by statutory changes weakening the party, particularly in the realms of campaign finance and primary elections. This weakening of the political party system has made parties less able to fulfill their traditional governing role in the United States.[3]

Building Regulation and the Political Party in Chicago

In this book I explore the role of the political party in the building regulatory process in Chicago. By focusing on the policy-making process in a strong city that still boasts a classic, American-style political machine, I have been able to examine the influence of the local Democratic party on the operations of government in a system that continues to be characterized by parties (or at least one party) that operate at "their fullest potential."

I shall argue that the political party based on material incentives, virtually the only strong party system in existence in America, is not an unmixed blessing from the point of view of democratically enacted, rationally administered public policy. More specifically, there is an inherent contradiction in party rule stemming from the fact that parties are essentially decentralized operations. While mayors in machine cities can centralize policy enactment because of the power that they hold as leaders of a powerful political organization, they cannot impose a rational administrative strategy for implementing their programs. The reason is that the very force that allows them to impose control on citywide interest groups—a party apparatus that is rooted in patronage—weakens the bureaucracy that must implement the policy solutions that emerge. In order to maintain their electoral bases, ward leaders must produce for their constituents, who are more interested in the distribution of outputs from the administrative process than in the policy-enactment process. In order to accomplish this, they make demands on bureaucrats, demands that conflict with the goal of smooth hierarchical implementation of programs. Moreover, the demands they make are directed at bureaucrats who are themselves a part of the party structure, since many city officials are active in ward politics.

The building regulatory process itself is inherently interesting as an attempt by local government to control the "built environment" of the city—the part of the urban environment that has been physically constructed by humans. As an attempt to regulate the behavior of private citizens, it joins a variety of city policies that limit the freedom of citizens in an attempt to realize common good. Hence policy impacts turn on the compliance of citizens who produce the built environment—architects, developers, housing managers, owners, and tenants—with the codes and ordinances that establish both the framework and the specifics of the regulatory system. As regulatory policy, building regulation and housing-code enforcement raise the issues of the distortion of incentives facing those who produce the built environment. Will housing be undersupplied because of the added costs of regulation? Will housing abandonment be encouraged by housing codes that raise the cost of maintaining older buildings? These issues have been thoroughly aired in the literature.[4] From the point of view of political analysis, it is to be expected that those who will suffer the costs of regulation will be active in the policy process; indeed, as I shall indicate, they are. The form of participation is, however, conditioned by the existence of a strong party structure in Chicago.

The administration of building and housing codes is also a city service. Code enforcement is delivered to neighborhoods by a system of inspections; violations of the codes found by inspectors are filed as cases in court. The adequacy of inspections and enforcement mechanisms is thus as important in establishing service impact as the particular wording of the codes and ordinances that are the legal basis of regulation. Because code enforcement can be disaggregated and delivered to separate neighborhoods, the question of service distribution cannot be avoided. Because inspections alone are not sufficient to gain the compliance necessary to achieve impact, it is necessary to examine the distribution of enforcement orders issued by the Building Department and housing court, as well as the distribution of compliances on the part of owners. Finally, because severe costs can be imposed by building regulation, the issue of corrupt enforcement colors the policy process, as we shall see.

The results reported here are based on four separate sources. First, I have assembled an extensive data set on the distribution of building regulatory services to wards. Over 150,000 separate cases of code-enforcement complaints, records of Building Department recommendations, and decisions of the housing court were merged to the city's fifty wards. This information was supplemented with information on the political structure, demography, and characteristics of the built environment. The second source was a questionnaire administered to all community organizations active in the building regulatory process; this was done to study the interaction, at the neighborhood level, between party structure and community organizations. Third, I conducted some forty-five in-depth interviews with participants in the building regulatory process. While these interviews centered on bureaucrats, I also interviewed housing-court judges, the corporation council, aldermen, and heads of interest groups involved in the process. Finally, I observed the building regulatory process in depth as a more or less unobtrusive observer.

The results from this study are, of course, not generalizable to all large American cities. Chicago is sui generis, the American anachronism of a political machine built on a patchwork of ethnic neighborhoods. But the entire impulse toward generalization in social science is misplaced insofar as it confuses theoretical generalization with statistical generalization. Any generalization from a single case study is of course a risky business. But case studies, even of deviant cases, serve to delimit the boundaries of accurate generalization by establishing the limits of variability in sociopolitical systems. Astronomers understand the value to astrophysical theory of detailed, quantitative study of particular events in particular regions of the universe; social scientists seem far less aware of just what rich and detailed case studies can contribute to general theory.

Such studies can, I hope, serve as a bromide to the tendency to overlook the old saw that everything carries with it a cost. The party structures in evidence in America today were weakened in part as a consequence of deliberate public policy decisions. The cost of such a weakening of party is evident in the lack of coherence and orderliness that characterizes policy making today. Yet any return to a strong party system would also entail costs; I hope that this study will indicate some of those costs.

Political Parties and Public Policy Making

The standard political science view of political parties in liberal democracies is that they are instruments for linkage and control.[5] They act to link the citizenry to the government by offering alternatives in popular elections, by mobilizing votes, and by relying on citizen volunteers to staff many party offices. They act as instruments of control by disciplining their members in legislatures, bureaucracies, and other public and quasi-public policy-making organs. By organizing elections and controlling the formulation and implementation of public policy, political parties are the primary institutions of governmental accountability in mass democracies.

What is too often forgotten in all of this is that American political parties have traditionally been decentralized organizations. While parties at the national level are probably stronger in relation to their local components than they once were, this has been more a result of the weakening of the local organizations than a strengthening of the national organization. As the American Assembly report notes, "If parties are weak at the community level, the levels above them will remain mere shells of specialists and technicians."[6]

There is much reason to be pessimistic about the potential for revitalizing local party organizations in America. Leon Epstein, in his seminal review of the role of political parties in Western democracies, notes that "only the old, large-scale, American-style distribution of the spoils of office provides the *material* incentive for any large amount of rank-and-file party work."[7] Yet the most effective material incentive available, patronage jobs, has been declining for decades under the onslaught of civil service reforms. And political parties in America, based as they are on coalitions of groups, are in a poor position to take advantage of other incentives that could induce citizens to contribute effort to the party cause. "Just as the necessity for broad appeals makes it difficult for a party to compete materially for members against economic interest groups, so breadth gives a party less solidarity or purposive attraction in competition with groups whose social or normative goals can be more narrowly defined."[8] Parties' lack of both material and purposive incentives has been compounded by changes in the laws governing election financing and the increase in the number of direct primaries, both of which have made it easier for candidates to bypass the party organization and appeal directly to the electorate.

The decline of political parties as organizational entities has paralleled a decline of political parties as orienting symbols for the electorate—a process termed *dealignment* by students of electoral behavior.[9] In this cultural milieu, in which social norms stress voter independence and ideological purity, it is difficult to determine causal direction. What is evident, however, is a decline of the control function of parties in government that parallels the decline of parties in the electorate and as organizations. Party discipline has become even more difficult to maintain in the Congress, and presidents have experienced increasing difficulty in holding the legislative party in line. Dealignment has occurred in government as well as in the electorate and in the organizational structures of the parties. This governmental dealignment has resulted in a decline in the ability of the party system to serve as a linkage between mass opinions and public policy.[10]

This decline in the linkage and control function of political parties at the national level has been paralleled at the state and local level. Local parties, weakened by the municipal reform movement in the early part of this century, have been further weakened by suburbanization and the inability of urban machines to integrate the large urban black electorate into their structures. In Chicago a factional struggle emerged after the defeat of Mayor Michael Bilandic in 1979, and Mayor Jane Byrne was not able to command the traditionally overwhelming machine majorities on the city council. Mayor Harold Washington is without a working majority on the council, although all members are Democrats.

Politics and Administration

The view of political parties as instruments of mass democracy is not widely shared in America. Parties have traditionally been viewed with suspicion in the American political culture. Depicted as manipulators of the baser motives of voters and chronic interferers with the smooth implementation of the popular will, political parties have never gained thorough acceptance in a culture stressing rational action by enlightened individuals. Widespread corruption and the domination of urban party structures by Catholic immigrants after the turn of the century further tarnished the image of party in the mind of the typical Protestant, rural American of the day.

Indeed, political parties, as they developed in America, had strong motive to interfere in the straightforward implementation of public policies. The need for material incentives, particularly patronage jobs, meant that party leaders were hostile to the idea of a neutral, professional bureaucracy for administering policies enacted by the political branches of government.

Classic public administration has viewed political parties as disintegrating factors rather than integrating ones. By interfering with the smooth implementation of public policies set by democratically elected legislatures, the peak policy-making institutions, political parties actually detract from democratic government, at least in the view of many past and present students of public administration. The norm of neutral competence in administration, as it has been labeled by Herbert Kaufman, has been the driving force of American public administration since the writings of Woodrow Wilson and Frank Goodnow in the late nineteenth century. Yet even Goodnow worried about the consequences for the control of policy administration if political parties were weakened without establishing a national, hierarchically responsible bureaucracy to replace them. While political parties, at least at their zenith in the late nineteenth and early twentieth centuries, did interfere with the ideal of the neutral administrative hierarchy, they also imposed some semblance of order on what Goodnow thought would otherwise be a "disorderly, uncoordinated, unregulated crowd of officers, each equal in actual power to every other, and each acting according to the dictates of his own conscience or the caprice of his own whims."[11]

These two competing conceptions—one lauding political parties as the primary instruments of mass democracy, the other condemning them as destructive of coherent policy making; one integrative, the other disintegrative—have not been unified into a general framework for thinking about party government. This probably stems from two factors. The first is a tendency of party scholars not to examine in very much detail the policy-making process, preferring to analyze the role of the party in the electorate, the organizational structure of party, and the effect of party organization in legislative assemblies. Samuel Eldersveld's recent comprehensive textbook on American political parties, for instance, makes no mention of parties' role in the administrative process and relegates the examination of party influence on policy outputs to six pages.[12] The second factor is the tendency of the public policy literature to "black box" the policy process in quantitative studies of the effects of party systems on policy outputs.

The Black Box of Policy-Output Studies

The impact of parties and other political institutions on governmental outputs has been a central concern of students of state politics at least since V. O. Key's seminal work *Southern Politics*. This research tradition has generated numerous studies evaluating the effects of party competition and other political variables on state expenditures.[13] In parallel fashion, political scientists interested in local government have assessed the impact of unreformed political structures, consisting of partisan elections, single-member districting for local council elections, and strong mayors, on local policy outputs.[14] Studies of local outputs in European cities have imitated the American concern with quantifying policy outputs and assessing the relative influence of political forces and socioeconomic factors in the determination of policies. European studies have been more concerned with the effect of party control than with party competition, generally hypothesizing that left-wing parties will raise local expenditures more than will right-wing parties. Substantial support for this hypothesis has been reported, especially on the Continent.[15]

While the issue of partisan control has not emerged as a major focus for research on the policies of American cities, it has been the occasional focus of research on state politics. The issue is whether partisan control alters the pattern of policy outputs beyond what one could expect from the economic resource base of the jurisdiction, since, all other things being equal, a richer jurisdiction is able to sustain a higher level of public expenditures than a poorer one. Thomas Dye reports that Democratic control of the office of governor had little effect on state spending patterns,[16] but Erikson indicates that party control of state government did affect state civil-rights legislation in the 1960s.[17]

Party control of government may, however, mean different things in different political systems. Party control in the one-party systems of the American South means something quite different from what it means in the "responsible party" system of Wisconsin. Even where parties are competitive in a state, party organizations can differ considerably. Some years ago, John Fenton contrasted the issue-oriented, class-based parties of Wisconsin, Minnesota, and Michigan with the patronage-oriented parties consisting of coalitions of regional and ethnic groupings in Illinois, Indiana, and Ohio.[18] As expected, the benefit-oriented parties of the lower Midwest produced different policy outputs than did the issue-oriented parties of the upper Midwest. Elling has shown that Wisconsin political parties fulfill more of their platform promises than do Illinois parties,[19] and Jennings finds that class-based party systems produce higher levels of welfare benefits than do systems based on patronage.[20] Nice shows that differences in the ideologies of state parties, assessed by voting patterns of state delegations to national conventions, are related to state public policies toward the have-nots, even when socioeconomic factors are controlled.[21]

While these studies have paid explicit attention to the influence of party systems (and other political variables) on policy outputs, they have not illuminated the process by which the translation of political inputs into policy outputs occurs. Nor could they be expected to do so. Only by employing some variant of the case-study method can one observe this translation process; this generally means sacrificing empirical rigor for theoretical insight and rich detail.

The policy-output studies compare the relationship between characteristics of party systems and policy outputs for different political systems. But party strength and organization also vary within a single political system. Within a single state, some county organizations are stronger than others; within a single unreformed city, several of a party's ward organizations will be stronger than others. In the latter case, the unit on which party strength is assessed (the ward) has no power to produce service. Hence the resources-outputs linkage is broken, and any relationship between the wealth of a ward, say, and the outputs received by the ward cannot be attributed to differences in wards' abilities to provide services. Rather, all demands for service must be channeled to a central decision-making unit—for most traditional city services, the municipality. The city as a whole, not the neighborhood, is responsible for taxing, spending, and service production.

Numerous studies of urban service distribution have been published in the last several years. Most indicate that the bureaucratic rules and procedures established for coping with the service-delivery task are responsible for observed patterns of distribution.[22] There is some evidence, however, that politics can interfere with the solidly bureaucratic service-delivery process. While Mladenka found no relationship between support for Mayor Daley and the level of sanitation, educational, recreational, and fire services received in Chicago wards,[23] Cingranelli does report such a linkage for police and fire services in Boston.[24] This study indicates that political forces can influence the bureaucratic procedures that normally account for patterns of service distribution. On the other hand, Mladenka's study suggests that politicized service delivery does not exist where one would most expect it, in the American city characterized by a political machine. Moreover, his observations of procedure and interviews with bureaucrats show just how powerful the bureaucratic impulse is, even in a machine city.[25]

Political Parties in Local Government

Although much contemporary political science research on the role of political parties in governmental decision making focuses on quantitative indicators of policy outputs, relegating the explicit mechanisms of influence to the unobserved "black box" of decision making, a handful of case studies do illuminate the darkness. Sayre and Kaufman, in their monumental study of government in New York, indicate that party leaders intervene in the governing process only on a narrow range of issues, primarily those relating to nominations and elections, patronage appointments, and requests from individual petitioners.[26] Banfield's study of public decision making in Chicago isolated a more essential governing role for the political party in a strong-machine city. The role of party leader gave the mayor political resources for enforcing (although not forging) policy settlements in a governmentally decentralized metropolis. Even though the party had no explicit policy positions on the decisions Banfield studied, it was not absent from the calculus of decision.[27]

Matthew Crenson, in his study of the manner in which cities dealt with the issue of air pollution in the 1960s, has issued a major challenge to the view of the political boss as a benign broker. Crenson found in his sample of forty-eight United States cities that industry's reputation for power was stronger in cities characterized by traditional machine politics, a relationship that could not be explained by variations in the concentration of blue-collar workers. Crenson further notes that the type of issue constrains brokerage politics—policies providing collective benefits are less useful to the boss in forging conditions than are distributive issues. Crenson's case studies of Gary and East Chicago indicate that the air-pollution issue was easier for reformers to get on the political agenda when the party organization was disorganized and the political party–business community linkage was fractured.[28]

Greenstone and Peterson have also been critical of the view of the urban machine as a benign instrument of coalition building and under-class participation. They examined the response of five cities, three machine (Chicago, New York, Philadelphia) and two reformed (Detroit, Los Angeles), to the federal government's community action program, a component of the so-called war on poverty. The type of policy settlement (proparticipatory or antiparticipatory) could not be predicted from city type, although in Chicago, the strongest machine city, the program was most controlled and the policy settlement most antiparticipatory. On the other hand, the political ideology of political leaders had important influences on outcomes, suggesting limits to the role of political institutions in policy settlements.[29] In his careful study of school politics in Chicago, Paul Peterson persuasively argues that Banfield's earlier focus on pluralist bargaining, with the political machine serving as a resource for imposing solutions, was confined to a narrow range of policy options because of prevailing ideologies. Moreover, both styles of decision making could exist within a single political system simultaneously: "Chicago politics in the late sixties was marked by both pluralist and ideological patterns of policy formation."[30]

The foregoing suggests that in local government the political party is directly involved in making decisions only on a narrow range of issues, primarily concerning nominations, elections, constituent services, and patronage. Even where the party is not actively engaged as a participant in the decision-making process, it is not irrelevant. Within the confines of pluralist bargaining, the electoral power of the local party structure serves as a resource for imposing and enforcing policy settlements on those groups who have some direct stake in the policy process. Where the party structure is weak, governmental leaders must turn elsewhere for the political resources that are necessary to govern effectively—or they will fail to govern effectively.

The political party in a machine city like Chicago, however, is part of a local culture that is rooted in ethnic exclusiveness. Hence ideology limits the range of policy options that may be considered by the political leader. Mayor Edward Kelly was not slated for re-election in 1947 by the Cook County Democratic Party after he supported an open housing provision and lost the support of European ethnic voters.[31] Mayor Richard Daley's revulsion at the "new politics" movement at the 1968 Chicago Democratic convention is legendary. In 1983, Harold Washington, a black Democrat, was elected mayor of Chicago in an election in which the majority of traditional white ethnic machine supporters voted for the Republican candidate, Bernard Epton. Paradoxically, then, the elements that give the machine style of government its strength—its pragmatic open style—may limit the options for policy action. In particular, a political machine may not be able to integrate the new participants in urban politics—blacks, Hispanics, women—into the decision-making process.

American cities still house large dependent populations, and many political actors continue to be motivated by material incentives.[32] Nevertheless, political machines may not be able to integrate these citizens into the policy process, either because of the limitations imposed by the political culture upon which the machine rests, or because of the decline of the material incentives needed to motivate party activists over the long haul. In either case, the role of the political party in local policy formation has been reduced, because the machine style of organization has not been replaced by an organizational style capable of structuring the local governing process meaningfully.

Chicago: The Built Environment

Chicago, with its three million citizens, remained the second largest city in the United States after the 1980 decennial census. It is also the largest political jurisdiction that has retained for so long the classic American-style machine form.

Machine politics, however, is not Chicago's only special characteristic. Observers also point to an economy that is part and parcel of the Midwest industrial crescent but which has a strong commercial and financial appendage to the industrial base. The result is a strong building boom in the downtown Loop area, but closed factories and abandoned buildings not far away. Chicago is the new commercial city with its glittering Loop high-rises and its regentrification along the lakefront, but it is also the aging industrial city losing firms and jobs to its own suburbs and to the Sun Belt. With job loss comes population loss; between 1970 and 1980 Chicago lost 11 percent of its population, while the metropolitan region gained 1.2 percent.

Figure 1.1 portrays this "two cities" phenomenon.[33] The map displays investment and disinvestment patterns in the city of Chicago as they affect the built environment. These patterns are assessed by the ratio of new construction to demolition permits issued by the city from 1976 through 1979. Investment in the built environment of Chicago is

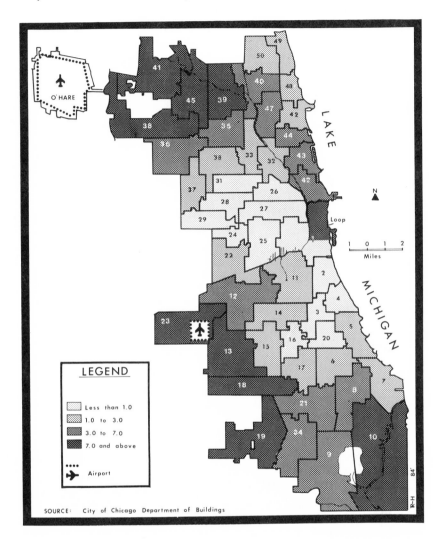

Figure 1.1. Construction Activity: Construction Permits Divided by Demolition Permits, 1976–1979.

concentrated in the outer city and the Loop, with disinvestment especially prevalent in the predominantly black wards south and west of downtown. The area north of the Loop, along Lake Michigan, is characterized by extensive high-rise development on the lakefront but extensive disinvestment a few blocks from the lake; these divergent tendencies do not show up clearly on the map. While new construction is concentrated in the lakefront communities of Lincoln Park, Uptown, and Lakeview, demolition is occurring in the black ghettos of Lawndale, Woodlawn, Englewood, and Garfield Park.[34] These neighborhoods also bear a disproportionate burden of the now-classic urban ills—unemployment, poor health, crime, fire. By 1980, Chicago's black population had reached 40 percent, and a growing Hispanic community meant that the city's European white population dropped below 50 percent (figure 1.1).

The forces of investment and disinvestment and their geographical expression, depicted in figure 1.1, impose constraints on what the local political system can achieve in regulating the built environment. Moreover, these investment patterns open opportunities for politicians to achieve goals for themselves and their constituents, but they effectively close other avenues for achieving goals. Between these extremes the patterns of investment in the built environment present political actors interested in achieving results a prior distribution of probabilities of success. Some outcomes will be relatively easy to achieve, given only minimal effort. Other goals will require extensive and continuous effort, and even then the desired result will be elusive. For example, it may be relatively easy to get an owner to repair a building where investment trends are favorable, but it will be uncommonly difficult to achieve the same end where extensive disinvestment is occurring. Hence, it is not enough simply to examine the politics of building regulation, lest we attribute a pattern of outcomes to political action when in fact economics is primarily responsible.

Chicago: Politics and Government

Although the government and politics of Chicago have been admirably described elsewhere,[35] a few remarks are in order here. Chicago is the classic unreformed city: a mayor-council form; council representation based on fifty wards; partisan elections for most city offices (although aldermen are elected on a nonpartisan ballot). Traditionally, Chicago had a weak mayor–strong council form of government, but the office of mayor has been formally strengthened twice in recent years. The first occurred in 1955, when Mayor Richard Daley took office and put into effect recommendations from a home rule commission's report. The office of mayor was further strengthened following recommendations from a second home rule commission presented to the city in 1972.

This second reorganization followed the inclusion of a home rule provision in the Illinois Constitution in 1970, and the granting to Chicago full home rule powers. The reforms increased the mayor's formal powers relative to budget, appointment, and personnel.

Formal governmental structures in Chicago have been dramatically modified by the most visible extralegal political organizations there, the political party structure. The powers of the mayor have been strengthened by a fusion of political and governmental powers, while the power of the city council has been concomitantly weakened. Mayor Richard Daley also held the position of chairman of the Central Committee of the Cook County Democratic Party. Mayor Michael Bilandic served as mayor only, sharing power in the party with George Dunne, president of the Cook County Board of Commissioners. Mayor Byrne also contented herself with serving as mayor of Chicago alone, although her power within the party was indicated by her role in replacing George Dunne with the Tenth Ward committeeman, Edward Vrdolyak, as party chairman in the spring of 1982.

The local presence of the national Democratic party is maintained in Chicago by the Cook County Central Committee, consisting of eighty elected committeemen, one from each of Chicago's fifty wards and one from each of the thirty townships in suburban Cook County. This structure is prescribed by state statutes governing party organization. The central committee collectively exercises political power in the county. Its two most important functions are making slates for elections, including endorsements in primaries, and allocating the vast patronage available locally (especially in the city of Chicago, Cook County, and the Chicago Park District, an independent government unit). Much of the power of the party in the government and politics of Chicago stems from these two activities, particularly the latter. Because the mayor of Chicago is able to control a large proportion of the patronage jobs in the county alone, he or she automatically is an important figure in party affairs. The mayor is also the most visible governmental figure in the Chicago metropolis, and this visibility is the source of substantial political power.

Within the ward organization the ward committeeman rules supreme. Because ward committeemen are elected in special primaries and access to the ballot is limited, it is very difficult to dislodge an incumbent committeeman. The committeemen control all party electoral funds and patronage positions allocated to their wards, and they appoint all precinct captains. The committeemen are responsible to the central com-

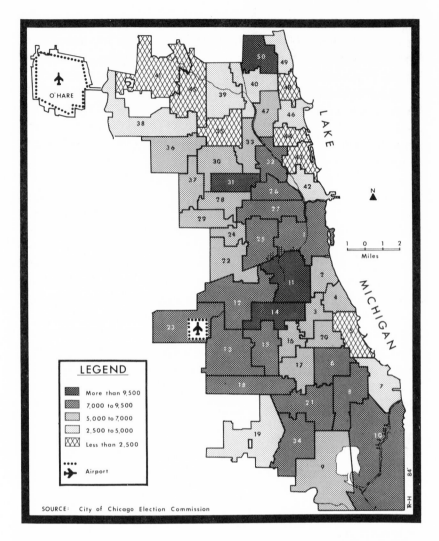

Figure 1.2. Ward Strength: Democratic Votes in Excess of Republican Votes for Cook County Sheriff, 1978.

mittee, first and foremost, for delivering votes in elections. They are also expected to support party decisions without question and to maintain effective ward organizations.[36]

Because of the very substantial power that is held by ward committeemen, the party structure is "not a monolithic, totalitarian dictatorship but rather a feudal structure,"[37] with each ward committeeman operating his or her own fiefdom. Variability in social, economic, and political conditions within wards as well as variability in ability, interest, and energy among committeemen means that the political productivity among wards varies dramatically. During the 1970s, for example, black electoral support for party candidates declined precipitously. Once the black wards on the city's south side, controlled by Congressman William Dawson, were the machine's strongest wards; today core machine strength is in the working-class, European ethnic wards on the southwest side of the city.[38]

There have been several attempts to categorize electoral blocs based on ward voting behavior.[39] None is entirely satisfactory, because there are many elections and many different ways to categorize the aggregate voting of citizens. Figure 1.2 offers a mapping of wards based on the number of Democratic votes in excess of Republican votes in the general election of 1978 for Cook County sheriff. A minor local office rather than mayor of Chicago or a state or national figure is used here in order to separate out the effects of candidates and issues that transcend the local organization. Moreover, the office of sheriff controls substantial patronage and is very important to the local party. The number of votes is used rather than the percentage by which a victory was achieved because votes, not percentages, matter to politicians. Enough votes must be garnered in Chicago to offset the large Republican vote that comes in from suburban Cook County. Hence, the electoral effectiveness of a ward organization is a combination of both turnout and vote direction.[40] Finally, the Republican nominee mounted a creditable campaign based on the ideology of urban reform. The map indicates that the strength of the Chicago political machine resides in the ethnically diverse wards of the southwest side of the city and near north wards along the Chicago River. It is weakest in the "reform" wards along Lake Michigan and in the suburblike wards on the far northwest side.

A Time of Transition

Most of the research upon which this book is based was conducted during the Bilandic and Byrne years. Michael Bilandic, alderman from Daley's own Eleventh Ward, was elected to fill out Daley's term after the mayor's death in December 1976. He was able generally to keep the Daley organization intact. In February of 1979 Jane Byrne, a protégé of Mayor Daley, defeated Bilandic in the mayoral primary. Byrne swept all black wards except the Twenty-seventh ("Skid Row") Ward, bossed by the city sewer commissioner, Edward A. Quigley; carried all the lakefront reform wards; and cut into Bilandic's pluralities in the machine core. Bilandic's machine support made the election close, even though voters expressed widespread dissatisfaction with the way city government had handled the heavy snowfall of that year. Although most ward committeemen supported Mayor Byrne on most issues, some have moved into permanent opposition. The most visible opposition faction was led by Richard M. Daley, son of the former mayor. The political machine of the Byrne era, never monolithic, was less centralized than it had been since the inauguration of Richard J. Daley in 1955.

Byrne, while careful to stress her ties to Mayor Richard J. Daley, attacked the machine politicians who supported Bilandic. After winning the Democratic primary, she commented that "the machine killed itself." Byrne attacked the city-council leaders, Edward Vrdolyak and Edward Burke, as heading an "evil cabal of men" and vowed that they would have reduced roles in her administration.[41] In governing, however, she increasingly turned to Vrdolyak, Burke, and other powerful ward committeemen. This alliance proved incapable of controlling the loyalties of many of the ward committeemen, and a strong factional structure emerged.[42]

Factionalism within the organization was evident during the Byrne years in endorsements for Democratic primaries, in city council votes, and in the replacement of George Dunne as Cook County party chairman with Edward Vrdolyak, a move engineered by Byrne, in the spring of 1982. Vrdolyak's support came from the well-to-do white wards of the far northwest. Dunne's support came from the core machine wards of the Daley-Bilandic era, especially the ethnic wards on the southwest side.

In the Democratic mayoral primary of 1983, Richard M. Daley and Harold Washington, a black congressman, challenged Byrne. Washington ran a strong reformist campaign, pledging to end patronage and dismantle the machine. The Democratic Central Committee gave him but lukewarm endorsement, and several committeemen from white wards openly endorsed his Republican opponent in the general election. Washington, putting together a coalition of blacks, lakefront reformers, and a small number of white ethnic voters in wards with loyal ward committeemen, won a tight victory in what was labeled by observers as one of the most racist elections in history.

While Washington was denouncing the machine, Vrdolyak, the consummate machine politician, was putting together an anti-Washington majority on the city council. The "Vrdolyak Twenty-nine" organized the council and ousted Washington's supporters from the committee chairmanships they had held during Byrne's reign. Washington refused to compromise, even going so far as not to attend the annual Democratic fundraising dinner in order to emphasize his reform credentials.

With a reform-minded black mayor and a city-council majority composed of white machine supporters, Chicago politics had entered a new era of factional strife. I evaluate the effects of these changes on the analysis presented in this book in a postscript.

Conclusions

Political parties have been embraced as carriers of the democratic creed and excoriated as corrosive of it. Yet for all the ink spilled over parties, we still know far too little about the specifics of their role in local government. A number of studies of policy output have suggested that the policies produced by governments where parties are strong differ from those where they are weak, but these studies are unable to provide the specifics of this linkage. Several case studies in United States cities indicate that the direct role of political parties in government is limited, but that the party serves as a resource for the chief executive in imposing policy settlements.

By examining the regulation of the built environment by government in Chicago, I hope to make explicit the linkages between public policies and the party structure. I examine both the manner in which policy is made and implemented and the distribution of service outputs to neighborhoods. Chapter 2 examines the process of policy making in regulating the built environment in Chicago. Major actors include the mayor, the party, functional interest groups, and city bureaucrats. Chapter 3 describes a second policy-making "system" centering on issues of management control—a policy system that activates different political actors—reformers, the press, and the FBI. Chapter 4 focuses explicitly on implementation and the administrative accountability in the Department of Buildings. Chapter 5 examines service distribution, and presents a model and an analysis of quantitative service data. The relative roles of party, community group, and bureaucracy are evaluated. Chapters 6 and 7 explicate features of this model, chapter 6 by examining the operation of the political party at the ward level as it makes claims for constituents, chapter 7 by studying the response of Building Department bureaucrats to the twin demands of hierarchy on the one hand and special treatment for politically powerful ward organizations on the other. The role of housing court in the enforcement process is the focus of chapter 8; because circuit court judges are slated for election by the party and many remain active in ward organizations after their elevation to the bench, political influence is not unlikely in housing court. Moreover, housing court is the scene of many battles between landlords, citizen groups, and city attorneys as the details of housing-code enforcement are worked out. A concluding chapter paints a picture of party government that incorporates the contradictions that are inherent in strong parties, American style.

2

Substantive Policy Making:
Party as Subsystem Cement

American social scientists examining the process of policy making in cities have spent a great deal of time and energy debating whether political power is pluralist or elitist. Does, as Floyd Hunter, William Domhoff, Michael Parenti, and others contend, an economic elite dominate politics in urban America? Or, as Dahl, Polsby, Wolfinger, and others contend, is power more widely dispersed, so that numerous groups have real opportunities to influence local policy outcomes?[1]

This particular debate is but one manifestation of a more enduring argument concerning the independence of the state from dominant economic forces. As Saunders has pointed out, Karl Marx spoke for the dependence of politics on economics, while Max Weber argued that politics was an autonomous sphere of action that was not reducible to economics. Through the action of politics, *any* class or group could control the state, and operate it for their interest. What American pluralists added to Weber was the element of balance: not only was the state autonomous, but it operated in a manner to ensure balanced, moderate outcomes. This occurs because of the existence of a fundamental value consensus among the politically active on the conduct of government and the role of elections as a meaningful check on oligarchical power. These two facets result, in the world of the pluralists, in a state that was neutral with respect to major economic interests. Saunders argues against rejecting Weberian analysis if one rejects the notion of a neutral state, maintaining that the state can be autonomous without being neutral.[2]

In this chapter I examine the process of substantive policy making for building regulations in Chicago. As we shall see, it offers a powerful example of an autonomous, nonneutral local state.[3] The case material will also provide considerable insight into two other aspects of the policy-making process. The first is the existence of both nonincremental reformism and institutionalized incrementalism within one policy sphere at different times. The actions of political leaders and policy entrepreneurs can dramatically alter the configuration of forces that characterize policy-making arrangements, and they can do so within a fairly short time. Because of these changes, it is dangerous to describe policy-making systems as incremental or nonincremental; even the most unstable policy system is capable of being institutionalized by the actions of political leaders.

The second point illuminated by this case study is the role of the leader of a political machine. In his careful study of political influence in Chicago, Banfield paints a picture of the political boss as a cautious deployer of political resources. Mayor Daley's position as head of the party allowed him to centralize policy making in an inherently decentralized system: "The political head, therefore, neither fights for a program of his own making nor endeavors to find a 'solution' to the conflicts that are brought before him. Instead, he waits for the community to agree upon a project. When agreement is reached, or when the process of controversy has gone as far as it can, he ratifies the agreement and carries it into effect."[4]

The present study suggests that Banfield's picture of the political head continues to have validity, but that he neglected a major political interest—that of government bureaucrats. As we shall see, the perspective of city bureaucrats is brokered along with other, private-sector interests in a policy-making process I term *subsystem corporatism*.

Development of Chicago's Building Codes

The part of municipal law that is termed the building code has two components. One, the building code itself, sets detailed specifications for new construction, including structural, ventilation, electrical, and plumbing standards. The other, the housing code, applies to the maintenance, repair, and occupancy of existing buildings.

Building codes stem from early concerns with fire safety. The first fire-safety law in the New World was enacted in New Amsterdam in 1647, when building surveyors were appointed to control chimney fires.[5] Chicago was incorporated in 1833, and one of its first ordinances established the office of fire warden.[6] In 1849 New York enacted the first comprehensive law regulating the construction of new buildings; this act served as the basis for subsequent building laws.[7] Chicago's Department of Buildings was established in 1875 and was given the power to enforce the elaborate building code enacted that year. The law required the superintendent of buildings to issue a permit before construction of a building could proceed.[8] Chicago's building code has been substantially revised periodically; the last thorough revision took place in 1949 under the supervision of William O. Merrill, a member of one of the city's prominent architectural firms.

Housing codes stem from the housing-reform movement that began in England in the mid-nineteenth century. The first English legislation, enacted by Parliament in the 1850s, approached the housing question via the common law doctrine of nuisance abatement.[9] The housing problem was thought to stem from the maintenance of unsanitary conditions by a limited number of individuals; the governmental remedy was to provide administratively for the removal of nuisances. When the housing-reform movement came to America, a similar conception of the problem was adopted. The housing reformer Lawrence Veiller saw the problem not as primarily one of the quantity of housing available but rather as a problem of externalities, in which a limited number of citizens imposed their unsanitary habits on the majority of slum dwellers: "The housing problem is the problem of enabling the great mass of the people who want to live in decent surroundings and bring up their children under proper conditions to have such opportunities. It is also to a very large extent the problem of preventing other people who either do not care or are unable to achieve them from maintaining conditions which are a menace to their neighbors, to the community, and to civilization."[10]

The housing reformers thus chose a regulatory approach to the problem of slum housing. The first laws regulated tenement houses only,[11] but housing reformers under the leadership of Veiller later began to press for comprehensive housing codes applying to all types of dwellings rather than solely those containing three or more families (which was the common definition of tenement house).

Chicago's initial tenement-house ordinance was passed in 1874, seven years after New York City passed the first tenement-house law in the United States. As in New York, housing-reform groups were instrumental in gaining passage of the act. The Chicago City Homes Association, a group centered around Hull House, successfully lobbied for a thorough update of the tenement-house law in 1901.[12] The Department of Health was made responsible for inspecting tenement housing, which was defined as dwellings containing two or more families; it thus regulated most of the dwelling units in the city.

In 1949, when the revised building ordinance was passed, a section on existing buildings replaced the tenement-house provisions of the earlier law. The Department of Buildings became responsible for enforcing the building code, including the section on existing buildings. A comprehensive housing code was added in 1956. As is typical of housing-code reform, the changes were pressed not by the residents of slums but by political elites on behalf of slum dwellers. In this case the code changes were sponsored by the Metropolitan Housing and Planning Council, a private planning agency subsisting on donations from businesses. William Hartman, a partner in the large downtown architectural firm of Skidmore, Owings and Merrill, and Allison Dunham, professor of law at the University of Chicago, wrote the code with little input from community groups or building owners. Mayor Richard Daley's approval ensured its passage by the city council with little dissent.

The authors of the new housing code clearly believed that they were acting on behalf of tenants, who had little recourse to the law under the existing building code. Mayor Daley requested that they undertake the task after a series of spectacular fires had raised the issue of the safety of Chicago's tenements. William Hartman, the code's senior author, commented to me: "I believed in this project. I was shocked by the lack of protection for tenants in this city at that time. Our concern was that there was no basis for establishing the responsibility of landlords to renters [in the existing code]. There was a building code, but that would be an obtuse use of it. We wanted to give the tenants a threat, something to pound the table with when they went to their landlords."

Through the 1960s, building regulation, in Chicago and nationally, was characterized by long periods of dormancy interrupted by brief periods of intense activity. Periods of rapid change invariably were stimulated by reform groups; often a major fire strengthened the reformers' cause.

The Modern Policy-Making System

Because of changing technology in building construction, and because of changing social expectations about what constitutes proper living arrangements, local building codes can quickly become outdated.

Buildings that conformed to the code fifty years ago generally do not meet modern standards. Hence building and housing codes must be revised frequently if they are to incorporate modern technology and changing social expectations.

As in other policy systems, a set of regularized relationships has developed among affected interests and government agencies. The substantive building-code policy system includes those professions and trades that are involved in designing, constructing, financing, and operating buildings on the one hand, and the public officials who are responsible for regulating these aspects of building on the other.

The system has both national and local components. At the national level, model building and housing codes have been developed by professional associations of code-enforcement officials, including the National Fire Protection Association (NFPA), Building Officials and Code Administrators, International (BOCA), International Conference Building Officials (ICBO), and the Southern Building Code Congress (SBCC). Many local jurisdictions have adopted one of the model codes as their own; others have adopted provisions from one or more of the model codes. Concerned with the crazy-quilt pattern of local building regulation, Congress established the National Institute of Building Sciences (NIBS) in Section 809 of the Housing and Community Development Act of 1974, to serve as "an authoritative national source to make findings and to advise both the public and private sectors of the economy with respect to the use of building science and technology in achieving nationally acceptable standards and technology."[13] In the 1970s the Department of Energy contracted with the model code groups and the National Conference of States on Building Codes and Standards (NCSBCS) to develop a model code for energy conservation.[14] This approach has also been used in the development of the Code Enforcement Guidelines for Residential Rehabilitation; the Department of Housing and Urban Development contracted with BOCA, ICBO, and SBCC for the development of these guidelines.

The policy-making system for modifying building standards has become increasingly nationalized, with the federal government providing more leadership in the field. Moreover, certain federal regulations and payment practices affect building standards in localities. This applies, for example, to Medicaid reimbursement for nursing homes. In order to be certified as eligible for reimbursement, nursing homes must meet federal standards, which affect both construction and maintena facilities. Housing inspections using national standards are required for federally subsidized housing.

The nationalization of building-code policy making is by no means complete. Large jurisdictions, in particular, engage in significant policy making, and innovations in local areas are often stimuli for modification of the model codes. Local officials serve in various capacities with the model code groups. For example, Chicago's director of rehabilitation serves on the Standards Review Committee of NCSBCS, and the commissioner of buildings during the period of this study served on committees for NIBS. Hence there exists a kind of loosely coupled national network that encourages considerable uniformity on local policy making.

Institutionalization

Nationalization of policy making, albeit with significant local discretion, is but one of two trends in building-code policy making. The second is the institutionalization of the policy system, the cementing of certain relationships among affected interests and bureaucracies. The political structures, legislatures and chief executives alike, seldom intervene in the process. The policy process is in the hands of technical experts in the regulatory bureaucracies and those groups and individuals who are most directly affected by the regulations.

During the early years of the development of building and housing codes, policy making was much more unstable. There seem to have been no regularized modes of policy making, and the process had a reactive character. At first builders, and later landlords and owners, fought the building and housing codes proposed by housing-reform groups and some public officials. The early history of building and housing regulation in cities was characterized by sporadic attention and significant "breakthroughs," generally when reform groups were able to arouse public opinion sufficiently to achieve a victory over the entrenched forces of contractors, developers, and building owners.

A policy-making system that has no institutionalized methods of access for affected interests cannot adjust to changing social circumstances and is destined to be wracked periodically by large, nonincremental changes, because demand for change must reach a high level before the issues of concern can reach the public agenda.[15] Institutional channels of access do not guarantee that policies will be adjusted continuously to changing circumstances, but they do serve to alert policy makers to alterations in demands for policies, whether or not the changes are made. Over time, building regulatory policy has settled down into a network of policy systems characterized by regularized relationships among local government agencies and concerned groups, such as architects, builders, developers, and leaders of building-trade unions. These local policy systems vary among themselves and are loosely connected to one another through national organizations that interact among themselves. As a consequence, policy has tended to evolve incrementally rather than sporadically, and changes in code-enforcement strategies tend to diffuse through the national policy network because of the activities of the national associations and the tendencies of smaller jurisdictions to rely on provisions from "model codes" sponsored by the national associations.

The Mayor's Advisory Committee

In Chicago the establishment of the Mayor's Advisory Committee for revising the building code may be seen as part of this process of institutionalization.[16] In 1964 Mayor Richard Daley, at the suggestion of his building commissioner, established an informal committee of architects, engineers, officials from the building trades, insurance underwriters, building managers, and officials from the Department of Buildings and the Fire Prevention Bureau of the Fire Department to serve in an advisory capacity on proposed amendments to the building code. The system worked for two years, with the mayor accepting fully the committee's recommendations and introducing them in the city council as part of his legislative program. It goes without saying that the council passed the proposals. Then, in 1966, the committee passed and forwarded a resolution to the mayor over the strong objections of the fire-prevention engineers, who felt that it significantly weakened the fire safety of buildings. The chief of the Fire Department, Robert Quinn, a close political associate and long-time friend of Mayor Daley, went to the mayor with his objections. Daley refused to support the resolution, and the committee died as a policy-making body when members perceived that their recommendations could be vetoed by disgruntled members who had access to the mayor's ear.

The committee was revived in 1969 at the suggestion of Joseph Fitzgerald, shortly after he was appointed as commissioner of buildings.

Since then every recommendation by the committee has been accepted by the mayor and passed by the city council.

In December of 1978 the committee was written into city ordinance. That ordinance requires that at least one member serve from each of the following categories: building contractors, architects, engineers, dealers in building materials, plumbers, ventilation experts, elevator experts, building laborers, insurance underwriters, and public service corporations; a representative from the Corporation Council and the chairman of the city council's Building and Zoning Committee also sit on the committee, as do representatives from the Department of Buildings, the Fire Prevention Bureau, and other city agencies. The committee is appointed by the mayor, who also designates its chairman.[17]

The committee itself works as a legislature. The commissioner of buildings chairs the committee, and the major work is done in subcommittee. The subcommittees (architecture, structure, materials, and so forth) hold hearings on proposed amendments; testimony is by invitation, although it seems fairly easy to get an invitation. A subcommittee report is forwarded to the entire committee, where a formal vote is held on the amendments. The amendments are submitted to city council, where the Building and Zoning Committee holds hearings; at this point in the process the outcome is already determined and opponents of the proposal offer objections only to get on the record. The amendments are forwarded to the floor with the recommendation of the Building and Zoning Committee that they pass; they generally do so on a unanimous vote. Even independent (antimachine) councilmen generally have gone along with the proposals, feeling that the process yields a better building code than if left up to the machine-dominated council.

The Mayor's Advisory Committee serves as a mechanism for compromise and conciliation on code amendments among affected interests. Occasionally a group that feels it is likely to be harmed by a measure may take its objection to the city council, but the objection is never sustained by the council. The reason is the mayor's almost automatic support for the proposals recommended to him by the committee. The former commissioner of the Building Department, Joseph Fitzgerald, who re-established the committee in 1969 and chaired it for ten years, claimed:

> Objections and problems are taken care of in the committee. I make sure of that. If there is going to be any objection, we warn the council.

The mayor introduces the committee's proposals to the council as a part of his program, and it goes right through. As long as I have been commissioner, the mayor has never objected to any measure. That is true of both Daley and Bilandic. I haven't had enough experience with Byrne to say.

Sometimes Daley would ask, "How much is this going to cost the builders?" We always consider that aspect and could tell him. He'd say, "Okay, go ahead."

Proposals for amending the building code invariably come from two sources: architects who have run into problems designing a particular building, or from code-enforcement officials seeking to improve or strengthen code provisions. Top code officials are in regular contact with their counterparts in other cities and with national associations, and this serves to bring new proposals to Chicago. Officials at the bureau level also bring to the committee proposals that result from enforcement problems in the field. Hence many, if not most, proposals for change come from bureaucrats themselves. Typical were the changes in nursing-home regulations drafted by the chief of institutional inspections. The state of Illinois had adopted for the construction of new nursing homes licensing regulations that were more stringent than city codes. The department set up a task force, which worked over the proposed changes and sent the results to the Mayor's Advisory Committee. There the changes received close scrutiny and were changed considerably. By the time the city council had completed its pro forma action, more than a year had passed.

The policy-making system for building-code amendments is largely in the hands of affected interests, representatives of those professions and trades that are affected by building-code amendments and the public officials responsible for administering them. This does not mean that the elected branches of government are totally removed from the policy process. First, ordinances are often redrafted at the insistence of Edward Vrdolyak, the chairman of the city council's Building and Zoning Committee. He is a substantive expert and is the key link between the policy-making and legislative processes. Second, the oft-noted alliance between the Democratic party machine and the business community in Chicago affects the code-amendment process by setting an overall tone ("Daley didn't like anything that made it harder to do business in Chicago," commented a bureaucrat in the Department of Buildings). Mayors of Chicago have ensured that this tone is maintained in code enforcement by making sure that their own preferences are taken into consideration before the committee considers proposals. Normally the chief executive has no explicit policy positions but rather is interested in making sure that any movement to toughen the code is tempered with a consideration of costs and that attempts to weaken the code do not go too far.

The probusiness tone is also reflected in the composition of the committee, which is appointed by the mayor. While all members of the committee represent interests affected by the regulations, not all affected interests are represented. The architects on the committee come primarily from large Loop firms in the business of designing sky-scrapers, shopping centers, and lakefront high-rises; the smaller firms concentrating on rehabilitation are less in evidence. No community groups or quasi-public redevelopment agencies are represented. ("Why not?" I asked a Building Department employee who served as a staff member to the committee. "We don't feel that it is conducive to a rational analysis of the situation," he responded.)

Whatever access community groups have had to the policy-making process has been indirect, through their contacts in the city's Planning Department, which does have representatives on the advisory committee. City planners tend to be more sympathetic to the attempts of the community groups to rehabilitate existing structures than do bureaucrats in the Department of Buildings or the particular architects and builders who have representation on the committee, at least in part because the planners are responsible for administering rehabilitation grants. One community activist pointed out that "the building-code advisory committee is not representative. There is no openness for citizens to become involved. The city planning people are involved and arranged for us to testify on illegal conversions. It was a farce of a public hearing; they had already made up their minds on what they wanted to do."

Yet community associations were substantially affected by the very stringent Chicago building code, at least until it was modified in 1982. The code itself operated to discourage rehabilitation, since extensive rehabilitation (as distinguished from repair) requires that the building be "brought up to code." This means that the structure must comply with modern construction standards rather than the more lenient existing building standards. If a community association secures a federal or state grant to upgrade a building, the building must be inspected by a team of building inspectors. Not only may the grant be rejected because bringing the building to modern code can be prohibitively expensive, but charges may be filed against the owner of the building as a result of the inspection.

In the past the committee has displayed a distinct inclination to support strong standards for new construction and to look very closely at attempts by some architects and developers to alter the stringent code provisions in order to facilitate rehabilitation of older buildings. Community groups and quasi-public neighborhood development corporations were excluded from the policy-making process, and the process leads to different outcomes than if they were offered direct access to the policy process.

Policy making has taken place far out of the limelight of public opinion. Journalists have shown little interest in the building-code amendment process. Occasionally the issue of a "rehab code" was featured by the press, but this is unusual. When building codes are covered by the press, the policy-making mechanisms are never discussed or critiqued. The press generally plays a limited role in building-code policies, partly because of the technical provisions involved and partly because building, electrical, and plumbing codes make dull stories.

Perspectives on Policy Making

The above description of the building regulatory process offers some support for a model of policy making that emphasizes the dependence of politics on economics. In Chicago the policy process has been heavily influenced by business interests, and large Loop-oriented business interests at that. Community groups have had little influence on the process.

Yet this model greatly underestimates the role of guild labor organizations and particular city bureaucrats involved in the building regulatory process. Bureaucrats represent interests in the policy process that are substantially at variance from the interests of business representatives, and these bureaucrats are often effective in getting their views enacted into public policy. This perspective has been termed *managerialism* to stress the independent role of public managers, who do more than represent a single class or simply balance competing interests.[18] Moreover, a simplistic model of elite dominance of the building regulatory process is unsatisfactory because the process does not uniformly benefit the capitalist class but rather fractures it.

Nationally, major policy initiatives were taken at the insistence of reform groups, spearheaded by a small number of policy entrepreneurs like Lawrence Veiller. A network of reform entrepreneurs ensured that policies would be diffused from New York to Chicago and other cities.

These housing reformers may have had ties to economic elites, but it is far from clear that they acted in the interest of those elites. It is true that one could argue that housing regulation is a form of social investment in the health of the proletariat. Housing reformers doubtless had that in mind. Yet in order to establish such an investment, reformers had to fight other segments of the capitalist class: builders, owners, and managers of buildings. The nineteenth-century reformer Jacob Riis put it this way: "It is to be remembered that the health officers, in dealing with this subject of dangerous houses, are constantly treading upon what each landlord considers his private rights, for which he is ready to fight to the last. Nothing short of the strongest pressure will avail to convince him that these individual rights are to be surrendered for the clear benefit of the whole."[19]

There was, then, no single overriding capitalist interest in the case of housing regulations. Moreover, it is far from clear that housing regulation was in the interest of *any* part of the capitalist class. Certainly a reading of the existing literature indicates no outpouring of support for housing regulation by industrialists, nor is there any today. Housing regulation was an early form of state interference with the ability of entrepreneurs to garner profits, a principle that neither industrialists nor builders of the day rushed to support.

Similarly, in Chicago the owners of existing buildings often have very different interests from those of architects, developers, or builders. These differences pale, however, when compared to the conflicts between all private-sector participants, pleading for less regulation, and the bureaucrats, wanting more.

A State Interest: Who Speaks for Fire Safety?

Even in the early stages of policy adoption nationally and in Chicago, city health officials pressed vigorously for stronger health codes—evidence of an emerging bureaucratic interest in tough codes, stringently enforced. In the settled policy system operating in Chicago, the only organized interests consistently supporting stringent construction standards are city bureaucrats, particulary fire-prevention officials. On the Mayor's Advisory Committee fire-prevention officials, with their uncompromising demands for what they call "fire safety," often find themselves in conflict with architects, builders, and city planners. The chief of the Fire Prevention Bureau noted: "On the Advisory Committee we are often alone. We are the ones who see the fires. There is tremendous ignorance in the design (architectural) community. They are not routinely schooled in fire safety. Fire safety costs money, driving the cost of construction up. The building code imposes restrictions on design creativity in what is essentially a creative field. They see us as 'bureaucratic dummies' telling them what they can and cannot do."

While fire-prevention officials believe that there is great public support for their efforts, they also recognize that such support is usually mobilized only after a tragic fire. One enforcement official commented that "great tragedies make it easy to get major changes through." Nevertheless, "there are continuous technical changes" that come before the advisory committee, and this is when the subcommittee work becomes, in the view of fire-prevention officials, vicious trench warfare.

The role of the commissioner of buildings in this trench warfare is to forge a compromise between the position of the fire-prevention officials and the demands of architects and builders to have a free hand in design and to keep construction costs down. "Everybody is in favor of life safety," commented the building commissioner, "but it costs money." The chief architect for the Department of Buildings claimed that "everybody would like a free [unrestricted] code, but the commissioner [of buildings] has to protect the public. The Fire Department usually sides with him."

The commissioner, then, forges compromises among represented interests, but he has an interest himself—a strong code promoting building safety. Costs of stringent code provisions must be considered because of a cost-conscious mayor, and so must the threat that an affected interest will refuse to accept the will of the committee—a stance that could destroy the committee as a policy-making organ.

Subsystem Corporatism

The managerialist perspective on local policy making has two variants, a weak form and a strong form. In the weak form, government officials have substantive policy interests, and they pursue those interests in the policy process. This is a phenomenon observed often enough in the American policy-making process.[20]

The strong form of managerialism is corporatism. Susan Clarke writes:

In contrast to the pluralist model, the corporatist model views . . . the state as an active participant, not a neutral broker. In this perspective, policy is rooted in objective interests with the state actively promoting specific interests rather than merely brokering exogenous pressures. . . . An autonomous state [attempts] to contain and manage incipient conflicts of interest and to formulate consensual policies in critical policy areas through incorporating affected interests into . . . decision structures.[21]

Let us leave aside the issue of the "objectivity" of state interests; for our purposes it will do to observe that bureaucrats often perceive themselves as pursuing an interest in the common good. It is of little utility to argue the objectivity of these beliefs. Certainly in the case of building codes, Chicago bureaucrats act according to what they perceive to be a compelling state interest: safety. Moreover, policy making is conducted in the corporatist mold, with powerful private interests structured into a formal policy process that is linked to the traditional structure of city government. The bureaucratic interest is incorporated into this policy process, but it is not determinative. Rather, the bureaucratic interest is brokered along with the interests of other participants. How much influence the bureaucrats' concerns with safety will have depends on the mayor's tolerance for imposing costs on builders and architects.

Most writers on corporatism have stressed the common interest of both private interests and the state in promoting economic development.[22] Yet safety is an interest that interferes directly with the profitability of private construction and limits the city's potential for economic development. The mayor is thus in a position of determining the balance between safety and economic development on an issue-by-issue basis. Clearly this mode of decision making protects the chief executive (and, consequently, the city council) from having to make hard choices by making sure proposed policy changes are acceptable to represented interests before they are forwarded to the mayor.

The corporatism of code enforcement is not the corporatism of peak associations of capital, labor, and government. While each is represented, it is a corporatism of trade unionists, housing capitalists, and city bureaucrats. It might best be called *subsystem corporatism*. Three aspects of the situation are important to note. First, major interests are structured formally in the policy process; they are not simply consulted informally. Second, potentially hostile interests are brokered in the process. This is not a case of cozy cooperation; real differences of opinion among groups are brokered. Finally, the local state has a compelling interest in fire safety; it is not simply a neutral broker among private interests.

Exogenous Demands

Although the process of making building regulatory policy in Chicago is substantially corporatist, nevertheless the policy subsystem does respond to exogenous pressures. There are two primary sources of demands on the advisory committee from the local community. The first is composed of architects who have run into problems with the code in designing buildings. These people are normally effective in obtaining serious consideration of their demands, although they may not be successful in getting them incorporated into the code.

The second source of demands is architects, builders, planners, and community groups interested in rehabilitation. The problem that these groups face is that, in the words of the city's director of rehabilitation, "there is an absolute trade-off: rehabilitation versus fire safety. There is no way around that." Older buildings are less safe than newer ones. Existing code provisions require that a building be "brought up to code" if the alterations exceed 50 percent of the reproduction cost of the building or if there is a change in occupancy classification.[23] This latter provision means that if an owner wished to remodel a three-story building with a store on the street floor, installing three flats by eliminating the store, he or she would have to bring the entire building up to current code standards, at a sizeable cost. City bureaucrats view these provisions as important tools for improving the housing stock. Community groups view them as roadblocks thrown up in the way of salvaging the city's aging housing and as incentives to abandon housing. Both positions clearly have merit.

Proponents of a "rehabilitation code," which would relax these stringent provisions through a variety of possibilities, never succeeded in getting their positions considered seriously. They ran into the bedrock opposition of city bureaucrats, allied in this instance with trade unionists who feared loss of work to "do-it-yourselfers." Mayor Jane Byrne finally appointed a blue ribbon committee, chaired by Joseph Fitzgerald, a former building commissioner, to write such a code. A major reason for the lack of success of the rehab forces had been that the Mayor's Advisory Committee contained no representatives of architectural firms or builders specializing in the rehabilitation of existing buildings; neither was there any representation of community groups. Nevertheless, their concerns became such an important public issue that Mayor Byrne felt it necessary to respond—at least by setting up a committee.

The Rehab-Code Breakthrough

In March of 1982 the city council approved the draft rehabilitation code as recommended by the blue ribbon committee and Mayor Byrne. The code revisions at that time also incorporated all requirements for existing buildings in a single place in the building code, minimizing cross-references to other sections of the code.[24]

The code revisions incorporated virtually all of the recommendations made by proponents of the rehab code. The most important changes relate to degree of hazard, adaptive re-use, the applicability of new-construction standards, and the establishing of a building board of appeals. The level-of-hazard provision made code provisions less strict where the likelihood of loss of life was lower. Hence a conversion that adds one apartment to a multiunit structure does not have to meet such stringent code standards as a conversion adding several apartments does. The adaptive re-use provision means that older buildings may be put to new uses even when they fail to conform to the requirements for the new occupancy category. (The old code provided that a conversion to a new occupancy category—from, say, commercial to residential—must meet modern code standards.) Third, the new code changed the so-called 25–50 percent new construction standard. Under the old code, if new work on a building exceeded 50 percent of the reproduction cost of the building, the entire building was required to meet new-construction requirements. When the cost of the work was between 25 and 50 percent of the reproduction cost, the work itself, but not the entire building, had to meet modern code standards. The new code specifies a set of criteria relating to the amount and intent of the alterations, with each category being treated separately according to change of occupancy and increase or decrease in degree of hazard.

Finally, the new code adds a seven-member board of appeals, which can hear matters of code interpretation and can grant exceptions to code provisions. More than anywhere else, the structure of the board of appeals indicates that these major changes in the building code have not disturbed the basic pattern of subsystem corporatism that has characterized the policy process. The board includes one architect, one engineer, one representative from the construction trades, one contractor, and three "public interest" representatives. The public interest representatives appointed by Mayor Byrne were the president of a savings and loan association, a second member of an architectural firm, and a Republican state legislator from Chicago.

The new rehabilitation code was a clean victory for the rehabilitation architects and contractors who had been shut out of the building-code amending process, while the bureaucratic advocates of stringent fire-safety provisions to prevent loss of life were the primary losers. The "absolute trade-off" between fire safety and rehabilitation had been decided in favor of rehabilitation.[25] All of the major code provisions altered by the rehab code were thought of by city code-enforcement officials as important vehicles for upgrading the housing stock. While they recognized the disincentives for rehabilitation, they felt that market forces were strong enough to provide safe rehabilitated housing for Chicagoans. The magnitude of the loss for code officials is also indicated by the lack of a representative of the bureaucracy on the board of appeals.

The Political Party as a Resource for Structure

A number of urbanists have noted that at least during the 1960s and 1970s, the policy process as conducted in many American cities increased in fragmentation and decreased in its ability to structure incoming demands. Yates labeled this state of affairs "street-fighting pluralism," while Wirt offers the term "hyperpluralism." Haider notes that in New York rampant pluralism did not operate to advance the general good. A financial crisis resulted from the inability of political leaders to limit the barrage of demands placed on them, and it caused the entry of participants, primarily members of the city's financial community, who previously had remained aloof from the fray of city politics.[26]

In Chicago, however, the making of building regulatory policy was stable and structured during this period, even though a number of issues became emotionally charged, particularly the rehabilitation-code proposal. Moreover, policy makers in Chicago tended to protect code provisions promoting fire safety even when such provisions discouraged rehabilitation. While building-code policy making tends to be dominated by professional associations of code officials nationally, rehabilitation made less headway in Chicago than in other jurisdictions.

In Chicago the regularized policy-making structure was maintained because of the mayor's extraordinary resources. Mayor Daley was head of the Cook County Democratic Party as well as head of government; his successors Michael Bilandic and Jane Byrne wielded disproportionate power in the party because of the prestige of the office and the patronage commanded by the mayor. Hence Daley, Bilandic, and, to a lesser extent, Byrne could count on overwhelming majorities on the city council in support of their programs. This meant in practice that no disaffected interests could appeal over the head of the mayor to the city council. Once a proposal from the Mayor's Advisory Committee secured the support of the mayor (which was virtually assured) the council's support was automatic, since the numerical superiority of the mayor's bloc was sufficient to discourage attempts to "end run" the process.

The party itself has no interest in substantive policy making. Rather, it acts as a resource for cementing the policy system and for ensuring that the participants in the process automatically take into consideration the policy preferences of the mayor. (As we shall see, the party has a far greater stake in code administration.)

The structure, cemented as it is by the resources provided by the political party, allows the chief executive to act as the capstone of a formal brokerage system that will automatically balance the bureaucratic interest in fire safety against the interests of architects, builders, and rehabilitators in a more flexible code. It is a prebrokered system, with the mayor never having to intervene to arrange or impose policy settlements.

There are, however, substantial costs associated with this structure. Neighborhood interests and the smaller architectural and construction firms active in rehabilitation were not represented in the formal process. Therefore the issues they champion were not addressed by the policy-making system. One danger in omitting such interests is that if they achieve sufficient independent power they can force consideration of their policy proposals by the wider political system, subverting the existing corporatist arrangement. The effect of this would be to transform the system from one producing incrementalist policy solutions to one characterized by long periods of inactivity interrupted by short, intense periods of change—a state of affairs that characterized building regulation before the 1960s.

Indeed, this is what happened when the rehabilitation forces were able to get their proposals considered by a commission that was not connected to the regular building-code amendment process. Mayor Byrne, lacking the consolidated power base of Daley or Bilandic, moved to placate the vocal rehabilitation forces by establishing the commission. Once the issue of rehabilitation code had been removed from the existing policy-making structure, victory by the rehabilitation forces was all but assured, and a major revision of the city's building code occurred. The political weaknesses of the mayor led her to open a tightly controlled policy subsystem to new participants. It would, however, be a mistake to interpret this as the infusion of new neighborhood-based forces into Chicago politics. Rehabilitation is a business, and new economic interests did break into the policy system. Moreover, the interests of certain community groups were furthered by this action. But the changes did not occur because of the demands of Chicago's poor renters and homeowners, nor did they address the problems of these groups. Indeed, the rehabilitation code may make neighborhood regentrification more attractive, leading to more displacement of the poor from their aging but attractive apartments.

It is likely that the policy-making process will return to normal, with the rehabilitation architects and contractors included in the system. The mayor is still powerful enough to impose the type of brokerage system in existence during the 1960s and '70s, and there is no reason that the interests of the rehabilitators cannot be included in a closed system of mutual marginal adjustment. If so, the system will continue to exclude representatives of Chicago's underclass and the renters supposedly aided by housing and building regulation.

3

Management Control
as Public Policy

All organizations, public or private, formal or informal, are concerned to some degree with internal control. Unless control is exercised over constituent parts, collective endeavors by the organization become impossible, and indeed, in the absence of control, organization may be a misnomer.

At some times in some organizations, however, concern over internal control becomes so intense that it consumes most of the attention of the management of the organization and can become an item of considerable interest to groups and individuals who are not members of the organization. An entire policy system can develop around the issue of internal control within the organization. Internal control can activate individuals and groups affected by actions of the organization more than the issue of the degree to which the organization is accomplishing its substantive goals.

In public agencies, concern with internal control occasionally so dominates the agenda of policy makers that management control becomes their public policy; they have little time left over to consider the substantive impact that their agency is having. Goals are displaced by means because the public managers of these agencies are held accountable for the control they establish rather than for the level of output their agencies produce. In some cases, the manager may find himself entwined in two separate policy systems, one of which is directed at substantive policy making, the other of which is concerned with the internal control procedures employed by the agency.

In this chapter I describe a second policy system, operating parallel to the substantive policy-making system described in chapter 2. The policy system that emerges around the issue of management control differs dramatically from the substantive policy-making system, both in its essential characteristics and in the political actors involved. Management-control issues become the grist of the policy mill, and problems of implementation suddenly become problems of policy formulation, because policy makers must fashion policy responses to perceived breakdowns in organizational control.

Governmental responses to allegations of corruption and other failures in management control tend to be highly symbolic, visible, and pieced together under tight time constraints. As a consequence, the new policy is usually drawn from the existing repertoire of policies. The organization turns not to innovative approaches but to "solutions" it already employs. Because the match between problems and organizational solutions is seldom perfect, the problem is often not solved. Moreover, the solution may be the source of other problems in the future. Ironically, however, the problem may allow the institution of solutions to other problems facing the organization. The response of Chicago's Department of Buildings to repeated corruption scandals has been increased central control of operations. This may do little to control corruption, but it does deal with the problem of discretion at the lower reaches of the organization, as we shall see.

Issues in Organizational Control

Control is not always a conscious activity of an organization. Behaviors may be coordinated through a variety of means; if behaviors are coordinated, then control must exist. Dahl and Lindblom have suggested that four social processes act to control behavior: the price system, hierarchy, polyarchy, and bargaining.[1] Of these only one, hierarchy, involves direct, intended control. The others are modes of interaction among individuals in which there is no central coordination. Individuals and groupings of individuals engage in actions in order to achieve ends, but are "constrained by an environment that consists of other people who are pursuing their goals or their purposes or their objectives."[2] The pursuit of objectives by individuals is also constrained by a framework of social norms that are understood by the participants. Social control can result from bargaining among individuals, but only if actors take the actions of others into consideration in their calculations, and only if the norms governing the situation are well understood by the participants.

An organization that is structured hierarchically and that relies primarily on command to coordinate the behaviors of its members generally seeks to control deliberately. Such an organization possesses an explicit control structure, which Etzioni defines as "a distribution of means used by an organization to elicit the performances it needs and to check whether the quantities and qualities are in accord with organizational specifications."[3]

In any organization the formal leadership structure is but one source of influencing members' behavior. When humans interact, a great deal of what Dahl and Lindblom call *spontaneous field control* occurs, even when interaction occurs within the constraints of a formally constructed hierarchical organization.[4] Spontaneous field control occurs when the unintended byproducts of a person's behavior include "signals about rewards and deprivations or even the rewards or deprivations themselves; these signals influence another person's expectations of rewards and deprivations."[5] That second person acts to receive the rewards or avoid the deprivations; the first actor has inadvertently controlled the behavior of the second actor. The problem for policy makers in a formal organization is that such control can occur outside the formal chain of command. It can also be an unintended byproduct of the activities of those in command. Leaders can create unrecognized incentives that lead to undesirable consequences (from the point of view of the leaders). Nonaction by leaders can easily lead organizational members to conclude that particular forms of behavior are condoned. In municipal service bureaucracies, for example, the failure of leaders to pursue corruption vigorously may lead members to believe that the corruption is condoned by management, even if management is unaware of the dimensions of the problem.

Competing Incentive Systems

Even if management did not send unintended cues to members, control and a smoothly functioning organization would not automatically follow. The set of incentives deliberately manipulated by management is only one source of rewards and deprivations that are considered by the organization's members; hence, these incentives are but one source among many that may influence the members' actions. These sources may provide sets of incentives that operate in the same direction as those provided by management, or they may directly compete with the incentives manipulated by management.

Competing incentive sets can stem from two primary sources, one of which is internal to the organization and one of which is external. Internally, central management may not be able to establish control over constituent parts of the organization for a variety of reasons. Bureaus or divisions within the organization, employee unions, or informal groups of members may have access to significant incentives with which to influence the behavior of members. If there exist differences of opinion over policy, it may not be clear that central management can implement its intended plans over the objections of constituent parts.

A second potential source for countervailing incentives exists outside the organization. It can be particularly powerful for the organizational member who spends most of the working day beyond the confines of the central office. Such "street-level bureaucrats" as policemen, social workers, public health nurses, and building inspectors spend much time interacting with people who have reason to try to influence the bureaucrats to act contrary to the policies of their organizations. Moreover, the organizations' policies may not be clearly specified for the particular situations that their members may meet in the field; in these circumstances the members must use discretion in interpreting and applying policy.[6]

Chicago's Department of Buildings (now the Department of Inspectional Services) has presented central management with both types of problems. The department consisted of two major divisions, the Division of Conservation, which was responsible for enforcing the housing code, and the Division of New Construction and Technical Inspection, which contained the technical bureaus responsible for enforcing the detailed construction standards of the code. The department is also responsible for approving construction and alteration plans and for zoning. The technical bureaus have traditionally been fiercely independent, and the Bureau of Electrical Inspection and the Bureau of Plumbing Inspection, in particular, had close ties to their respective metropolitan guild labor organizations. Further, virtually all work in both divisions was performed in the field, leading to classic problems of supervising "street-level bureaucrats."

While many discussions of organizational control treat conscious, planned coordination as a prerequisite for achieving goals, this is not invariably the case. Some system of control is necessary, but that control need not be central and hierarchical. A decentralized, nonhierarchical organization can nevertheless be effective and productive.[7] It may happen that the organization is forced into initiating more control even though it is doing a good job in achieving its substantive goals. If, for example, a building inspector demands tribute for approving a project but will not approve a project that is below code standards, the code will be enforced even though corruption is rampant. Demands that the corruption be curbed are independent of whether the building code is adequately enforced.

The Dual Policy System

An organization plagued by problems of internal control may find that its internal processes have become a public policy issue. In these circumstances the agency must somehow contend with two dimensions of public policy: the substantive and the internal. Problems of control can no longer be dealt with as means of achieving a substantive goal; the means have become ends. Such a process is termed *goal displacement* in the theory of organizations. The typical treatment of the phenomenon of goal displacement stresses the divergence between the motives of the individuals who make up the organization and the stated goals of the organization. Individuals have scant motives to achieve organizational goals, but they have strong reasons to be concerned with the manner in which the organization operates. Aaron Wildavsky has suggested a further reason for the concern with means rather than ends: oftentimes public organizations cannot achieve their stated ends.[8] So they focus on what they can affect: the means that ideally would contribute to ends but do not because of the difficulty of the goals set for them. If the health of the country's citizens cannot be affected by the existing health-care system, then at least we can achieve equal access to that system via government insurance and clinics for the lower class.

Organizations caught up in a dual system may become concerned with means not because of the failure to achieve substantive objectives and not because of the lack of organizational will, but because they are forced to. Demands for control can be stronger, more vehement, and more sustained than demands for substantive goal accomplishment. Moreover, failures of control may be more visible and measurable than failures in substantive goal accomplishment. Finally, goal achievement is a function of social circumstances as well as agency action, while internal control is clearly the sole responsibility of the agency itself. It is hard to hold building departments solely responsible for the decayed housing stock that characterizes many American cities, but it is reasonable to hold them responsible for keeping their inspectors from extorting tribute and accepting bribes. If an inspector is caught and indicted for bribery, the act is far more symbolic of the failure of municipal government than is the apartment fire that could be due to the failings of tenants, managers, or owners as well as of lax building inspectors.

The Second Policy System: Management Control

All public organizations have occasional problems with the control of constituent parts, but only occasionally do the internal problems of an organization become public business. When control is the issue, rather than the achievement of substantive goals, an entirely different policy system is activated. Different actors tend to be involved, and the modes of policy making characterizing the management-control policy system can differ considerably from the modes associated with the substantive system. Policy making in the management-control system tends to be *regularized, adversarial, unstable,* and *nonincremental.*

Regularity occurs because the same actors can be counted on to put control issues on the public agenda. These actors have motive to raise the control issue, and, since they occupy roles within institutions that reward the raising of the control issue, there is a regular supply of incentives to exploit the issue. These policy entrepreneurs can gain if they raise the issue of control, just as surely as the participants in the substantive policy system stand to gain from raising issues of substantive policy change. The difference is that the policy entrepreneurs who raise the internal control issue benefit by simply raising the issue; a solution is not necessarily in their interest and can often be opposed to it. If a public agency quickly solves an internal control problem, the issue cannot be exploited later by the entrepreneur.

The policy entrepreneurs who activate internal control issues are seldom bureaucrats. Sometimes a "whistle blower" will emerge from the depths of the bureaucratic hierarchy to accuse his fellow workers or superiors of malfeasance or misfeasance in office, but even when this happens there have to be other actors outside of the blower's agency who are willing to exploit the situation.

Because local governments are most directly involved in delivering services to citizens, because their employees are inherently difficult to supervise, because the outputs of local government are often so difficult to measure (and their performance is therefore difficult to measure), and because of the political history of machine rule in many cities, local governments serve as the stages for most of the dramas of management control. Of course, the term *management control* is never used; it has little symbolic value, adding nothing to the drama. Rather, the discourse revolves around corruption, discriminatory enforcement, and misuse of power.

The issues are raised in these terms because it is in the interests of key actors to phrase them in this manner. The primary actors responsible for raising the issues of corruption and control in local public agencies include journalists, federal and state prosecutors, reform groups, and community associations. In some cases relatively powerless groups attempt to thrust the issue onto public consciousness in a classic maneuver to expand the arena of conflict. Michael Lipsky has portrayed the use of protest and publicity by the poor to gain substantive ends.[9] This is not normally the case. Issues of management control are raised most often by advantaged groups and favored institutions: the press, reform groups appealing to middle-class distaste for petty governmental corruption, and prosecutors who have their eyes on judgeships or other higher political offices.

The central role in the policy system that is concerned with the business of exposing problems of corruption and control in government is occupied by the media. In his study of corruption scandals in police departments in four cities, McGlennon found that in each case local newspapers, collaborating with department informers, were the source of the revelations.[10]

The *adversarial* character of policy making in the management-control system stems both from the role orientations of the major participants and the fact that casting the control problem as a morality play yields them substantial benefits. The role expectations of investigative reporters, professional reformers, and prosecutors all stress the adversarial character of their positions. It is part of the job to be ever vigilant to uncover wrongdoing, to put your adversary in the worst light possible, and to push for total victory—compromise is unacceptable, at least in lore.

Benefits also accrue to the policy entrepreneurs if they are successful in portraying themselves as the embodiment of good and their adversaries as the personifications of evil. The appeal to the moral sentiments of citizens is nowhere more intense than in the corruption exposé.

Policy making in the control system is regularized but *unstable*. The actors are known in advance, but the timing and severity of their allegations are not. As McGlennon notes, "The corruption itself does not generate administrative crisis; rather, it is the revelation of corrupt practices which triggers the crisis."[11] At some point the external pressure associated with the allegations presented by the press (whether investigative reporters are the source of the allegations or not) becomes so intense that action must be taken, or at least policy makers think that action must be taken. Something must be done, so something is done; that something may or may not be related to the problems raised by the press.

Policy responses by public officials are both *reactive* and *nonincremental*. They are reactive because the responses have seldom been thought out thoroughly beforehand and are often adopted on the spur of the moment. The normal response in crisis is to turn to an option already available but not heretofore utilized. March and Olsen have viewed organizational responses to environmental changes as available all along, and the response is pulled out of the repertoire ("garbage can") to fit the problem.[12] So while policy making may be reactive, it is not random. Rather, it is constrained by existing options available to the agency.

Nonetheless, policies do tend to be nonincremental. City officials feel that it is necessary to demonstrate some definite, authoritative action to deal with the problem. Small changes in existing policies will not convince the public that decisive action is being taken.[13]

Douglas Yates has described urban policy making as "fragmented and unstable. Most especially, it is reactive; urban policy makers are constantly rushing from one small crisis to another, constantly remake and undo decisions, and often search blindly for some solution that will work."[14] While this description does not fit substantive building-code policy making at all, it does describe management-control policy making, at least when issues of control reach the public agenda.

Management Control and Building-Code Enforcement in Chicago

Control problems associated with the enforcement of building codes are threefold: *corruption, differential enforcement,* and *lax enforcement*. The most acceptable definition of *corruption* is the most narrow, the one used by Gardiner and Lyman in their studies of corruption in local land-use regulation: "the acceptance of money or other material rewards in return for preferential treatment."[15] These authors emphasize that corruption can be explained by three factors: the opportunities available (and their lucrativeness), the incentives and disincentives for corruption, and the expectations set by the organization and political culture with respect to corruption.[16]

Scandal and allegations of corruption, differential enforcement, and laxity are nothing new to Chicago's Building Department. Abbott noted the incentives and opportunities for corruption in code enforcement:

> The provisions of the building code . . . are highly technical, and their administration therefore lays the inspector open to many temptations. The builder or contractor and the "materials man" are under pressure to expand the dimensions of the building and to scrimp in the quality and quantity of the building materials. It is so easy for the inspector who approves the plans to make apparently slight concessions, or for the inspector who is observing the building in course of construction not to visit the site at the moment when the violation is apparent, that the organization and maintenance of the Department's work on a basis of honesty and efficiency have been very difficult.[17]

Abbott cites a 1910 study by the city council that found the administration of the Building Department the weakest in the city administration, an evaluation that many Chicagoans would concur with today. In the modern Building Department, housing-code enforcement functions have been added, opening a new avenue for venality. One architect who had studied codes for the local chapter of the American Institute of Architects commented:

> For old buildings, there is a system in operation. Maybe it is an old building with transients living in it, full of violations. The building inspector gets a few dollars, finds a few violations, which covers him. The owner does a little work, puts up a few screens. The building gets into court, the inspector testifies that the owner is doing work, the judge continues the case. He probably thinks to himself that the poor transients have a place to stay, at least, and if he is too tough they will just close the building.

Department officials have three standard lines when confronted with allegations of corruption. First, corruption is not as widespread as the allegations indicate, especially in certain bureaus (the Division of Conservation as opposed to the new-construction bureaus). Second, inspectors are to blame less than the owners, contractors, and builders, who are an almost inexhaustible source of bribes. Commissioner Fitzgerald claims that "in 99 percent of the cases, it is the owner or contractor who is laying it on the inspector. If he takes it, he is wrong; I don't condone it. But so is the owner. In the FBI cases in the Electrical Bureau, they gave the contractors immunity, on the theory that the inspector is implicitly 'coercing' them." (FBI investigations in the Electrical Bureau resulted in twenty-nine indictments in the fall of 1978.)

Finally, officials point to policies adopted to control corruption. The centerpiece of the attempt to limit corruption is a sophisticated computerized management-information system that facilitates routine workflow and allows management to check the degree to which routines are violated. This is supplemented by random reinspections of inspectors' work and a "get tough" attitude toward those who are caught engaging in corruption or dereliction of duty.

Differential code enforcement is the application of different code standards to different individuals or neighborhoods. Code standards are set legislatively or through administrative interpretation for all neighborhoods and for all individuals, yet uniform enforcement can have perverse effects. Owners in certain neighborhoods are generally very responsive to attempts to enforce the housing code—particularly in those neighborhoods where rents ensure a substantial profit for landlords or where property values can be expected to increase. Money expended in correcting code violations can be recovered in increased rents or selling values, since the real improvements will be reflected in the rents the market will bear. Owners in marginal or declining areas will be far less likely to repair their properties, however, since it is unlikely that rents can be increased. If enforcement is pushed too stridently, the result may be increased housing abandonment, as landlords conclude that the increased expenditures associated with correcting code violations cut too deeply into profitability. These considerations have led to a debate over whether regulatory housing policy is worth the effort.[18]

There thus may be sound policy justifications for developing differential code-enforcement programs, perhaps concentrating on those neighborhoods which can be salvaged rather than on slum neighborhoods or stable high-income or "regentrifying" ones. If municipalities exercise appropriate care, differential enforcement programs are probably stitutional.[19]

Differential code enforcement can, however, easily shade over into preferential code enforcement. If management established the program, questions would soon be raised about why the poor and black renters are being slighted in the enforcement programs. The Chicago press is convinced that certain strong machine wards get better service as it is, and these are the lower-income, white, stable or gradually changing wards that might benefit most from a program of differential enforcement. If management leaves it to the discretion of inspectors in the street, instances of preferential enforcement are bound to occur as inspectors perceive that management's attitude toward the issue is tolerant.

The official policy of the Chicago Department of Buildings is to deny vehemently differential enforcement, setting a standard of uniform enforcement throughout the city. Central management wants as little discretion at the street level as possible. When I asked one of the five district directors of the Division of Conservation (which is responsible for enforcing the housing code) whether it was his policy to rely on the inspectors' discretion in writing citations, he emphatically responded: "No way. I tell them: If you see it, write it up. None of this playing God. Let someone higher up in authority decide what to do—the supervisor, or (preferably) the courts."

Nevertheless, both differential enforcement and differential impact result. Differential enforcement results from workload expectations and the "occupational hazard" of being a building inspector. One of the district directors commented: "A boxcar figure is that each inspector can do approximately nine buildings a day, but you send him into a twenty-flat building, and that is out of the window. And some of these complaints [by citizens] in the far southwest of the city are 'gutter bitches'— often just a drive-by. Some of those ethnic communities over there, they will complain if their neighbor has a blade of grass out of place." If an inspector spent his time writing up the minor violations in the slum twenty-flat he would drop behind in his work, and soon find himself in hot water with his superiors, who are sensitive to the problem of "loafing inspectors."

The second factor leading to differential enforcement in practice is the occupational hazard that inspectors are exposed to. The deputy commissioner said that inspectors might "get conditioned to an area, and not notice violations. It becomes a conditioned reflex. Where there are real problems, you just pick up the major stuff."

Differential impacts result both from the differential enforcement that occurs in practice and from the propensity of some classes of owners (those possessing profitable buildings) to comply more readily than others (owners of marginal buildings). There is uniform agreement among Building Department officials and housing-court personnel that the occasional slumlord is not the critical problem in housing-code enforcement; rather, it is the marginal owner who cannot raise the money necessary to make repairs. The court is generally unwilling to act too harshly against these owners, fearing that the housing might be abandoned. Delay is not only possible; it is the norm.

The final problem of control is *lax enforcement*: doing a uniformly poor job of enforcement everywhere. Lax enforcement makes almost as good newspaper copy as does corruption or differential enforcement, especially in Chicago, where the search for "payrollers," who spend much of their on-the-job time working for the ward organization, is a local pastime. Such vigilance makes management sensitive to the issue and offers incentives to institute procedures to check on what inspectors are doing in the field.

Mirage and Response

In the late 1970s, the Building Department suffered a seemingly endless series of embarrassing corruption scandals. In 1978 alone, a number of new construction inspectors were indicted and convicted for allowing work without proper permits for a "fee." Then twenty-nine electrical inspectors were indicted and convicted for extortion. The deputy chief of the Electrical Bureau was indicted for extortion and racketeering; he was convicted in the summer of 1979 by a federal district court and sentenced to three years in prison. The bureau chief quietly retired. The Electrical Bureau convictions were obtained by the Federal Bureau of Investigation, which was concentrating on white-collar crime at the insistence of President Jimmy Carter. Cooperating contractors, wired for sound, recorded the incriminating comments of electrical inspectors. Particularly revealing comments by the deputy chief included boasts of how much money he had extorted over the years, and his contempt for those relatively few electrical inspectors who acted legally.

The most spectacular corruption scandal broke on Sunday, January 8, 1978, when the *Chicago Sun-Times* began its series on bribery and tax evasion uncovered by its undercover operation of a tavern on North

Wells Street. The newspaper operated the tavern, christened "The Mirage" for the sting operation, jointly with the Better Government Association, a reform organization. During the next month, Chicago's attentive public was treated to journalistic exposé of the finest sort, including pictures of city inspectors accepting payoffs from the phoney bar owners. A television camera installed by CBS News documented the action and brought Chicago's Building Department national publicity.[20]

The public response of the department officials was to cry foul. This was entrapment. In private, they shook their heads. "Burt Herrera. He was a *good* inspector. I don't understand why he did it—if he did do it. It is their word against his." Publicly, however, no words of condemnation of the press were uttered by officials of the city government—this was too sensitive an issue to get in a war of words. How was the damage to be contained?

Mayor Bilandic announced a program to deal with corruption—a new Office of Professional Review to uncover wrongdoing in city inspectional departments, a hotline for citizens to report corruption, major reorganizations in the Building Department, and new inspectional procedures, including team inspections, for license applications. The response was designed to attract attention, to convey the impression of major governmental action, and it did.

The Mirage caused real policy changes in the Building Department. Out of the "garbage can" came the responses, all of which involved significant centralization of decision making. A deputy commissioner was appointed to oversee the technical bureaus that had formerly reported directly to the commissioner, and a new division, the Division of New Construction, was created—a new layer of bureaucracy between the technical bureaus and central management. The new division was staffed by an assistant commissioner whose primary task was to extend central management control into the technical bureaus. This involved initiating a computerized information system and a system of random checks on the work of inspectors. The bureau chiefs complained to the commissioner of "gestapo tactics" and argued that the random checks that supervisors must make of the stops their inspectors make (the assistant commissioner checks the work of the supervisors) cut into the already scarce resources available for doing the job required. Resistance of the chiefs had been weakened by the electrical and new-construction scandals, as well as the Mirage exposé and the investigation being conducted by the FBI in the Ventilation Bureau, and the aggressive assistant commissioner for new construction used that weakness to his advantage.

Teams

Reorganization was not the only response to the Mirage. A re-evaluation of licensing procedures took place, and, on instructions from Mayor Bilandic, the city initiated a new policy for license inspections. Rather than sending out inspectors from the various bureaus and departments individually, teams of inspectors are dispatched. Each license application triggers a different set of inspections. A team for a tavern inspection, for example, consists of a building inspector, a plumbing inspector, a health inspector, and a fire-prevention inspector; the electrical inspection is still conducted separately. This involves coordination of three city departments, which is time consuming. Tavern owners lose money while the teams are scheduled. Inspections are extraordinarily tough, as each inspector seeks to demonstrate his own competence before his fellow inspectors. The result has been the denial of a high proportion of license applications. During the first six months of 1979, the Building Department alone refused to grant licenses to well over half of the applicants. Moreover, the increased cost of making the mandated improvements without the income that a license would bring caused severe financial difficulties for many owners.

Innovative ownership arrangements became the vogue in the local tavern business. Instead of buying a tavern outright, a prospective tavernkeeper would simply lease the business from the present owner; the present owner would remain the license holder but would otherwise be uninvolved in the business. Because license inspections are conducted only when ownership changes or a new establishment is opened, this arrangement avoided the burdensome and expensive team inspections— and also avoided the payment of the license fee.

Figure 3-1 presents a time series for the license applications received by the Building Department for the years 1974–79. The data are seasonally adjusted because of the uneven manner in which license applications come in. The data go no further than December of 1979 because the Institutional Inspections Bureau, responsible for coordinating license inspections, was reorganized out of existence at that time. That bureau was the only source of information on license applications in city government; incredibly enough, the Revenue Department, which was re-

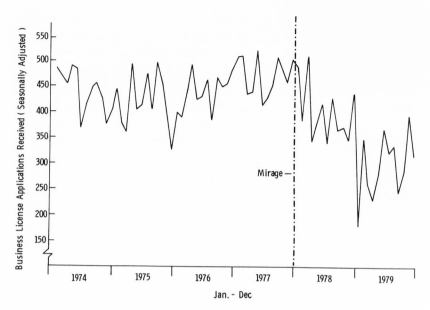

Figure 3.1. Business License Applications Received by the Building Department.

sponsible for accepting license applications, kept no records on its operations. The data in figure 3-1, then, cover only applications that required an inspection by one or more of the Building Department bureaus; this includes, however, the vast majority of cases.

The data demonstrate the steady decline of license applications after the institution of the team inspections in January of 1978. The decline was not instantaneous, primarily because it took time for the new business arrangements to diffuse through the network of owners of small businesses, their lawyers and accountants. The targets of regulatory activity had adjusted their behavior to the new realities of city inspections, but they had done so gradually, not instantaneously.

The adjustments of small businessmen to the new arrangements began to pose problems for the city as the revenues from license applications declined, and pressures for change built. The team inspections were the heart of the problem, yet it was impossible to end them without appearing to soften the stand against corruption. Finally a solution was devised: if the license applicant would sign an affidavit that he or she would complete the construction and repairs that were necessary to bring the premises up to code, the license would be released. A case would be filed in housing court, as was already standard procedure. By agreeing to issue licenses without full compliance the city relinquished an important tool of code enforcement, one doubly important given the general view among Building Department bureaucrats that housing court is an unsatisfactory enforcement mechanism.

In the meantime, the executive director of the Better Government Association claimed that the only thing that had changed as a result of the team inspections was that it was more expensive to bribe inspectors. A "double-back" operation was uncovered, with dishonest inspectors returning to taverns threatening to change their reports. (The escalating price of the bribe may not be all bad. If owners are less willing to pay the inflated price, they may be more willing to testify against the corrupt inspector, and the risk for the inspector "on the take" may increase. Perhaps the goal of such reforms ought to be to increase the going price for an inspector.)

Feedback and Reform

No reform is ever isolated in its effects. Whenever a policy is instituted or a procedure is changed, it will have unintended consequences. The reason is that the reform changes the incentives that individuals both within and outside the organization face. In one respect, the policy of team inspections was a brilliant strategy: it utilized the incentives faced by inspectors to limit undesirable behavior. By sending inspectors out together, city officials had in one stroke made corruption less likely and good inspections more likely. Street-level discretion was narrowly circumscribed, and city codes were more rigorously enforced.

But the high quality of inspections changed the relationships between the Building Department and the small businessmen who were the targets of the regulatory action. As the costs of compliance increased, the incentive for avoiding the costs of compliance also increased. Hence owners, facing financial strain, developed new business arrangements to avoid the increased costs imposed by the improved performance of government. Finally the city capitulated: in order to avoid the losses of revenue caused by the innovative actions of owners, the city divorced licensing from compliance with the building code.

Aaron Wildavsky has labeled such feedback effects "policy as its own cause." A policy change causes a future change in the policy via complex feedback effects. Such problems may always plague government attempts to affect social affairs; all government actions interact in complex ways with the policy environment. But such problems are especially likely in the unstable and reactive policy-making system that characterizes management control.

Reorganization: The Ultimate Standard Response

During the late 1970s the Building Department, with its constant corruption crises, had become an embarrassment to city government. Its reform was high on the agenda of Jane Byrne as she assumed the office of mayor of Chicago in the spring of 1979. By the fall of that year, a major reorganization of city inspectional services was in place. The Department of Buildings became the Department of Inspectional Services, and William Duggan, a former police inspector, was appointed commissioner. Mayor Byrne had chosen to replace the substantive expertise of Building Commissioner Joseph Fitzgerald, an architect of whom she was personally fond, with a policeman whose mandate was internal control.

In addition, a major shift of functions was instituted, primarily with the aim of reducing the inspectional responsibilities of the Department of Buildings. The responsibility for cycle inspections of the twenty-eight thousand buildings that must be inspected annually was transferred to the Fire Prevention Division of the Fire Department, as was the responsibility for institutional inspections. The Lead Poisoning Bureau was transferred to the Department of Health, while rodent control went to the Department of Streets and Sanitation.

In a particularly bizarre move, fire-prevention inspectors were made responsible for building inspections (structural, electrical, plumbing, and the like) as well as fire-prevention inspections and complaints generally. However the Department of Inspectional Services was made responsible for building complaints on the buildings not requiring annual inspections, even though identical skills are required in each situation.

This particular division of responsibility was the result of an attempt by the mayor to solve the problem of an oversupply of firemen. During the fall of 1979, fire officers went on strike in an attempt to force the city administration to bargain collectively. The city responded by hiring new firemen to replace the strikers; Mayor Byrne promised to retain all firemen hired and trained during this period. When the striking firemen returned to work, the city found it had far more fire officers than needed. The solution was to add responsibility to the Fire Prevention Bureau; this also removed functions from the corrupt Department of Buildings and placed them in a well-run and professional Fire Department.

Unfortunately, the result was disaster. Uniformed fire officers felt that crawling around buildings looking for faulty plumbing was far beneath them. Fire prevention has never been a choice assignment in the department; building inspection was even less desirable. The number of city building-code violations dropped from 11,500 in 1979 to a mere 400 in 1980 for the 28,000 buildings that fell under the responsibility of the Fire Prevention Bureau each year. "We have had a few bugaboos in our new program," Fire Prevention Chief James Newbold commented.[21]

The reorganization of functional responsibility is perhaps the most favored response of new policy makers. Reorganization is highly visible as a demonstration of the political leader's concern with management control. Moreover, the theory behind reorganization is sound: moving functional responsibilities from an agency with entrenched problems to one efficiently administered can effect improvements. Unfortunately, the assumption of new responsibilities almost always causes the agency great difficulties in simply performing the routine functions of the agency losing responsibilities. No reorganization is ever solely benign in its effects.

Moreover, the reorganization of the Building Department suggests the far limits of the politics of management control. City officials were willing to sacrifice substantive expertise for control, as indicated by the replacement of Fitzgerald, who was perceived to be lax on the issue of control, with Duggan. They also seemed to be willing to tolerate substantial declines in the quality of work and increases in the cost of inspections (fire inspectors were paid considerably more than building inspectors) in order to solve control problems. The enforcement of the building code was far from the minds of city officials as they wrestled with the immediate problems of corruption in the Department of Buildings and labor unrest in the Fire Department. As a consequence, that function deteriorated.[22]

The Policy Response: More Bureaucracy

The response of the Building Department to the Mirage and new-construction and electrical scandals, and the rapid reorganization of the city's inspectional services, illustrates the sporadic, unstable policy making that characterizes the management-control policy system. Centralizers in an organization need dramatic events brought to the department as a *public* issue in order to break the resistance of entrenched groups. This facet of the management-control policy system creates significant tensions among the centralizers. On the one hand, they identify with the agency and decry what they view as unfair allegations against the department. On the other hand, their projects are significantly aided by the exposés and allegations, since they can use them as levers against entrenched interests in the agency. Scandal becomes a centralizing tool.

Since the timing, exact nature, and severity of the crisis cannot be predicted beforehand, the responses of the agency tend to be drawn out of the repertoire of the potential responses without much forethought. It is not unusual for such responses to create large problems for the agency later, as did the institution of team inspections for the Chicago Building Department and the assigning of responsibility for building inspections to the Fire Prevention Bureau. Since most of the battle will be fought in symbolic terms, the response must be dramatic. Something must be done to convince the critics that the crisis is being adequately dealt with, and only large changes have the potential for doing that. Hence policy making in the management-control system tends to be nonincremental (at least from the viewpoint of the agency).

While agencies' responses to external demands for increased control are varied, they all embody one central characteristic: they are bureaucratic solutions to the problem. Hierarchy is stressed; routines and procedures are instituted; record keeping becomes more important; division of labor occurs; the organization spends a larger proportion of its time on control activities. This increasing stress on regularized, predictable behavior can lead to problems with clients of the agency, as well as with organizations that have regularized relationships with the department. Commissioner Fitzgerald, commenting on the tendency of bureaucracy to beget bureaucracy, put it this way:

> Take this [building] permit thing. You try to stop the bad guys by putting in checks. They figure a way around the check, and you put in another check. And so on. Meanwhile the normal person has to go through the same checks, and get frustrated. You begin to get complaints from architects—it takes too long to get a permit, there are too many

checkpoints. So you review the system of checks, drop some that everybody has found a way around.

Then, all of a sudden someone says there is a building that is not going up right, and it's not. So you put in the checks again.

As Merton pointed out, and as March and Simon emphasize, increasing demands for regularity and predictability in behavior lead to increasing bureaucratization.[23] This often causes other unanticipated consequences, including making the whole process more difficult for clients of the agency. More central control, since it proceeds by increasing the bureacratic tendencies of the agencies, is not an unmixed blessing.

Conclusions: The Politics of Management Control

Issues of management control in public agencies not infrequently reach the community's political agenda. The local corruption scandal, the public payroller, the lax inspection crew can all be raised to the level of active public concern by the efforts of the mass media. The implementation of public policy, in such circumstances, has become public business.

Because issues of internal management control can lie dormant for long periods of time, only to erupt suddenly and unexpectedly, policy making on issues of management control is reactive, unstable, and nonincremental. Nevertheless, although the particular timing of management-control issues is not predictable, the major actors are. The media have an interest in raising these issues, and the heads of the affected agencies and local elected leaders must respond. Hence the system is regularized, if unstable.

The long periods of dormancy in a management-control policy system mean that a great deal of inertia characterizes the particular distribution of administrative discretion that exists in a public agency. Discretion may exist at the street level, the bureau level, or at the top of the administrative hierarchy. Of course, some discretion occurs at each of these levels, but the particular distribution of discretion is different for different organizations and for an organization at different periods of time. Nivola describes a code-enforcement process in Boston that involves far more street-level discretion than exists in Chicago. In Boston, few of the management-control procedures instituted in Chicago exist (or existed at the time of Nivola's study).[24] Hence there seems to be a substantial difference in the distribution of discretion in the code-enforcement agencies of the two cities.

When policy makers are presented with public allegations of faulty internal control, they respond with options that occur within the organization's response set. Almost invariably this involves increased bureaucratization. Management institutes procedures to centralize decision making. In order to do this, procedures must be instituted that, first, limit the discretion of the constituent parts of the organization and, second, monitor how well constituent parts are complying with the policies of central management. Hence management institutes work routines, checklists and forms for the performance of duties, systematic information systems capable of establishing an audit trail, and direct, random observations of employees' performance. The twin goals of such procedures are to ensure standardization of effort and to locate responsibility for actions not in conformance with central policies.

When Chicago policy makers were faced with a series of corruption scandals in 1978, their response was to bureaucratize. Each measure was designed to increase internal control by increasing the predictability of administrative processes and by establishing a locus of responsibility for actions taken by the organization. Each response involved more bureaucracy: an additional layer of administration in the Division of New Construction; the extension of the computerized management-control system, limited before to the Division of Conservation (which was responsible for enforcing the housing code); the institution of random checks on inspectors' work by supervisors; the employing of inspector analysts to root out wrongdoing on the part of inspectors; the institution of standardized reporting forms in new-construction bureaus. Resentment on the part of the bureaus, long used to extensive discretion based on expertise and a tradition of organizational decentralization, was extreme. Only the severity and longevity of the corruption scandals in the new-construction and licensure bureaus allowed the extension of central control into these bureaus.

Nevertheless, centralization may not solve the problem caused by the scandal. An administrator may be able to increase predictability and control in an agency without eliminating corruption. He or she may well be able to increase the costs of corrupt actions by making detection more probable, but this is not the major effect of the reforms. The major effect is to alter the distribution of policy discretion in the organization.

Increased central control not only alters the existing relationships among the constituent parts of the organization. It also alters the relationships that exist between the organization and groups and individuals that interact with it. The changes in inspectional procedures following the Mirage revelations caused increases both in the control exercised by the organization via the mechanism of mutual surveillance and in the quality of inspections. The increased quality of inspections imposed increased costs on license applicants. The imposition of increased costs on the small business owners who were the targets of regulation encouraged them to seek to avoid the costs by avoiding inspections. This could be done by establishing ownership arrangements that avoided triggering the dreaded team inspections.

The Building Department, faced with the choice of devoting more resources to the problem (by, for example, inspecting every tavern and restaurant at license-renewal time rather than solely when a new license was applied for) or altering its procedures, chose the latter. By agreeing to approve licenses on affidavit, officials relinquished an important code-enforcement mechanism and permanently altered the relationship between the department and the small businesses who were the most frequent targets of licensure inspections.

In the substantive policy system described in chapter 2, the political party played a major, if relatively invisible, role. The mayor's control of the party structure gave him or her a critical resource in imposing policy settlements. On internal control issues, however, the party plays a very minor role. The mayor turns to bureaucracy, not to brokerage politics, for solutions to the rapid access of internal control issues to the policy agenda. Chapter 4 examines the impact of such bureaucratization on the agency.

Management Control, Democratic Accountability, and the Distribution of Discretion

At least since the writings of Woodrow Wilson[1] and Frank Goodnow[2] in the late nineteenth century, public policy making and policy administration have been viewed as separate processes—or at least separable processes. The dichotomy between administration and politics has formed the basis for the claim of a scientific public administration in which public bureaucracies are neutral implementing mechanisms for the explicitly policy-making branches of government.

The ideal of a separate public administration has provided much more. There is, according to at least one school of thought, a definite "democratic utility of a disciplined hierarchy."[3] The political, or policy-making, branches of government are responsible for policy formulation, while the executive agencies are responsible for implementing these policies. The policy-making branches are electorally accountable to the citizenry, while the executive agencies are hierarchically accountable to the policy-making branches. Emmette Redford has labeled this model of the policy process "overhead democracy."[4] Even though most writers have recognized the overhead democracy–disciplined hierarchy model to be at best only roughly approximated in any political system, the model has nevertheless attracted numerous defenders over the years.[5] If political parties are to link policy makers to the electorate via the "overhead" institutions, it is necessary for bureaucrats to refrain from substantially modifying legislative policies or adding new policies at their discretion.

The notion of a separable public administration came under severe attack following the Second World War. Paul Appleby attacked the politics-administration dichotomy, and with it the overhead democracy–disciplined hierarchy model, in no uncertain terms: "Public administration is policy-making. But it is not autonomous, exclusive, or isolate policy-making. It is policy-making on a field where mighty forces contend, forces engendered in and by the society. It is policy-making subject to still other and various policy-makers. Public administration is one of a number of basic political processes by which this people achieves and controls governance."[6]

Five years after Appleby's claim that public administration was both policy making and politicized, Norton Long frontally assaulted the notion of overhead democracy and the value-free administrative science of Herbert Simon: "The view of administration as sheerly instrumental, or even largely instrumental, must be rejected as empirically untenable and ethically unwarranted. The rejection will entail abandonment, on the one hand, of Herbert Simon's quest for a value-free administration and, on the other, of the over-simplified dogma of an overloaded legislative supremacy."[7]

In more recent times, students of public policy making have noted that public policies are not self-implementing. Public bureaucracies do not neutrally implement public policies enacted by the policy-making branches of government. Rather, bureaucrats at all levels of government have input into the policy process, and the resulting policy oftentimes looks dramatically different because administration involves both policy discretion and a political process.[8]

Discretion

The relative roles of politics and administration in public bureaucracies hinge on the degree of discretion bureaucrats have in their activities. While earlier students of politics in administration focused on the discretion of agency heads and bureau chiefs, a more recent literature has emphasized the influence of individuals at the bottom of the formal hierarchy.

The case that extensive discretion exists at the street level has been made most forcefully by Michael Lipsky.[9] As public employees interact with citizens in the field, far from their supervisors, they are subjected to intense stress that causes them to adjust to the demands of the immediate situation. These adjustments are often contrary to organizational policies. Because coping interferes with the implementation of policies set at the top of the formal hierarchy, Weatherly and Lipsky claim that "in a significant sense, street-level bureaucrats are the policy-makers in their respective work area."[10]

Not all observers agree that street-level discretion invariably exists, at least to the degree implied by Lipsky. First, bureaucrats, street level and otherwise, may conceive of their roles as neutral implementors of policies set by the political branches of government or by people higher up in the bureaucratic hierarchy. The norms of their professions may serve to enhance administrative control. In the second place, commands may be obeyed because subordinates accept the authority of superiors to issue such commands and, in the absence of reasons to the contrary, obey them. In the view of Chester Barnard, subordinates maintain a zone of indifference with respect to what they are asked to do; so long as a command from above falls within that zone, it will be obeyed.[11] Third, street-level bureaucrats, in coping with stress, may well deny decision-making discretion. If a client understands that the administrator must follow the rules of the agency, then the client may reduce demands on the administrator. Moreover, the administrator is relieved of the responsibility of judging the individual merits of the client's case. This retreat from discretion, as Lipsky terms it, reinforces the influence of the hierarchical command structure on the street-level bureaucrat. Fourth, any organization has a set of sanctions, positive and negative, that act to induce members of the organization to contribute to it. In a public bureaucracy these include such positive inducements as promotions, salary increases, and status allocations, as well as such negative sanctions as suspensions, transfers to less desirable duties, demotions, and terminations of employment. Finally, a substantial amount of organizational behavior is governed by decision rules that are not questioned by members of the organization. Cyert and March have termed these simple operating procedures *task performance rules*.[12] These rules conserve organizational effort by allowing similar treatment of similar stimuli. They also limit the decision-making discretion of administrators.

The literature on public organizations is also replete with normative critiques of bureaucratic discretion. The overhead democracy–disciplined hierarchy model has served as a standard for those who champion majoritarian democracy. Its neat lines of accountability stand in stark contrast to the patchwork of iron triangles, policy systems, and disaggregated policy making that results from the granting of decision-making authority to administrative agencies by legislatures.[13] Not surprisingly, the literature on implementation implicitly (and sometimes explicitly) uses the overhead democracy–disciplined hierarchy model as a normative standard. Richard Elmore complains that "the dominant view that discretion is, at best, a necessary evil, and, at worst, a threat to democratic government pushes implementation toward hierarchically structured models of the process and toward increased reliance on hierarchical controls to solve implementation problems."[14]

The organizational locus of policy discretion is related directly to the issue of administrative accountability. If management can control the activities of lower-level bureaucrats, administrative accountability exists, and the overhead-democracy model has validity. Hence the locus of policy discretion in supposedly neutral bureaucracies is an issue of central importance to the theory of democracy.

Yet the issue has always been one of balance. Roland Pennock notes that "the problem of the relative merits of the certainty and impartiality of the settled rule as against the greater flexibility and potential nicety of adjustment of official discretion, must be almost as old as government."[15] And Pendleton Herring gives what must be a classic statement of the problem when he writes of the predicament of the bureaucrat:

> Special interests cannot be denied a voice in the councils of state, since it is their concerns that provide the substance out of which the public welfare is formulated. On the other hand, a well-coordinated and responsible bureaucracy is essential if the purpose of the state is to be attained. The solution of the liberal democratic state must lie in establishing a work relationship between the bureaucrats and special interests—a relationship that will enable the former to carry out the purpose of the state and the latter to realize their own ends.[16]

As is clear from chapter 2, bureaucrats have an important influence on policy making in Chicago. Along with the affected interests, they serve in formal positions in the major policy-making body for building regulation: the Mayor's Advisory Committee for Building Code Amendments. Moreover, many code changes come at the suggestion of bureaucrats in the Building Department and the Fire Prevention Bureau.

The bureaucratic role in policy making does not end with participation in the policy formulation and legislation process. Formal policies are invariably elaborated, augmented, and altered by administrative policies. By administrative policy I mean those intraorganizational policies made in the process of administering state statutes and city codes. Here, too, the influence of special interests plays an important role. Builders, building owners, contractors, renters, and community groups constantly plead for relief from the formal codes and ordinances governing construction in the city. In Chicago bureaucrats claim to have little discretion in interpreting the building code. In interviews bureaucrats uniformly denied that they had discretion, stating that only the courts could grant exceptions to the strict interpretation of codes. Yet the voluminous literature on bureaucratic discretion and street-level bureaucracy suggests that much policy (at least of the administrative variety) is made by those agency employees who are in most direct contact with citizens.

This chapter presents an analysis of those administrative operations in Chicago's Department of Buildings that relate to the twin issues of administrative accountability and management control. The findings presented here suggest substantial modification of both the standard model of disciplined hierarchies and the discretion-riddled street-level bureaucracy. In the first place, it is a serious mistake to view public sector organizations as consisting of central management on the one hand and unsupervised street-level bureaucrats on the other. In all modern organizations, functional divisions of activities mean that subparts of the organization develop interests that do not invariably correspond to the interests of the agency as a whole (as defined by central management). Not infrequently central management has to contend simultaneously with substantial discretion in bureaus, among middle managers within bureaus, and among the street-level bureaucrats directly responsible for service delivery. This means that the issue of management control is far more complex than the top-versus-bottom view commonly presented in the street-level bureaucracy literature.

In the second place, although the issue of controlling the actions of street-level bureaucrats is certainly a real one, agency heads and bureau chiefs have far more impact on what lower-level bureaucrats do than conventional academic wisdom would suggest. Agency policies do govern the actions of bureaucrats in the field as well as in the office; that management conditions what it asks in its directives to employees on what it believes employees will accept does not change that fact. Moreover, it is possible for dedicated managers to improve management control—if that is what they desire and if they are willing to commit resources to that end. As indicated in the previous chapter, opportunities for increasing central control can follow corruption scandals, so that even if corruption is not limited, predictability and hierarchy in an agency may well be increased.

Finally, operations in the department suggest that extensive patronage powers are not conducive to establishing hierarchical control. Municipal reformers long argued this point forcefully. The modern counterargument is that patronage is necessary to facilitate policy implementation by allowing a mayor to remove those bureaucrats who are subtly thwarting program aims. As we shall see, there exists strong motive for political chief executives to use patronage to achieve political, not administrative, goals.

Management-Information Systems

The control structure of an organization must consist of a method of obtaining valid and reliable information on the performance of the organization's constituent units and some way of enforcing performance and output specifications. A good management-information system must include, first, information that is organized so that decision makers can comprehend it. Too much information is as useless as too little. The information must also pertain to aspects of the organization that can be affected by the actions of policy makers. Wildavsky complains that PPBS (Program Planning Budgeting Systems) and zero-based budgeting are not cost-efficient because they provide information that is wrongly organized and therefore cannot be used in the process of allocating expenditures.[17]

One ought to distinguish between information that is organized so that it cannot, in principle, be useful and information that is useful in diagnosing problems but that cannot be acted on because of constraints, whether the constraints are monetary or political. Management cannot do everything it would like. Nevertheless, reliable information is a prerequisite for controlling the subparts of an organization.

Any management-information system must have three characteristics if it is to aid organizational control. First, it must accurately mirror the flow of work in the organization. Second, the system must establish the locus of responsibility for a particular action. If a bureau is responsible for taking an action (for example, making a reinspection or filing a court case) and the action is not taken, the management-information system must be capable of indicating the organizational locus of the failure to act. Third, the system must provide a reliable set of records to compare with what employees say they are doing.

This requires, first and foremost, an accurate system of record keeping. Second, it requires a method of summarizing the vast quantity of information generated in the process of delivering services so that it is useful for management. As Anthony Downs has noted, it is unnecessary for superiors to monitor all of the behaviors of subordinates. Control may be established by monitoring a sample of subordinates' behaviors, so long as subordinates do not know which behaviors are being monitored.[18]

A satisfactory management-information system will allow the monitoring of problematic behaviors. This is normally done by case "aging." When one bureau finishes its action on a case and transfers responsibility to another agency, case aging begins. This may be done on a daily or a weekly basis. Case aging stops when the bureau takes an appropriate action on the case. For example, if an inspectional bureau is supposed to make a reinspection on a case, aging begins when the case is forwarded to the bureau and ends when the bureau returns its report on the reinspection.

Management can easily discover which cases have not received action and, theoretically at least, can find out why. Management needs to monitor only cases that have not received action. This approach circumscribes discretion at the bureau level, because inspectional bureaus lose the power to hold up approval until compliance is achieved (or until tribute is extracted). Responsibility for obtaining compliance is also shifted out of the inspectional bureaus to a more central location in the organization. In the Chicago Building Department, this central location was the Compliance Bureau, which was responsible for holding compliance hearings and filing court cases.

Passive management-information systems, based on the records generated in the process of service delivery, solve only some problems of organizational control. In particular, it is not possible to monitor the *accuracy* of bureau action. In order to monitor the correspondence between records and action, central management must institute more active systems for acquiring information. The most common form of active information acquisition for control purposes is the random checking of employees' work. This is done by having a supervisor reinspect a site already inspected by an employee, and comparing the results.

Passive information systems allow computerization, enable management to concentrate on problems and ignore the smoothly functioning parts of the organization, and allow substantial centralization of function, especially the transfer of discretion from the bureau level to central management. They also allow central decisions about what sort of inspectional report will be linked to particular organizational responses.

Identical inspectional reports should not generate different organizational responses, and the passive informational system allows management to enforce such standardization of response.

Passive systems, however, cannot link what street-level personnel are doing with what they are reporting. If the records are invalid, the system will be invalid. Moreover, it is possible to sow the seeds of distrust in the system. Supervisors in the Division of Conservation, for example, would occasionally send out inspectors to a location but then fail to file the completed report. When the aging system showed an "open" inspection, the supervisors would produce the inspectional report from their own files, claiming that the computers had "failed again." In one of ten of such cases, there might be venality, but supervisors protected themselves by handling properly the other nine. Such shenanigans caused more than one bureau or division chief to keep a parallel card-file system on the progress made on cases under his supervision. This completely duplicated the computerized management-information system but provided the chief protection against computer errors and limited the potential corruption of supervisors and assistant bureau chiefs.

Management Information in Chicago

In 1969, in the wake of yet another scandal in the Building Department, Mayor Richard Daley replaced Building Commissioner Sid Smith with Joseph Fitzgerald, a young deputy commissioner who had worked his way up from ventilation inspector on the basis of his considerable ability. The story circulates around the Building Department that the new commissioner, during his first week in office, dropped by the construction site of a multistory office building. Sticking his head into the construction shack, Fitzgerald is supposed to have said, "Hi, I'm the new commissioner of buildings." "Geez, commissioner," came the reply, "I didn't expect you so soon. I don't have the envelope ready for you yet."

Not only had Fitzgerald inherited a department that had the worst reputation for corruption in city government, he also faced an organization that was decentralized in the extreme. The department consisted of inspection bureaus and a plan-examining operation; the inspection bureaus included the Division of Conservation, responsible for inspecting existing buildings and enforcing the code; the Bureau of Institutional Inspections, responsible for inspecting institutional establishments such as hospitals, schools, and large restaurants; the technical bureaus (New Construction, Electrical, Ventilation, and Plumbing), responsible for supervising new building and alterations; and the Bureau of Dangerous and Dilapidated Buildings, responsible for inspecting buildings slated for demolition by the housing court. The technical bureaus, in particular, have traditionally asserted their independence, generally claiming special competence in interpreting the code. The Electrical Bureau has been able to sustain a special claim of autonomy. It does not interact with other bureaus in the department regularly; for example, it is responsible for conducting its own compliance hearings and filing its own court cases. This function is centralized in the Compliance Bureau for all of the other bureaus. Moreover, William Hogan, the chief of the bureau for years until his retirement in the wake of a corruption scandal, also served as the president of the Chicago chapter of the International Brotherhood of Electricians. This link reinforced the special claim of competence made by the electricians.

Central administrators in the department spoke bitterly of the independence of the technical bureaus and were not completely unhappy with the corruption problems there. The director of administration commented that corrupt behavior in the Electrical Bureau was "condoned and perpetuated by leadership. That prima donna attitude on the part of inspectors—it has been indoctrinated. If you don't get the cooperation of the leadership, how can you get it from the men?"

Soon after Fitzgerald took office in 1969, he instituted a sophisticated management-information system that gave central management the ability to monitor workflow. It also had the effect of centralizing decision making in the department by limiting bureaus' discretion. Hence it has been bitterly resented by the technical bureaus. The system allowed the establishment of procedures that could subsequently be monitored to see if they were being followed. Computerization of records allowed the establishment of an aging system and a coding system for both inspections (Conservation Division only) and recommendations.

The procedure for existing buildings is diagrammed in figure 4.1. Department action is activated by a citizen's complaint, a referral from another city department or Building Department bureau, or by the cycle inspections conducted by the Conservation Division. In the first two cases the information is written to a computer file, along with the date the complaint or referral was received. The complaint is "aged" from that date and, after a certain number of weeks has passed, begins show-

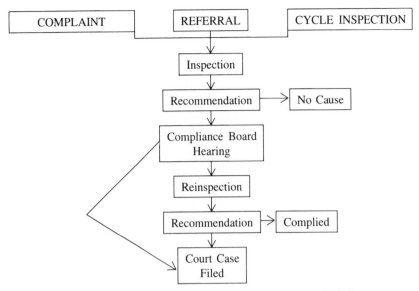

Figure 4.1. Building Department Procedures for Existing Buildings.

ing up as an open complaint on reports to central management. An inspection kills the aging of a complaint.

Inspectors in the Conservation Division use a numbered checklist that contains code violations; once an inspector learns the list, he need only check off the appropriate violations he finds in the field. The technical bureaus have resisted the establishment of such discretion-limiting devices in their bureaucratic turfs, derisively calling them "idiot sheets." On completion of the inspection, the inspector gives his report to his supervisor, who assigns a "recommendation code." This six-point code determines future action—whether the case is dropped, goes to the department's compliance board for an administrative hearing, goes to municipal court, or goes to chancery court. (The majority of cases on which there is further action go to the compliance board initially.) After the compliance board hearing, the case goes back to the responsible bureau to conduct a reinspection (presuit inspection). At this point a second aging system is activated, which is killed when the reinspection occurs. If the violation still exists at the time of the reinspection, the case must be sent by the inspectional bureau to the Compliance Bureau, which must file a court case.

The system limited the discretion of the functional bureaus in four ways. First, no longer could a bureau chief, supervisor, or inspector get rid of a complaint; separate records existed on the computer. Second, no longer could a chief or supervisor give some owners extra time to comply or "lose" the reinspection sheet; reinspections are aged. This included the extra time granted to the friend of the precinct captain as well as the little old lady who would have to do without food or heat in order to comply; the aging system cannot distinguish between discretion for good and discretion for ill. Third, the discretion of bureau chiefs and supervisors to determine appropriate action was circumscribed. The standardized inspection sheet and recommendation code linked findings by inspectors to organizational response in a standard manner, so that minor violations would not, for example, result in a court case.

Finally, the system provided independent records for reinspections after the compliance board's administrative hearing. This limited a favorite tactic of corrupt bureau chiefs and supervisors: demanding payment *after* the administrative hearing and before a court case was filed. If payment was received, the file would not be returned for court action. Yet since no inspector had actually ruled the violation to be in compliance, no charges of corruption could be sustained. The files were just "lost." As the chief of the Compliance Bureau commented, "You'd be surprised how many cases were lost from those little carts that took the cases between here and inspectional bureaus."

The key bureau in this process is the Compliance Bureau. It is small and central; it thus became the mechanism through which centralization of decision making took place. It was the organizational lever in the management-control system. Any loss of discretion by the functional bureaus meant that the Compliance Bureau's workload would increase, because the cases normally held up by the bureaus would now go to the Compliance Bureau. As long as the information system was having the desired effect, an increase in workload of the Compliance Bureau would have to result.

Figure 4.2 diagrams the number of new cases scheduled for compliance hearings, at six-month intervals through a twenty-year period. As expected, a dramatic leap in the number of Compliance Bureau cases occurs in the second half of 1969, when the system was instituted. (The large number of hearings conducted in the second half of 1977 reflects a special smoke-detector inspection program.) Before the institution of the system, the number of cases handled by the Compliance Bureau had been declining for a number of years, a fact that can most likely be explained by an increase in the discretion exercised by the functional

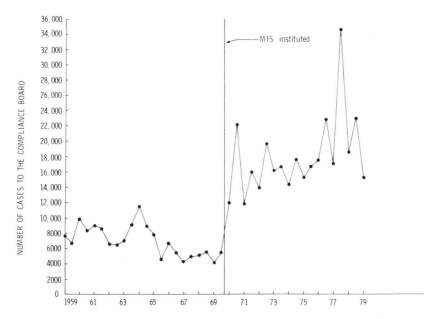

Figure 4.2. Number of New Cases Scheduled for Compliance Board Hearings.

bureaus. They were just not sending their cases to the compliance board. After the system was instituted, they were forced to send their cases there or suffer the questions of the commissioner's staff, who were sure to notice the backlog of complaints.

The increase of Compliance Bureau cases did not stem from a transference of caseload from the courts to the Compliance Bureau. That is, bureau chiefs were not filing cases directly in court before 1969 and using the Compliance Bureau thereafter. As Figure 4.3 shows, the number of court cases filed jumps after 1969 (the number would be expected to remain constant if the Compliance Bureau were just being used as an intermediate step). The figure also demonstrates a truism often ignored by decision makers in a single organization: you cannot reform one organization without affecting others. Court dockets, already strained, became hopelessly overloaded during this period. Housing-court judges heard over two and one-half times as many new cases in 1970 as in 1969, and the number of cases filed has remained high.

Figure 4.4 most dramatically illustrates the decline in discretion exercised by the functional bureaus (except the Electrical Bureau, which continued to file its own court cases and hold its own compliance pro-

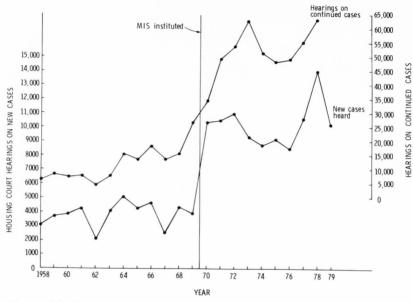

Figure 4.3. Number of Housing Court Hearings.

ceedings). These are the cases recorded by the Compliance Bureau as awaiting reinspection after compliance hearings. The Compliance Bureau's memorandum files indicate that as early as 1962 the bureau chief was concerned that case files sent to bureaus for reinspection were never returned to the compliance board for court action or with a notation that the bureau had found substantial compliance. The chiefs of the inspectional bureaus were deciding, on a case-by-case basis, when to allow extra time for compliance and what would be judged as substantial compliance. The lack of a central information system meant that bureau chiefs could claim that they had acted on particular cases and forwarded the results to the Compliance Bureau, and that Compliance Bureau files failed to show this was not their fault.

A variety of corrective actions were tried, none of which apparently worked, until the management-information system was instituted. Responsibility for taking the next action could be clearly pinpointed; there could be no dispute over whether the Compliance Bureau or the inspectional bureau had failed. Suddenly, after 1969, the backlog of cases awaiting reinspection disappeared. The bureaus began to conduct the

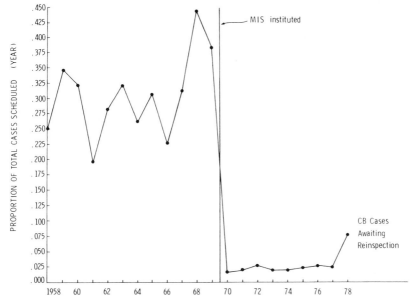

Figure 4.4. Number of Compliance Board Hearings Awaiting Reinspection at Year's End.

reinspection and forward notification of the action taken to the Compliance Bureau according to specified procedure.

Figures 4.2, 4.3, and 4.4 document the dramatic changes in internal operations caused by the institution of the management-information system. Bureau-level discretion was clearly circumscribed, and decision making was centralized. Whether these changes are associated with changes in relationship at the street level is a different matter. Wildavsky notes that organizations change what they are able to change and subsequently claim that they have changed what needed changing. What evidence is there that corruption declined, preferential treatment was limited, and enforcement was less lax? Evidence is difficult to obtain, but most observers of the Chicago scene believe that the Building Department has improved and that there is less corruption and preferential treatment than twenty-five years ago. To attribute these changes to the management-control system may well be a mistake, however, since conditions generally have improved in city government. Gone are the days, in the words of a Conservation Division district director, when "people were sent in the field and, in effect, told, 'You are paid two thousand dollars. Now steal six thousand dollars.' '' Increasing pay and professionalization have substantially changed the traditionally patronage-laden Chicago civil service. Patronage workers are a smaller and smaller component of the city's work force. Moreover, the modern ward committeeman must control his "boys" if he wishes to combat the declining party loyalties of voters. Things may be better less because of conscious management control than because of general changes in the political system.

Central Control in the Technical Bureaus

Just as an earlier scandal gave the department's central management the leverage to institute a computerized control system for housing inspections, the Mirage incident described in chapter 3 allowed the commissioner to extend control into the technical inspection bureaus. With appointment of an assistant commissioner for new construction the commissioner had his man in charge of the technical bureaus. For the first time, the chiefs of the technical bureaus would not report directly to the commissioner; they resented what they viewed as a demotion. The new assistant commissioner had the primary duty of increasing hierarchical accountability in the technical bureaus.

Before this time, the technical bureaus had been linked to the central information system through the complaint-aging device, and all technical bureaus except the Electrical Bureau had been linked to the compliance board through the computerized reinspection system. There was, however, no use of standard inspectional forms or recommendation codes in these bureaus. Central management knew the timing of workflow but had no way of enforcing standardized performance. In the absence of standard reporting on inspections and on the actions taken, outputs could not be linked to the findings of inspectors in a uniform manner.

Central management had long felt that this system accorded far too much discretion to the bureau chiefs. The new assistant commissioner for new construction commented:

> The new construction bureaus were fiefdoms before Brick [his deputy] and I came in. We are trying to gain more cooperation, teamwork. But you walk a tightrope here. Certain policy should be made at this [the division] level, but you must not diminish the bureau chief's authority. The type of inspection, what passes, the number of inspections per in-

spector, all are at the bureau level. Reporting, supervisor checks of inspectors' work, are at this level. The rule I use is that they must be
consistent in what they pass.

The key to management control, according to the assistant commissioner, was the establishment of an audit trail that gave the locus of
responsibility for an action: "The problem we have now [in the new-
construction bureaus] is that there is often no audit trail. You can't prove
wrongdoing even if you sense it. And that is partly by design. We want to
change that, establish a clear audit trail. You have to be able to get back
to the guy that approved the job."

By instituting a system that allowed consistency checks and was
capable of establishing the organizational locus of responsibility for an
action, central management had put in place an adequate passive information system. An active component was also added, with random
checks of inspectors' work by supervisors and the use of inspector
analysts to examine the work of suspect inspectors and to check on the
supervisors checking on inspectors.

The active component allowed the direct evaluation of inspectors'
work. The assistant commissioner claimed that "if there is a discrepancy
between the inspector's report and ours, it can be three things. He's
incompetent. He took a bribe. He was never there." While most problems came from inexperienced or incompetent inspectors, management
believed that it could control corruption and lax enforcement through the
random check system.

Discipline

Even if a management-information system is effective in detecting
malfeasance and lax enforcement, there still must be a reliable method
for disciplining inspectors to ensure control. Even in Chicago, the disci-
plinary process is tortuous, at least for employees on civil service. The
charges must be documented by the director of administration of the
department, who then makes a recommendation to the commissioner of
buildings. The commissioner must take the case to the Law Department
for formal charges. The case is taken by the corporation counsel to the
Department of Personnel, which prosecutes the case, calling on build-
ing-department personnel for testimony. While it is somewhat simpler to
terminate an employee who holds a provisional appointment, one must

be careful that such an employee does not have good political connections. Actions against such individuals can cause problems for departmental management.

The department has terminated a number of inspectors because of charges of incompetence or malfeasance, but it is likely that this is partly due to the extreme sensitivity to charges of corruption by departmental administrators. According to the director of administration, "We have never failed to get rid of a corrupt or unproductive employee. You just have to carefully document the charge."

Computers and Control

In what is by far the most comprehensive analysis of the use of computers in local government, Kraemer, Dutton, and Northrop discuss the impact of computerization on performance, on personnel allocation, on budgeting and account systems, on the routine processing of cases and service demands, and on policy analysis. Yet the authors present no analysis of the use of computers in controlling the behaviors of the individuals and units that make up the organizations that deliver local services.[19]

Managers of service-delivery organizations, however, face problems of organizational control daily. Although most of the literature has focused on the problems of controlling the behavior of street-level bureaucrats, most service-delivery agencies also face problems of controlling the actions of bureau chiefs and division heads. It is likely that computerized information systems are often instituted or extended not to improve performance or to increase efficiency but to effect control. Certainly that was the case in Chicago's Building Department. While efficiency in processing cases was a desirable outcome, it was not the primary motive for the institution of the system.

More important, the argument that computerization would increase the agency's efficiency was not enough to convince the independent bureau chiefs to cooperate in establishing a management-information system. The commissioner attacked the weakest part of the organization first: the Conservation Division, where technical expertise was lowest and where trade-union power was nonexistent. The Conservation Division also had most to gain in the efficiency promised by computerized operations, since it processed most of the complaints from citizens. The system was not extended into the technical bureaus for almost a decade;

only the seemingly unending scandals of the late 1970s broke the resistance there.

The Monday Massacre: Patronage and Political Accountability

Many political scientists have considered that the ability of a political leader to implement his or her programs has been severely curtailed by the decline of patronage positions in government. Patronage allows a mayor to replace recalcitrant bureaucrats with loyal supporters of the mayor's program, at least in theory. Civil service, on the other hand, has the effect of locking in opponents of new policies. Bureaucrats can be fired only for cause, and most civil service systems end up protecting employees who are busily subverting the new policies—again, in theory.

All this presupposes that elected leaders use patronage as a lever to implement programs. But the dynamics of machine rule mitigate against mayors' having programs in the first place. Machine politicians are good at negotiation and compromise, in the use of material incentives to achieve compliance, and in linking neighborhood demands to government outputs. They are not so good at urban programs. Hence it is highly unlikely that patronage was ever used systematically to insure the implementation of programs.

As we shall see in chapter 6, patronage is allocated in Chicago according to vote productivity. It would nevertheless be possible to change patronage allocations in order to achieve governmental ends simply by searching out and dismissing a program's opponents. Machine politicians, however, are most concerned with electoral success, not with the success of particular programs (as long, of course, as things don't fall apart completely). Hence changes in patronage allocations are most likely to occur during factional squabbles over the selection and support of candidates.

Machines tend to run smoothly during periods in which one "boss" is able to maintain hegemony, but they often break down into squabbling factions in the absence of strong leadership. After all, the ward structure and decentralized governmental structure of Chicago (and most other machine cities) favor factionalization. Only where one person is able to control the loyalties of party chieftains, normally by gaining control of patronage, do machines run smoothly. During a succession crisis, patronage is most likely to be used to punish political enemies.

The Cook County Democratic Organization has experienced just such a succession crisis. Mayor Jane Byrne had trouble centralizing the disparate elements of the machine, and several of the ward committeemen went into permanent opposition. Most prominent among Byrne's opponents was Richard M. Daley, Eleventh Ward committeeman and former state senator, who in the primary election of 1980 defeated Byrne's handpicked candidate for state's attorney of Cook County. Byrne then threw her support to Bernard Carey, the incumbent Republican—an indication of just how deep the factional split was. In a stunning upset, Daley narrowly defeated Carey in a countywide contest in the November general election, which saw Reagan sweep suburbs and deeply cut into the normal Democratic vote in the city.

The factional split had broken out into the open during late 1979. Byrne had decided to endorse Senator Edward Kennedy's intraparty challenge to President Carter, and she wanted to line up the support of the ward committeemen for the coming Illinois presidential primary. Most ward committeemen fell reluctantly in line, but Daley and Thomas Hynes, Nineteenth Ward committeeman, defied the mayor. As the primary approached, it became clear that Kennedy was enormously unpopular among Chicago voters, and other ward committeemen became restive. In order to stave off any further defections, Bryne announced the "vising" of all city workers who lived in the Eleventh or Nineteenth wards and occupied management positions in city government, an act that came to be known as the "Monday Massacre."

On January 3, 1980, twelve mid- to high-ranking administrators in the building department were terminated by order of the mayor. Most occupied positions that were exempt from civil service regulations, but all carried civil service titles with them into their exempt positions. Ward activists and the politically indifferent were indiscriminately terminated. Opponents of the mayor's new reorganization plans for the department continued in their positions, while supporters of the mayor's changes were fired, and vice versa, in a desultory pattern. There was, in a word, no linkage between programmatic considerations and the action.

Because most managers also carried civil service titles (mute testimony to the ability of machine activists to make sure their personal interests come before the interests of the machine), they could not be fired from city government except through the proper procedure. They were forced to accept the reduced pay and responsibility of their highest civil service position. In the Building Department the victims of the Monday Massacre were given meaningless tasks and were assigned desks far from their former bureaus.

The ward organizations sued, in one of those ironies that seem to pervade Chicago politics, under a federal district court decision that prohibited firing municipal employees for political reasons. Nine of the twelve "vise victims" in the Building Department joined the suit (those not joining were politically inactive). In an out-of-court settlement, the city agreed to place the plaintiffs back in their original positions or in equivalent ones.

In this particular case, one of the few incidences of such a dramatic use of the power of patronage to enforce executive decisions, the mayor used resources not to maintain administrative control of bureaucrats but to influence the political decisions of ward committeemen. Patronage was used in an attempt to achieve political, not administrative, centralization. In eras during which the mayor lacks the ability to centralize the political party apparatus, he or she will be tempted to use governmental resources to do so.

Conclusions: Management Control and Policy Discretion

There are sound reasons for allowing little discretion in public organizations. The model of agencies as disciplined hierarchies has long captured the imagination of students of public administration, and it fits into a coherent theory of democratic government. There are, however, also sound reasons for allowing discretion. Organizational rules and policies may not fit a particular situation requiring a decision. The strict application of the rules may not be in the best interest of the organization or the client. It may be almost impossible to achieve complete hierarchical control, and this may become a justification for not spending too many scarce resources on it.

Public organizations may be characterized by a particular *distribution of policy discretion*. The amount of discretion can vary both vertically and horizontally in an agency. Some organizations achieve tight central control. Others are composed of managers and street-level personnel, with managers unable to achieve much operational control over employees. Still others are more complex: policy discretion is located at the street level, at the top, and at the bureau and division level as well. Moreover, some bureaus may possess more autonomy than others; the technical bureaus in Chicago's Building Department had more discretion than did the Conservation Division.

While the particular distribution of policy discretion in an agency is partly a function of organizational tasks and the particular cluster of policy responsibilities assigned to an agency, it is also a function of the philosophy of agency management and the resources that management is willing to devote to imposing central control. No manager of any local service-delivery organization is likely to be able to establish complete central control. On the other hand, he or she is not simply at the mercy of street-level bureaucrats and bureau chiefs. Throughout his tenure as commissioner of buildings, Joseph Fitzgerald tightened the vise of management control over the bureau chiefs and street-level inspectors who made up his department. Yet the entrenched technical bureau chiefs were able to frustrate his attempts to extend central control into their fiefdoms until major scandals destroyed their effectiveness. Moreover, the control system was expensive and consumed resources that could have been used in tasks more directly related to goal accomplishment.

While hierarchical control in a service agency has much to do with the ability of an elected chief executive to implement smoothly his or her policies, it is not clear that patronage is relevant to this ability. Patronage is the bedrock of a strong party system and gives a mayor the resources to control policy formulation and legitimation. It is not a resource useful in the process of policy implementation, however, because mayors in machine cities are unable or unwilling to use patronage to punish opponents of program implementation.

As the Monday Massacre illustrates, mayors are most likely to replace bureaucrats who cause political problems, not problems of implementation. Because removal was unrelated to either competence or willingness to implement new programs, the direct use of the patronage power in this case was actually corrosive of both organizational control and service efficiency. In later chapters I argue that strong parties are corrosive of hierarchical control in a second way. By causing patronage appointees to be overly sensitive to demands from ward organizations for services, strong parties force those appointees to ignore procedures implementing central control.

This chapter has emphasized the effects of the formal control system on bureaucratic behavior. Because of the special problems of control that existed in the Department of Buildings, administrators were forced to rely heavily on these explicit means of control. In organizations less plagued with such visible lapses in organizational control, the formal control structure may receive less emphasis. Indeed, most bureaucrats probably obey the dictates of central management less for reasons of explicit incentives, whether negative or positive, than because of general role expectations concerning appropriate bureaucratic behavior. Even in Chicago many bureaucrats constantly stressed this generalized culture of obedience in denying their own discretion in administering the codes.

The sources of hierarchical control may lie in the bureaucratic culture or in the formal control structure of the organization; in either case the heads of public agencies have access to powerful incentives for achieving cooperation by organizational members. The use of these incentives is neither absolute nor free; like any resource, they may be used up, and their use generates opportunity costs. Nevertheless, organizational decentralization and street-level discretion are not immutable facts of life in urban service agencies. Rather they are both obstacles to disciplined hierarchies and overhead democracy and aids to organizational adjustment and response flexibility.

The emphasis on increasing internal control described in this chapter should lead to increasing bureaucratization in the performance of agency tasks. Yet the insistence on more hierarchy, predictability, and procedural neutrality runs counter to the demands by party ward organizations and organized community groups for special attention. Neighborhood democracy and overhead democracy clash. The next three chapters examine the clash between the norm of procedural neutrality and bureaucratic decision making on the one hand, and party and community group demands for preferential treatment on the other. As we shall see, these demands usually are directed at altering bureaucratic priorities. Because city bureaucrats operate in a world of scarce resources, they formally allocate outputs according to rules, such as keying outputs according to judged severity of the problems they face. Community groups and ward organizations want their problems solved first, leaving other neighborhoods to fend for themselves.

Chapter 5 presents a quantitative analysis of the relative influence of ward organizations, community groups, and bureaucratic procedures in the distribution of building-regulation outputs. Chapter 6 examines in detail how ward organizations are able to produce service outputs for their constituents. Chapter 7 examines the effect on the internal operation of the Building Department of the conflict between neighborhood-based demands for preferential treatment and hierarchically imposed bureaucratic decision rules.

5

Service Distribution

Recent urban policy research has documented the connection between procedurally neutral bureaucratic decision rules and the distribution of urban public services.[1] These rules, adopted primarily to deal with the repetitive tasks that urban public service bureaucracies must perform in making services available to citizens, have the unintended consequence of determining what groups and neighborhoods receive what levels of service.[2] This research has discredited what Lineberry terms the "underclass hypothesis": because of lack of political power or because of ingrained discrimination, neighborhoods inhabited by the poor and minority groups get less service, or the service they do receive is poorer.[3] The wealthy do not seem to be able to gain service benefits consistently, and there is no evidence to indicate that electoral coalitions account for variations in public services. The primary explanation for service distribution is bureaucratic rather than political.

Yet politics, particularly politics played out in a bureaucratic milieu, concerns perhaps more than anything else using and manipulating rules for group or individual gain. Some groups are doubtless better than others in making use of bureaucratic procedures to gain their ends. If these groups are linked to urban neighborhoods, and if they are successful in using bureaucratic procedures to obtain services, then their neighborhoods will receive more or better services than would be the case if the bureaucratic decision rules operated without interference.

Intermediary groups link citizens to government. As government becomes more and more bureaucratic, these intermediary groups increasingly must deal with complex organizational structures to obtain desired benefits. Yet it is an open question whether such groups are able to do so. In most cases citizens are on their own in dealing with public bureaucracies, interacting with agency officials directly rather than going through an intermediary process. In that case, the citizen is likely to be treated most bureaucratically, and will receive service according to service-delivery rules, unhindered by the influence of intermediary organizations. On the other hand, intermediary organizations—parties, interest groups, and even independently acting elected officials—may be able to take advantage of bureaucratic procedures to secure benefits, or even to change the rules or alter their impact.

This chapter analyzes the role of intermediary groups in the building-regulation process in Chicago, using data from city agencies and other sources. The primary issue is whether citizens are linked in any meaningful way to the service bureaucracy through mediating structures, and whether these linkages, if they exist, affect the distribution of services to the neighborhoods represented by these organizations.

Citizens' demands for services come through a limited number of channels. These include the party organizations, community groups, and elected officials; citizens may also contact the service bureaucracy directly. The efficacy of these mediating structures will, of course, vary with a city's political and governmental characteristics. Party officials are not likely to be effective where party structures are weak, and elected officials chosen from wards may be more important channels of citizens' demands than those chosen at large. The major advantage of studying these linkage processes in Chicago is that each of the major intermediary groups is alive and well; hence we may estimate their relative efficacy in at least one city.

Municipal Regulatory Agencies

Municipal regulatory agencies engage in activities aimed at changing the behavior of the individuals who are the targets of the regulatory action. Government uses coercion to induce compliance and can threaten the loss of property or liberty. These regulatory activities include enforcing the building code, the housing codes, and the environmental code, as well as fire prevention.

All municipal regulatory agencies possess the following: (1) a method of acquiring information defining the universe of potential targets; (2) a process for determining targets requiring action; (3) a process for determining the intensity of agency effort to be used in attempting to achieve compliance; and (4) a standard that indicates when compliance has been achieved. In the language of policy analysis, the process of local regulation involves inputs (1), efforts or outputs (2 and 3), and outcomes or impacts (4).

Levers of Action. Urban intermediary groups are primarily interested in impact, in solutions to neighborhood problems. The difficulty lies in finding and using the processes likely to have maximum impact.

Intermediary groups may intervene in three ways to raise the level of services delivered to their neighborhoods. First, they may stimulate demands on government and thus stimulate action. If a service agency is attuned to responding to citizens' demands for service, a group can improve service to its constituents by increasing demand.

In the second place, intermediary groups may be able to take advantage of special attention rules, either explicit or implicit, that result in better service for some neighborhoods.[4] If agencies are more sensitive to demands from neighborhoods represented by strong party organizations or community groups, then the linkage between citizens and municipal outputs will be strengthened. This violates bureaucratic procedural neutrality or what is often termed the norm of neutral competence.[5]

Finally, intermediary groups can facilitate government regulatory programs by intervening in the compliance process. It may be possible to convince the targets of government action to comply with agency directives. Rather than intervene in the bureaucratic process, the group tries to influence the target. This situation has been termed *coproduction*.[6]

Hypotheses

Intermediary Groups. To make full use of the data gathered, I shall set up several research hypotheses, develop a model based on these hypotheses, and then use the data to test the model.

If intermediary organizations are stronger in some neighborhoods than in others, and if they are effective in securing services, then those neighborhoods will be disproportionately benefited. Hence our first interest is in relating the organizational strength of intermediary groups to neighborhood social conditions. Using the existing literature on urban parties, we may hypothesize that party organizations will be stronger in neighborhoods composed of citizens of southern or eastern European stock, where citizens are relatively poor, but where there are relatively high proportions of homeowners.[7]

The literature on neighborhood support for community organizations is less precise, partly because of the variety of urban community organizations. There are organizations for homeowners and for middle-class renters, as well as for the poor. It seems sensible to assume that community organizations will be strong where party organizations are strong. This would be the case if the neighborhood political culture tends generally to support organizations. In addition, it seems reasonable to hypothesize that community groups are particularly active in housing-code enforcement where there are numerous renters. These hypotheses may be stated briefly as follows:

HYPOTHESIS 1. Party organizations will be stronger where there are concentrations of European ethnic homeowners of low to moderate incomes.

HYPOTHESIS 2. Community organizations will be strong (a) where the party is strong, and (b) where there are numerous renters.

Citizen Demands. By initiating demands for service, or by stimulating citizens to do so, urban intermediary groups can affect the service-delivery process. One key question concerns whether intermediary organizations have a stimulative or substitutive effect on the demand process. Are there more demands where such organizations are strong than in demographically similar neighborhoods where they are weak, or are the demands that would normally be forwarded to service agencies anyway simply channeled through linkage organizations? Of course, a final possibility is that organizations have no effect whatsoever on the demand process.

To a substantial degree, the demands from urban neighborhoods directed at municipal service bureaucracies are based on need. There are generally fewer demands from neighborhoods that have little use for housing-code enforcement activities than from neighborhoods plagued by deteriorating housing. This is true even though those neighborhoods with proportionally fewer demands are characterized by higher income and levels of education, both of which are associated with high social and political participation.[8] What effects do intermediary organizations have on a process that would doubtless occur regardless of what community groups, party organizations, and other urban linkage organizations do? The hypotheses concerning citizen demands may be stated briefly as follows:

HYPOTHESIS 3. Citizen demands for government action will be more numerous where intermediary organizations are strong, all other things being equal. (This is the stimulation effect.)

HYPOTHESIS 4. A high proportion of citizen demands will be mediated by party organizations and community groups where these groups are strong. (This is the substitution effect.)

Agency Outputs. Municipal agencies distribute services according to certain internal decision-making processes. The literature suggests three types of decision making in these agencies: the decision-rule hypothesis, the attention-rule hypothesis, and the street-level discretion hypothesis.

The decision-rule hypothesis holds that municipal service agencies employ standard bureaucratic decision rules in deciding where to direct effort. These decision rules are procedurally neutral and do not openly benefit or harm any particular person or class of persons. However, these decision rules can be biased toward some citizens in their operation.

Two decision rules seem particularly likely to be adopted by code-enforcement agencies (and probably by most municipal regulatory agencies). The agency may respond to citizen demand, or it may respond to (agency-defined) need for service. Response to citizen demands is likely because such demands are an inexpensive method of acquiring information for the agency. They indicate where potential code violations or other service problems exist. All other things being equal, using this decision rule implies that more service effort will be directed at high-demand neighborhoods.

Response to agency-defined need means that neighborhoods with decaying housing stock will receive more government service. In Chicago, responses are often determined by the wording and the administration of the municipal housing code. While agency personnel are required to exercise considerable judgment regarding code violations, inspectors and supervisors are not supposed to exercise much discretion. If a violation is identified, personnel are supposed to follow standard procedures for all areas of the city.

If bureaucratic decision rules are the sole basis for agency action, then the only way that intermediary groups can influence service delivery is to stimulate citizen demands. The decision-rule hypothesis can be stated as follows:

HYPOTHESIS 5. More government effort will be directed at neighborhoods (a) with more demands for service; and (b) with deteriorating housing stock.

It is also possible that some municipal bureaucracies openly employ certain rules that are not procedurally neutral. Agencies may be more sensitive to contacts from some sources than others and thus follow attention rules.

Some research on Chicago has suggested that consistent machine support is linked to the provision of public services,[9] but, as Dornan has pointed out, the empirical research clarifying the linkages between process and distribution has not been undertaken.[10] If there are such linkages, they must exist in the form of either explicit or implicit attention rules within service agencies. Only through such attention rules can the repetitive tasks involved in delivering services accumulate to benefit politically active neighborhoods.

The fact that intra-agency attention rules link political support to receiving service means that different agencies within the same city can be programmed with different attention rules. Mladenka found no evidence of linkages between neighborhood political support and levels of service provided by four Chicago service agencies, but there are three reasons to suspect that these agencies were not as susceptible to political influence as the Building Department.[11] First, three of the agencies Mladenka studied deliver services from fixed facilities (parks, schools, and fire stations), facilities that cannot be moved around in response to changes in the successes of political coalitions. Second, two of the four agencies (the Fire Department and the Board of Education) adopted strong civil service provisions long ago and enforced them. These agencies had few patronage positions. Presumably, attention rules based on political support are more common in agencies containing numerous patronage positions. Third, none of the agencies he studied deal with individualized citizen contacts; demand-driven agencies seem more likely to be open to political influence, all other things being equal. Finally, Mladenka performed no multivariate analysis, so that there is some question whether his analysis was sensitive enough to discern political effects.

Managers of Chicago's Building Department are of two minds on the issue of attention rules. On the one hand, it is fashionable to claim that complaints receive equal treatment. On the other hand, the department maintains special desks for handling the complaints forwarded by community groups and by aldermen. Moreover, quite a few officials in the Building Department are also active in ward organizations, so they may be especially sensitive to demands from party officials.

Attention rules may also exist for the characteristics of citizens. White, middle-class neighborhoods may get better service than do poor black neighborhoods. While this thesis has been generally discredited by research, it is worth testing once more in an agency in a heavily political environment.

In order to distinguish the attention-rule hypothesis from the decision-rule hypothesis one must control for the effects of the latter when studying the former. Hence I control for citizen demands and the condition of the housing stock in this analysis. The attention-rule hypothesis may be stated in this manner:

HYPOTHESIS 6. More agency effort will be directed at neighborhoods with (a) strong party organizations; (b) strong community organizations; and (c) concentrations of economically well-off white citizens, all other things being equal.

It is possible that a service organization will use neither standard decision rules nor attention rules. In his study of street-level bureaucrats, Lipsky suggests that agency personnel will develop routines that run counter to agency policies.[12] They may, however, also develop routines that actually enhance agency policies. If street-level bureaucrats do develop routines that subvert decision rules established by agency executives, then the service received by neighborhoods may not be reliably related to citizen demands, or the condition of the housing stock, or political support. Indeed, this is exactly the interpretation that Nivola puts on his finding that in Boston code enforcement does not vary systematically with socioeconomic differences among neighborhoods.[13] Thus we may suggest a counter-hypothesis to the attention-rule and decision-rule hypotheses, the street-level discretion hypothesis:

HYPOTHESIS 7. All relationships between agency outputs and (a) condition of the housing stock, (b) demographic characteristics of citizens, (c) the number of citizen demands, and (d) the strength of intermediary organizations will be statistically insignificant, and all correlations will be low.

Of course, there are many other reasons that such relationships would be weak. If they are strong, however, substantial street-level discretion would be ruled out in accounting for the pattern of service distribution.

Impact. What is the impact of code enforcement? The most straightforward hypothesis is that compliance with an agency's efforts to improve housing conditions is directly related to the intensity of the agency's effort. But certain neighborhood conditions may also be more conducive to agency efforts because owners there will comply more readily than elsewhere. Homeowners, for example, may be more likely to comply than absentee owners of large apartment buildings. Hence, we must control for such neighborhood conditions.

> HYPOTHESIS 8. Compliance with an agency's directives will be more extensive where the agency makes a greater effort to obtain compliance, all other things being equal.

Finally, intermediary groups could intervene at this stage by trying to get recalcitrant owners to comply with the directives of the Building Department and housing court. This activity has been termed coproduction because citizens are able to get more service despite a constant level of government outputs. Where intermediary groups are strong, they are more likely to be able to intervene successfully with owners.

In Chicago, concerned citizens' groups and ward organizations may intervene in two ways. First, they may intervene formally by testifying in housing court; judges report that aggressive testimony from citizens is likely to bring decisive action. The representatives of citizen organizations report that it is very difficult to get judges to act decisively against violators, but they agree that their activities often do make the difference. Second, intermediary groups can intervene by informal means. Citizen groups have been known to keep the pressure on known "slumlords." So have certain ward organizations. While slumlords have influence in some ward organizations, there are more voters who are offended by bad buildings than voters who own them. The coproduction hypothesis may be stated as follows:

> HYPOTHESIS 9. Compliance with agency directives will be more extensive where intermediary organizations are strong.

The Basic Model

These hypotheses may be translated into a single recursive causal model, capable of being tested empirically. Figure 5.1 presents the model. The model contains no reciprocal causal linkages or feedback loops. The justification for this simplification is that the actions of the building regulatory process are unlikely to alter the overall charac-

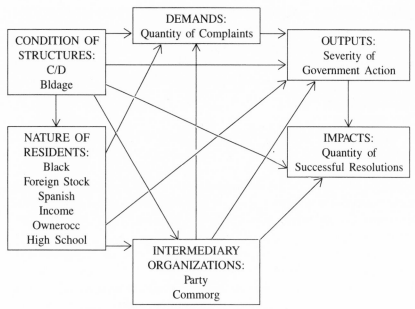

Figure 5.1. Basic Model of Code Enforcement Process.

Note: Definitions of terms appear in the appendix to this chapter.

teristics of neighborhoods except over a long period of time, while these characteristics should affect the output and impact variables immediately. All of the hypotheses may be directly tested by estimating the links in this model using ordinary least squares regression analysis, with the single exception of the demand-substitution hypothesis. This hypothesis implies a test on proportions, while all other hypotheses imply tests on levels or quantities of variables, so that a separate regression analysis must be conducted.

The key endogenous variables in the model are the quantity of citizen complaints concerning alleged targets of the regulatory process, the severity of government action taken, and the impact of the government action, or the degree to which the situation was resolved. Exogenous variables include, first, the characteristics of the targets of regulatory activity: for code enforcement, these are the objective conditions of buildings. A second set of exogenous variables includes characteristics of residents of city neighborhoods. These characteristics should not influence service delivery independently of the concentration of service targets, unless special attention rules make service bureaucrats more attentive to demands from, say, higher-income neighborhoods. Intermediary organizations provide a potential link between neighborhood characteristics and government services. Each set of variables potentially affects service delivery at each stage—citizen demand, government action (outputs) and impact.

The Data

To provide an empirical test of this model, I have analyzed computerized records collected by the Chicago Building Department between 1975 and 1979. These records have been supplemented with measures of the strength of intermediary organizations and housing and population characteristics of city neighborhoods. The variables used in this study and their sources are listed in the appendix to this chapter.

Records from the Building Department served as the data base for estimating citizen complaints, agency outputs, and service impacts. I geo-coded the records to Chicago's fifty wards (1970 boundaries) by first aggregating addresses of the buildings that were targets of departmental action to census tracts, and then aggregating tracts to wards. Because the department maintains separate computer files for each of its functions, each file had to be geo-coded to wards separately. I used four files: the complaint file, which tabulates incoming contacts; the recommendation file, containing the recommendations for agency action made by supervisors after inspections have been made; the permit file, which tabulates information on construction permits issued, and the master file, which contains more enduring characteristics of buildings, such as structural features and number of dwelling units.[14]

Buildings and Residents. I have assessed the conditions of buildings in wards by two separate measures. The first is the age of buildings, derived from the master file. These are inspectors' estimates and thus are not fully reliable, but there is no good alternative. The U.S. census estimates of ages of buildings also are not altogether reliable; moreover, the census estimates do not contain sufficient variation for an older city (structures built before 1940 are tabulated together).

The second measure is the ratio of the number of new construction permits issued to the number of demolition permits issued, 1976–79. These data are reliable, and they indicate the process of neighborhood investment and disinvestment. The variables indicating the demographic characteristics of ward residents come from standard census sources.

Party Ward Organizations. Where ward organizations do well elec-torally, they are likely to have the resources to channel citizens' demands for service more effectively.[15] Kemp and Lineberry argue that it is not enough for a ward organization to turn out a high percentage for the machine-backed candidate in an election.[16] Rather, it is the actual number of votes that is important—particularly the number of votes by which the machine's candidate exceeds the opposition candidate. The index of ward organizations' strength used here is based on the deliv-erability index developed by Kemp and Lineberry, which takes into consideration both turnout and direction. The best wards, from the organization's perspective, are those that both turn out large numbers of voters and support the organization's candidates without fail; Kemp and Lineberry term these wards "deliverable."

Of particular interest to the Democratic party organization are the offices at the bottom of the general election ballot, such as Cook County board chairman, county tax assessor, and sheriff. Since these are county-wide offices, the organization must turn out enough voters to offset traditional Republican allegiances in the suburbs—taking advantage, of course, of the natural inclinations of city voters to support the Demo-crats. These county offices control substantial patronage. City precinct captains often request that voters support the candidates for minor office even if they desert the party candidates for governor or senator.

The measure of ward power used here is the number of Democratic votes for Cook County sheriff in 1978, minus the number of Republican votes, divided by the percentage of ward population under the age of twenty-one (to standardize the measure on the potential electorate). Not only is this office extremely desirable to the party organizations, but also the Republican challenger in the 1978 race ran a strong reformist, anti-machine campaign. The focus on this race isolates the organization's ability to deliver votes and eliminates as far as possible the effects of national, state, and local trends, as well as the personality characteristics of candidates (particularly those of candidates for mayor of Chicago).

Community Groups. I estimated the strength of potential community-group influence from information obtained from telephone interviews with community organizations registered with the Department of Build-ings, and referrals from the contacts made with these organizations. The department's list included many organizations that had ceased to exist but included nearly all community groups active in the code-enforcement process. The list was supplemented with organizations listed in a widely circulated directory of community organizations.[17] This process yielded fifty-two organizations whose personnel indicated that they regularly engaged in code-enforcement or housing-conservation activities. The boundaries reported by the organizations were used to merge the information gleaned from the survey to wards on an area-weight basis.

The measure of the role of community organizations in code enforcement is an estimate of their potential for influence. In order for a group to exercise influence, it must possess resources for influencing outcomes, and it must make the effort to influence the process. The influence potential of a group regarding a particular objective can be defined as the group's resources times its efforts toward an objective. The measure of the influence potential of community groups in the code-enforcement process used here is the resources possessed (the number of years the organization has been in existence times the number of full-time equivalent paid staff) times the number of code-enforcement activities engaged in (referring complaints, recording violations, initiating complaints, testifying in housing court). This measure is admittedly imperfect, yet it does include indicators of the bases of community groups' influence.[18]

Model Estimation

The first step in estimating the model of figure 5.1 was to examine a matrix of intercorrelations among independent variables to check for potential multicollinearity. The matrix indicated that two problems existed, one very severe. First, the percentage of black and percentage of foreign stock correlate .95, so that, practically speaking, it will not be possible to obtain independent estimates for these two variables. Percentage of foreign stock was therefore dropped from the stock of independent variables. Second, the two variables assessing the conditions of structures in wards correlate .79. Little construction occurs in old neighborhoods. All other correlations are below .65 in absolute value.

Since the model is recursive, ordinary least squares regression analysis may be used to estimate the equations implied by figure 5.1. The general approach used in estimating regression equations was to regress each dependent variable on the variables which figure 5.1 indicates should serve as independent variables, drop those that do not reach standard levels of statistical significance (.05), and then re-estimate the equation. Variables were dropped in a backwards stepwide process in order to guard against collinearity effects as far as possible.[19]

Findings

Intermediary Group Strength. Our first interest in model estimation is assessing the social and economic determinants of intermediary-group strength. Relevant regression equations are presented in table 5.1. The equation for party strength in table 5.1 indicates that the Democratic organization is strong where incomes are lower, where owners occupy their homes, and where new construction is low. When these factors are controlled, there is no direct influence from the racial composition of the ward.

The specialized strength of community organizations in code enforcement tends to follow party strength, as is indicated in the second regression equation of table 5.1. Community organizations also tend to be strong where there are relatively many renters. Here is where the specialized character of the influence potential doubtless plays a role; community organizations involved in code enforcement may act on behalf of tenants against landlords.

The Demand Process: Stimulation Effects. Stimulation effects exist when intermediary groups are able to generate demands beyond what would be generated by citizens acting independently. If we regress service demands on ward characteristics and the variables assessing intermediary-group strength, the regression coefficients for civic groups and ward organizations will be positive and statistically significant only if these groups add complaints beyond what could be predicted from information about the characteristics of buildings and their occupants alone. Stimulation effects are estimated by using the incidence of contacts from the Building Department's complaint file to assess demand.[20] Logarithms were taken for citizen demands; such an approach is particularly appropriate when the dependent variable is a count of discrete occurrences.[21] The final equation is presented in table 5.1.

Variations in complaint incidence are strikingly predictable from the three significant independent variables, as is indicated by a coefficient of determination for the equation of .72. The three significant variables are the measure of neighborhood investment (C/D), which is negatively related to the incidence of complaints; the proportion of owner-occupants in the ward, also negatively related to complaints; and the

Table 5.1. Model Estimation

Strength of Intermediary Organizations

Party = 238.08 − 0.019 Income + 2.403 Ownerocc − 5.152 C/D
t: 6.41 − 4.31   5.32   − 2.77
Partial r   − .54   .62   − .38
          R^2 = .445; F = 12.32

Commorg = 130.25 + 0.913 Party − 2.284 Ownerocc
t: 2.30   2.24   − 2.33
Partial r   .31   − .32
          R^2 = .170; F = 4.81

Demands: Stimulation

Log (Complaint) = 1.014 − 0.033 C/D − 0.012 Ownerocc + 0.0025 Party
t: 9.76 − 2.48   − 4.13   3.04
Partial r   − .34   − .52   .40
          R^2 = .719; F = 39.19

Demands: Substitution

% Commorg = 2.061 + 0.0048 Commorg − 0.0346 Bldage
t: 3.18   4.71   − 2.87
Partial r   .57   − .39
          R^2 = .338; F = 12.00

% Official = 0.841 + 0.061 Party − 0.080 Black
t: 0.56   4.63   − 4.23
Partial r   .56   − .52
          R^2 = .399; F = 15.63

Agency Outputs: Incidence of Severe Actions

Log (Severe) = − 1.389 + 0.198 Log (Complaint) + 0.022 Bldage + 0.003 Party
t: − 10.83   4.84   7.54   4.94
Partial r   .58   .74   .59
          R^2 = .878; F = 110.68

Impact of Agency Action

Repair = 0.411 + 0.165 Severe + 0.002 Party
t: 4.75   4.15   1.95
Partial r   .52   .27
          R^2 = .538; F = 27.35

Source: Compiled by the author.

Note: All variables are as defined in the appendix, except:

  % Commorg: Proportion of complaints from ward coming from community organizations.

  % Official: Proportion of complaints from ward directed at an alderman or building department official.

strength of party organizations, which is positively related to contacting. The variable assessing community organizations was not significant.

Complaints are high, then, in wards where neighborhood investment is low, in wards with high proportions of renters, and in wards where the party is strong. In Chicago the party is an independent source of complaints about code enforcement, but community organizations do not generally stimulate demands beyond what would be generated anyway.

The Demand Process: Substitution Effects. Substitution effects can be studied because of the system of source codes maintained by the Building Department. The source codes provide information on the channel through which the complaint comes into the department. While there are a number of categories, the most important are the Building Department's complaint desk, the Mayor's Office of Inquiry and Information, community organizations, aldermen, referrals from other city agencies, and direct contact with code-enforcement officials.

The vast majority of complaints (89.6 percent) are direct, unmediated contacts with government.[22] Yet the totals mask wide variability. In the Eleventh Ward, a machine stronghold, only 28.8 percent of contacts with the department were unmediated, but in the four black wards on the west side of the city, 98.2 percent of contacts came directly from citizens.

Do citizens rely more on intermediary organizations to channel demands on city agencies where these organizations are strong? The reliance on a channel of access may be measured by the percentage of complaints whose source is that channel. If we regress this variable on ward characteristics and strength of intermediary organizations, we expect the coefficient for the latter to be positive and statistically significant. The results are shown in table 5.1.

The first equation presents results for reliance on civic organizations as a linkage channel. It indicates that there is a substitution effect; complaints whose source was a community organization are a higher proportion of all complaints in wards where community organizations are strong. Independently, there is a tendency for citizens to rely more on community organizations to forward their complaints to the Building Department where buildings are newer.

Party ward organizations may also serve such a substitutive function in the demand process, as may the ward aldermen. While the Building Department records complaints from aldermen, it does not do so for complaints coming from ward organizations. Interviews with department officials indicated that party officials were likely to transmit their complaints about code enforcement directly to line officials—particularly bureau chiefs and the heads of the geographic districts in the Conservation Division, which handles the majority of complaints. The measure I have employed to assess the reliance on party as a complaint channel is the percent of complaints whose source is an official of the Building Department. While some of these complaints were not party-generated, most were.

When the Democratic party organization controls the aldermanic seat, the offices of the alderman and those of the organization are linked. During 1978 only three independent, antimachine aldermen, and no Republican aldermen, sat on the council. Because it serves no useful purpose to segregate complaints handled by the alderman from those handled by the ward organization, I have combined complaints from these sources in the final measure.

Table 5.1 contains the regression equation for substitution effects. Party strength is positively related to the degree of reliance on city officials to transmit complaints; where the party is strong, citizens rely on city officials, both elected and appointed, to handle their complaints about code enforcement.

Agency Outputs. The relevant equation for outputs is in table 5.1. There the dependent variable is the incidence of more severe agency actions taken in 1978 as a proportion of housing units in the ward. A severe action is deemed to have been taken when a case was either sent directly to housing court or to the department's compliance board, which is an internal hearing procedure for cases that do not immediately threaten health or safety. Housing court, of course, may or may not move expeditiously against violators, but the court at least possesses legal sanctions to act; the agency does not. Logarithms were taken for the dependent variable; the table presents the final equation after insignificant variables were eliminated.[23]

The equation indicates that street-level discretion does not affect the overall distribution of agency actions. The incidence of severe actions is highly predictable from the three significant variables in the equation (incidence of complaints, age of buildings, and strength of party organization); the coefficient of determination indicates that almost 88 percent of the variability in agency outputs can be explained.

The bureaucratic decision-rule hypothesis is strongly supported by the equation. Both the number of complaints and the age of buildings are significantly related to severity. High-complaint neighborhoods, and, independently, neighborhoods composed of older buildings, receive stronger responses from the agency. Moreover, as is indicated by the partial correlation, the age of buildings is the most important determinant of agency outputs.

Finally, the attention-rule hypothesis also receives support. There is no indication of discrimination on the basis of race or class, since these variables are insignificantly related to agency outputs. Moreover, communities with active civic organizations are not better served. However, wards with effective ward organizations do receive special attention. Even with other factors controlled, wards with strong party organizations receive more agency services than do wards not so blessed.

The Impact of Agency Action. Citizens are not particularly impressed with government action, unless that action solves problems. A precondition of impact is compliance; only if a building owner complies with a directive from the Building Department or an order from housing court can results be achieved. I have used the number of permits taken out in response to an order from the Building Department as an indicator of compliance.[24]

The final regression equation for compliance is presented in table 5.1. Only the variables assessing agency outputs and the efficacy of ward organizations are significant determinants of the extent to which owners comply with building-code violations by taking out repair permits. The two variables measuring conditions of structures were not significant, surprisingly; one would think that owners in deteriorated neighborhoods would be less likely to take out such permits. An agency's effort is directly related to outcomes; the more numerous the severe actions taken, the higher the level of compliance. Neighborhood problems are more likely to be solved if the agency's effort is extensive.

A more interesting finding, however, is the influence of party. Even when other factors are controlled, party—that is, strong ward organization—emerges as a determinant of compliance. The relationship is not as strong as others in the model, but is statistically significant (for the one-tailed test that is appropriate when directionality of regression coefficients is implied by theory).

Conclusions and Interpretations

The Ubiquitous Party. The most consistent finding to emerge from this research is the influence of the political party structure at all stages of the service-delivery process. Indeed, the complex network of variables

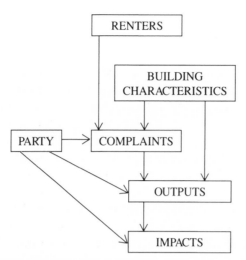

Figure 5.2. Statistically Significant Links in the Model of Figure 5.1.

that were initially postulated as affecting code enforcement collapses into the simple model diagrammed in figure 5.2. Of all the variables entered into the different stages of the model, only the strength of ward organizations is significant at each of the stages of the code-enforcement process: the citizen-contact stage, the output stage (assessed as the incidence of severe actions taken), and the impact stage (assessed as the extent to which building owners comply with directives involving structural alterations). Community organizations do not match the party in stimulating citizen demands, intervening in the internal procedures of the service bureaucracy, or helping to produce service.

Penetrability and Uncontrollability. The standard finding in the study of urban services is that bureaucratic decision rules are primarily responsible for the distribution of services to urban neighborhoods. That neighborhood-based political organizations are able to use such rules for community gain does not contradict the basic thesis: a neutral bureaucracy can exist in a political environment. Yet the findings presented here indicate that the local party structure can influence service provision independently of the system of standard agency operating procedures. This state of affairs does not characterize all bureaucracies in strong-party systems, as Mladenka's study of Chicago demonstrates.[25]

It may be possible to explain the degree of neighborhood-based political influences in a service-delivery process by three factors: the nature of the governmental system in which the agency operates; the penetrability or openness of the agency to political influence; and the nature of the agency's service product.

Reformed governmental systems, including nonpartisan elections, ward constituencies, council-manager governments, and strong civil service systems, are more likely to provide service primarily through bureaucratic channels. Reformism seems to lead to decreased responsiveness to aggregate demands.[26] This finding, which is derived from cross-city research, can probably be explained by the internal decision-making processes of urban service agencies.

Even in machine cities, agencies vary in the degree to which they have been reformed. Certain characteristics of agencies make them susceptible to political influence. Just as reformed institutions blunt the effect of political demands, the reform of individual agencies tends to close them to political influence. The most important reforms include stringent enforcement of civil service requirements for positions, merit- or seniority-based promotions, and protection from arbitrary (politically based) firing. Such provisions give bureaucrats the power to ignore and even rebuke political forces. Indeed, the replacing of attention rules with decision rules is one key ingredient in the recipe for governmental reform.

Finally, an agency's degree of responsiveness to political forces is affected by the nature of the service it offers. Some agency services can be altered only marginally in the short run. The distribution of park land, for example, is virtually uncontrollable in a built-up city; this is also true for fire stations and library branches, as well as other capital-intensive services.[27] Past decisions are more influential than present policy in distributing service. Present political forces can have but marginal impact.

Where services are controllable and where political forces can more easily penetrate the organization, the connection between political forces and urban outcomes is likely to be strongest. In reformed cities, and in relatively impenetrable municipal agencies, one is likely to find a pattern of bureaucratically determined outcomes.

Incentives and Linkage. Even in penetrable agencies, only strong external forces are likely to be able to influence service outcomes over the long haul. While political parties can provide linkages between urban neighborhoods and urban government, community organizations are not likely to provide long-term stable connections between citizens and governments.

The powerful inducement of patronage distinguishes the efficacy of party from that of community organizations in distributing urban services. Community organizations, with their small paid staffs and volunteer labor, cannot provide the day-to-day incentives that are necessary to keep government agencies constantly in touch with citizens. It may be true, as Johnston has stated, that "jobs leave much to be desired as organization-maintaining incentives" because the "lumpiness" of jobs as rewards prevents direct tradeoffs between patronage and performance.[28] But patronage jobs are far better than volunteer positions as incentives. As we shall see in the next chapter, the distribution of patronage is the link between electoral success and success in the service-allocation process.

Appendix
Variables Used in Estimating the Model

1. *Condition of Structures*

C/D: The ratio of construction permits (new, additions, alterations) to demolition permits issued by the Department of Buildings (1976–79).

Bldage: Average age of buildings from the Department of Buildings master file. (The file contains all buildings in the annual inspection program and all those inspected since the file was established in the early 1970s.)

2. *Nature of Residents*

Black: Percentage nonwhite, 1970.

Foreign Stock: Percentage foreign stock, 1970.

Income: Median family income, 1970.

Owner occ: Percentage of owner-occupied dwelling units, 1970.

Education: Percentage completing high school, 1970.

Spanish: Percentage with Spanish surnames, 1970.

3. *Intermediary Organizations*

Party: $(D - R)/\% \, 21$, where D = number of votes for the Democratic candidate for Cook County sheriff, November 1978 general election; R = number of votes for the Republican opponent; and $\% \, 21$ = percentage of residents over 21 years in 1970.

Commorg: Resource $\times$ Effort, where resources = number of years in existence $\times$ number of full-time equivalent paid staff, and effort = number of code-enforcement activities engaged in (referral of complaints, initiation of complaints, recording of violations, testifying in housing court).

4. *Quantity of Complaints*

Complaint: Number of cases handled by the Department of Buildings during

1978, minus certain referrals not generated by citizen contacts, divided by 1975 estimated population.

5. *Severity of Government Action*

Severe: Number of cases in which the Department of Buildings initiated serious measures (the case went to the compliance board or to housing court) against the building, divided by the number of housing units.

6. *Impact of Government Action*

Repair: Repair permits issued by the Department of Buildings as a result of a violation notice (1976–79), divided by the number of housing units.

SOURCES: City of Chicago Department of Buildings computer files; City of Chicago Department of Planning, *Chicago Statistical Abstract,* pt. 4, 1970 Census-Ward Summary Tables, Chicago (1973); Board of Election Commissioners of Chicago, "Election Summary Statistics," mimeographed (1978); Survey of community organizations made by the author; Chicago Area Geographic Study, "Population Estimates for the Chicago SMSA by Census Tract and Community Area within the City of Chicago, 1975" (Department of Geography, University of Illinois, Chicago Circle, n.d.)

6

Service Delivery and the Political Party

In Chicago strong ward organizations are able to get more building-regulation services for their wards than are weaker organizations. They are able to do so for three reasons. First, they claim more of the available services. Second, they are able to get officials in the Building Department to establish attention rules that favor them. Finally, they coproduce services by intervening in housing court and directly with landlords.

The previous chapter unequivocally demonstrated the power of the party in the service-delivery process, or at least in the building-regulation process. In many ways, however, the analysis presented there raises as many questions as it answers. Just how do ward organizations avail themselves of the standard decision rules in order to maximize service benefits? All we know from the previous chapter is that ward organizations that do well in elections also generate more service demands than do wards that are more anemic electorally. How are attention rules established, and what accounts for their continuance?

To begin to answer these questions, we will look in two places: outside government, at the operation of the ward organizations themselves, and inside government, at the manner in which the party influences process of delivering building and housing regulatory services.

The Party outside Government

One of the classic myths about the urban political machine is that it provided extensive welfare benefits for voters and that the growth of the welfare system during the 1930s and after thus helped to end the reign of the machine politicians. This is not really the case. It is true that in the past urban machines did possess substantial monetary resources when compared to today's party organizations. These funds came from the contributions of patronage workers who understood such "voluntary" contributions to be a condition of employment. Even today Chicago's patronage workers purchase numerous tickets to political rallies, ward dinners, and the like. One minor official in the Building Department estimated his expenses for such affairs ran three to five hundred dollars per year. Yet the resources of the parties were (and are) quite limited and could not be used to support all constituents in need. Harold Gosnell, writing of the Chicago machine in the 1930s, noted: "Since the political parties in the United States have very limited financial resources of their own, it is necessary for them to rely upon the governmental agencies to supply most of the needs of their constituents who are in want. They act as brokers for the various governmental services filling the gaps left by the red-tape provisions of the bureaucrats. Party workers refer their voters to the proper authorities and try to claim as much credit for themselves as possible."[1]

The role of service intermediary is deeply imbedded in the structure of the urban political party. The need for this function is no less today than it was during the massive waves of immigration that occurred during the heyday of the machine. Urban populations are more dependent than ever on government. Increasing bureaucratization of government and the extreme fragmentation that characterizes most American metropolises mean that a partisan advocate would be as useful to the citizen as ever. The decline of the machine cannot be attributed to the decline in the need for intervention in the service network by partisan advocates.[2]

Patronage

Political parties are organizations whose goals are, quite simply, electoral successes. Patronage workers, local government employees whose jobs can be made contingent on political performance, contribute to that goal in two ways. First, they engage in standard electoral activities such as canvassing, working the polls, and getting voters to the polls. Second, they act as service intermediaries between citizens and government.

Milton Rakove describes the work of a modern precinct captain in these words: "Most of the work of a good precinct captain in providing services to his constituents is not fixing tickets, bringing officials, or getting special favors for people, but rather ascertaining the individual needs of his people, communicating those needs through proper channels to the proper authorities, and providing help to those who are unable to find their way through the massive layers of bureaucracy in twentieth century American government."[3]

Precinct work is hard work. Were the job of precinct captain merely to mobilize the voters at election time, then it would not be impossible to staff the precincts on a purely voluntary basis. But precinct work is much more than that. The job of service intermediary is a grueling, demanding job that requires constant attention to the needs of citizens. It is absolutely necessary that the precinct captain or his assistants be in continual touch with potential voters.

What incentives do the party workers that staff the precinct have to perform this work day after day? Many, of course, simply enjoy the work; many others would just as soon use their spare time in other pursuits. One young precinct captain told me that he had obtained his position with the Chicago Park District only after he gave up applying to the district personnel office and went to his ward committeeman. His job, like many others in the city, came because of his precinct work, and he surmised that the job would not last long if he chose to stop doing political work: "I don't really like politics. I wouldn't do it if I didn't have to keep my job. . . . I always figured that politics had a lot of corruption, manipulation. But I figure that I'll just do the job as best I can, and try to be honest. When citizens have problems, I don't promise them anything. I just see what I can do. I go to the [city] department, the alderman, the committeeman. . . . I'd like to live in Evanston, but I cannot because of my job, this work."

Because of the leverage that party leaders gain because of patronage jobs in their control, the entire political structure is threatened by the institution of civil service systems. Yet civil service systems have been adopted in most of America's large and medium-sized cities. In Chicago, where a civil service system exists formally, numerous employees are kept on "temporary" assignment to allow the flexibility needed for patronage operations. Even there, true civil service systems have been instituted for the police and fire departments. Moreover, courts have imposed on recalcitrant machine politicians civil service provisions governing the hiring and firing of public employees.[4]

In the absence of the very material incentives of jobs and promotions, the ability of party leaders to get officeholders to perform political work is limited. By establishing standard criteria for hiring, and prohibiting politically based firing, civil service systems threaten to undermine the political machine by eliminating the core incentives that party leaders have to use in encouraging party workers to produce. This incentive also works at a higher level: if a party boss is able to threaten a ward leader with loss of his patronage, he can get the leader to comply with his wishes—including the policy proposals of the boss. He who controls the patronage controls the policy-making apparatus. Hence, the practice of patronage has a centralizing effect on the operation of a political system.

Not all precinct workers will immediately stop working with the institution of a civil service system, but the system gives them a resource to fall back on if they decide they have had enough of working the precinct. As Len O'Connor has written, with the initiation of civil service in Chicago "telephone calls poured in from angry citizens to the ward boss, because the man who worked the 'precint' was no longer interested in repairing sidewalks, removing trees, or getting grandpa into Cook County Hospital—now that he was under Civil Service and damned well didn't have to 'stay political' if he didn't care to."[5]

The Allocation of Patronage to Wards

The intermediary role of party in the service-delivery process does not stem from any direct interest of party leaders in services. Rather, that role is undertaken because it is a means to a more important end: winning elections. Intervening on behalf of constituents in the service-delivery process is part of a package of incentives available to party leaders that can be used to influence voters. Traditional party loyalties, personal loyalty to the precinct captain, exchanging favors, and assistance in finding jobs join aid in obtaining services in this package of incentives. This intermediary role can be performed more effectively where the ward organization controls numerous patronage positions. The more government workers available to staff the ward headquarters and to work the precincts, the more citizens' problems can be handled by the party. Hence the allocation of patronage to wards is likely to determine the magnitude of the intermediary effort by the party. We have already seen that electorally strong wards are able to act more efficaciously as service intermediaries. The issue at hand is whether patronage allocations explain this linkage.

Patronage is the lifeblood of machine organizations. It sustains the ward organizations in their electoral activities and not infrequently becomes the subject of squabbling among ward leaders. The "stripping" of the patronage of a ward leader is one of the most severe sanctions that a party "boss" can impose to bring a recalcitrant chieftain in line. Without patronage a ward leader has few material incentives with which to motivate his precinct workers; without precinct workers, his electoral performance will decline.

Ward leadership is able to build successful organizations only where there are sufficient patronage jobs available. Not all ward organizations with numerous patronage positions are able to build electorally successful organizations. Many face voters who are independent-minded and hostile to the organization. Others face apathy. The decline of partisan loyalty as an accepted cultural norm has hurt party organizations everywhere they exist. Some ward committeemen are simply better than others at translating the resources available to them into electoral success. Nevertheless, the existence of patronage is a necessary if not sufficient condition for building strong party organizations at the ward level as well as city-wide.

The Cook County Democratic Organization controls somewhere between twenty and thirty thousand patronage positions in the various governments in metropolitan Chicago—the city of Chicago, the Park District, the Sanitary District, the Forest Preserve District, and the various boards and agencies of Cook County.[6] The ward committeeman, the party official for the ward, controls the patronage assignments in his ward. Formally, at least, patronage positions are assigned to wards (and suburban townships) by the Cook County Democratic Central Committee, which consists of the ward committeemen from the fifty wards in the city of Chicago and the thirty township committeemen from the suburbs. The power of a committeeman depends on his ability to deliver votes in elections; hence, "the real power is wielded by a bloc of committeemen from the inner city wards in Chicago, the black and white working-class river wards on the north, south and west sides of the city which carry heavily for the Democratic party in elections."[7]

In principle, then, patronage jobs are allocated to wards according to their vote productivity. Yet there are many reasons in practice that party leaders might want to violate that principle. The desire to bolster a ward whose electoral results have been anemic, considerations of friendship and personal loyalty, and the necessity to negotiate with the legal officeholder formally holding the appointment power can all interfere with the strict allocation of patronage according to electoral merit.

In the literature of political science there are only two systematic investigations of the allocation of patronage by political parties. Frank Sorauf studied the changeover in personnel in highway jobs that occurred in a rural Pennsylvania county following a Democratic electoral victory in 1954. Sorauf found that the party actually had to recruit people for lower-paying jobs, that many Republicans in skill-dependent positions were not replaced because of their roles in keeping the organization running, and that personal friendships rather than partisan merit often formed the basis of allocation.[8]

A second study investigated the allocation of federally funded CETA summer-employment positions to wards in New Haven, Connecticut. In that study Michael Johnston found that the positions were over-allocated to the Democratic party machine's core wards at the expense of other wards. Johnson concludes that friendships, personal reciprocities, and ethnic networks are as important as strict performance criteria in allocating jobs.[9]

Patronage Allocation: An Empirical Estimate

Studies of patronage allocations are scarce because of the extreme secrecy that party organizations maintain with regard to their patronage rolls. Not surprisingly, there is no available listing of patronage positions in Chicago on a ward-by-ward basis. Hence patronage allocations must be studied indirectly. The U.S. Census tabulates the proportion of persons within an enumeration district who work for local government. Because these figures include both those in patronage and those in civil service positions, they are not direct estimates of patronage allocations.[10]

We may, however, approach the problem by adjusting the local government employment figures for wards so that they approximate patronage allocations. Then we can use the adjusted figures to examine ward-by-ward employment patterns. The adjustments are accomplished by reasoning as follows. Government employment of the civil service variety requires certain characteristics of the work force but will most certainly exclude political productivity. Different job classifications will of course require different skills, but the overall level of employment in a ward can be explained by such factors as education, income, and race (the latter because many local government jobs are of the menial variety, and discrimination in the labor market tends to direct blacks into such positions). Hence if we can remove the influence of such factors, we can

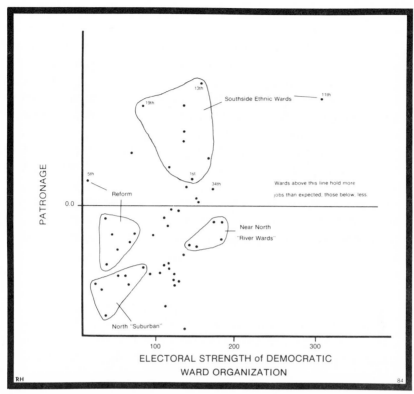

Figure 6.1. Estimates of Patronage Allocations to Democratic Ward Organizations and Electoral Strength of the Ward.

> *Note:* Patronage estimates are derived by regressing local government employment in 1970 as a percentage of ward population twenty-one years of age and older on certain demographic variables. The final equation included race and income as significant predictors (both in a positive direction). Patronage estimates are residuals from this equation.

be reasonably confident that remaining variation in the number of local government jobs reflects patronage assignments plus any other idiosyncratic factors that influence the number of jobs in a ward.[11]

In figure 6.1 I have plotted the adjusted employment figures against the measure of electoral strength of wards. Recall that this measure is indicative of the vote productivity of wards for the important minor offices at the bottom of the general election ballot. The plot shows a clear relationship between employment and vote productivity: the better the electoral showing of the ward, the more patronage positions have been assigned to the ward (making the plausible assumption that our adjustment technique was successful). We can conclude that political productivity is a factor in allocating patronage positions to Chicago wards.

Yet we can glean much more out of the figure. There is a clear split in the machine's best wards. That is, at equal levels of political productivity, there are substantial differences in patronage allocations. This fact alone would not mean much; jobs, as Johnston has indicated, are "lumpy" inducements and are hard to move around in response to electoral fortunes.[12] The most productive wards, however, divide themselves into two clear groupings, and one group gets substantially more patronage than the other. The south and southwest side white ethnic wards that have generally been considered the "core" of the machine, at least during the late Daley and Bilandic years, have been awarded substantially more patronage than equally productive near north side wards. Several of these near north wards have changed from majority white to majority black during the last two decades, yet white ward committeemen and precinct captains remained in power. Many of the precincts in these wards were staffed by captains who drove from their homes in other, whiter wards. In the Twenty-seventh Ward, Ed Quigley, city commissioner of water and sewers, was political overlord of a poor black ward; Bernard Neisten performed a similar function in the Twenty-ninth Ward.

Several other north side wards of mixed ethnicity do less well than comparable south side wards: the Twenty-fifth Ward of Alderman Vito Marzullo and the Thirty-first Ward, longtime bailiwick of the former city council leader and Richard Daley associate Thomas Keane (who was convicted of mail fraud in 1974) both have fewer jobs than their vote productivity would indicate.

These differences reflect patronage allocations that are not based on political productivity. These differences could be rooted in ethnic ties (the southwest wards are—or were until very recently—solidly white and ethnic), racial discrimination, or "friends and neighbors" considerations.

The political power structure in the westside black wards is far different from the southside black wards, where Congressman William Dawson built a powerful submachine in the '20s and '30s. There blacks have held power continuously, without a white political superstructure. In general, these wards are less politically productive than the black wards on the northwest side, with the clear exception of the Thirty-fourth Ward of Wilson Frost, the powerful chairman of the city council's Finance Committee under Bilandic and Byrne.

Just before the 1979 mayoral primary that propelled Jane Byrne into City Hall, a *Chicago Tribune* political columnist, Richard Ciccone, wrote a column accusing Mayor Michael Bilandic of designing a "southern strategy": "The plan devised by Bilandic and his political strategists—Thomas Donovan [mayoral aide in charge of patronage], Edward Bedore [city budget director] and [State] Senator Richard Daley—has been to strip the once formidable Northwest side organizations of key governmental posts. Appointees from these groups have been replaced, without exception, with loyalists from the 10 or 12 South and Southwest Side wards that surround the all-important 11th Ward."[13] Ciccone lists the critical wards as the Tenth, Eleventh, Thirteenth, Fourteenth, Fifteenth, Eighteenth, Nineteenth, Twentieth, Twenty-first, Twenty-second, Twenty-third, and Thirty-fourth. His evidence concerns the slating of elective offices; in a number of cases candidates from these wards replaced officials from northside wards on the party slate.

Figure 6.1, however, indicates that the south side had captured the lion's share of patronage allocations long before Bilandic moved to replace elective officials from the north side (recall that the data presented there were gathered in 1970). Apparently it had been the long-standing policy of the Daley machine to favor the key south side wards with patronage appointments even though certain northside wards were just about as politically productive (with the distinct exception of the Eleventh, which, interestingly enough, has *fewer* patronage positions than its extraordinary political productivity would indicate).

A second interesting split occurs in figure 6.1, this time among the machine's weakest wards. The wards that cluster along the lakefront, and have a tendency to vote for independent Democrats, hold more patronage positions than do the "suburban-like" wards away from the lakefront. The staunchly independent Fifth, for example, home of the University of Chicago, holds substantially more patronage positions than one might expect from its voting behavior (it is the worst ward for the machine). This split may have less to do with patronage allocation policies than with the unattractiveness of many patronage positions to the relatively well-off residents of the far northwest wards. The lakefront wards, on the other hand, are composites of wealthy high-rise dwellers, young professional "regentrifiers" of old buildings, marginal working class, and the destitute. Many residents in these latter two groups find patronage positions far more attractive.

Since the election of Jane Byrne as mayor, the strict control of patronage maintained by Daley, and to a lesser extent Bilandic, has declined. Moreover, Byrne was engaged in a running squabble with certain south side ward committeemen, most prominent among them the Eleventh Ward committeeman, Richie Daley, and the Nineteenth Ward committeeman, Thomas Hynes. Hence it is reasonable to expect that this pattern of patronage allocation has changed recently, with fewer jobs going to the south side. Nevertheless, the data here present strong testimony that, while political productivity is a major consideration in patronage allocation, factional differences also play a key part.

The Party as Intermediary: Citizen Contacts

How do ward organizations deploy their patronage workers in order to handle citizens' grievances, and how do they get the attention of city bureaucrats? Lineberry and Watson have written that machine politics "depends on a very close interface of citizens with city government."[14] Yet a poll of Chicagoans found that over 40 percent of the respondents to the poll had never even met their precinct captains, and only a little over a third had called on the party to help in solving a problem with city services.[15] How can the party serve as intermediary when so few citizens have regular contact with the organization?

There are three answers to this question. First, the figure of one-third who have contacted a party official is comparatively high. Other surveys of citizen contacting indicate that well under 30 percent of citizens in other cities have ever taken complaints about service to city officials.[16] Chicagoans seem to call on political officials more often than citizens of other cities call on government in general. Machine politics may well engender a spirit of participation that stimulates citizens to contact both party officials and city officials generally. For example, Lineberry and Watson report in a survey of citizens in five Chicago wards that over 25 percent of respondents had contacted city government in the previous year alone.[17]

In the second place, citizens do not have to complain to party officials in order to benefit from their work as service intermediaries. In well-run ward organizations, at least, it is common for precinct captains to take initiative in handling service problems. A Twenty-fifth Ward official commented: "If I see a building violation, I'll turn 'em in to the Building Department. Turn 'em right in. Of course, you try to work it out with the owner, contact him, ask him, 'What are you going to do about it?' If he doesn't give you an answer, you just turn him in. After all, it is a violation."

Occasionally such intermediary services are developed into programs by the ward organization. The most successful of these is the Eleventh Ward organization's Code Enforcement Program. Established in 1970 by Richard M. Daley, it consists of two thorough inspections of buildings in the ward per year, one in the spring and one in the fall. Careful records are kept at ward headquarters, so that problems can be continuously monitored; suspected violations are turned in to the Building Department. One Eleventh Ward official described the program in the following terms: "We check every block, every street; we even do the alleys, because we have lots of barns that were converted to garages plus apartments on top, and we have a lot of trouble with these. We make copies of plats—we mark houses that are in housing court and get people down to testify. There is nothing of architectural interest in the neighborhood; in fact, its an ugly neighborhood. But it is clean, and free of crime, and we are trying to keep it that way."

A final reason that the party can act as intermediary even though many Chicagoans do not know their precinct captains is that the party organization works far more effectively in some wards than in others. Lineberry and Watson report a great deal of variation in the willingness of citizens to get in touch with party officials in order to solve problems with city services, with the highest percentage of respondents willing to call party officials in the Eleventh and Twenty-fifth wards, both strong machine wards.[18]

We may examine differences in reliance on the party as a service intermediary using data from the Building Department. The department maintains a system of source codes that tabulate the source of the contact with the department. Most of these contacts come from citizens either directly to the department or via the Mayor's Office of Information and Complaints, a centralized information and referral bureau of the city. Other contacts are referrals from other bureaus. Still others come from aldermen or civic groups. Finally, some come directly to particular Building Department officials. Table 6.1 presents these contacts for 1978 and 1980.

Of particular interest to us are the mediated contacts, which are those that come from aldermen, from civic groups, or from code-enforcement officials. These contacts are mediated, since the citizen is not interacting directly with the service bureaucracy but has requested aid from a politi-

Table 6.1. Citizen Contacts with the Building Department, 1978 and 1980

	1978	1980
Direct Contacts		
Building Department's Complaint Desk	37,067	44,589
Mayor's Office of Information and Complaints	15,050	13,066
Mediated Contacts		
Aldermen	2,373	1,871
Civic Groups	1,859	465
Code Officials	1,852	1,219
Referrals		
Daily Fire Report	1,982	1,732
Fire Prevention Bureau	2,973	472
Rodent Control	31	6
Electrical Bureau	1,235	104
Elevated Blood Lead (Health Department)	4,206	470
General	8,802	6,350
Special Programs		
Lead Paint	681	37
Chicago Housing Authority	381	121
Survey	——	1,486
Heat Complaints* (25,660)		
TOTALS	78,492	71,988

*Heat complaints are handled via a separate administrative process; figures not available for 1980.
Source: Chicago Department of Buildings, Management Information System.

cal official or community group. This includes, surprisingly, the contacts that were directed at departmental officials. While some may simply be irate neighbors of the officials, the vast majority of these contacts have been forwarded by a ward organization to the official, who may himself be active in ward affairs. Hence complaints attributed to code officials indicate that ward organizations are the actual source of the complaint. A particular target was Art Moisan, district director in the Conservation Division of the department, and an Eleventh Ward official himself. He was the recipient of the results from the Eleventh Ward code survey, for example. In order to protect his organizational position, Moisan read the complaints he received into the management-information system before sending inspectors to examine the complaints. This would ensure an organizational record of the complaint and action.

Table 6.2. Source of Contact with Chicago Building Department by Ward Type

Source of Contact	Strong Machine (6 Wards)	Weak Machine (15 Wards)	North Side (7 Wards)	Reform (6 Wards)	South Side Black (12 Wards)	West Side Black (4 Wards)
Alderman	5.7%	5.5%	7.5%	3.5%	1.9%	1.4%
Community organizations	18.3	0.9	0.8	1.9	0.7	0.1
Code-enforcement officials	23.2	0.1	0.3	0.1	0.1	0.3
Direct citizen contacts	52.8	93.5	91.3	94.4	97.2	98.2
Total complaints	7,484	14,129	6,013	8,917	15,932	4,910

Note: Ward type is based on the voting behavior of the ward as assessed by the standard measure described in chapter 5, and the demography of the ward. A full explanation may be found in Bryan Jones, "Buildings, Bridgeport, and Back of the Yards: The Role of Intermediary Organizations in Public Service Delivery," Paper presented at the Annual Meeting of the Midwest Political Science Association, Chicago, April 19–21, 1979. Referrals from other government agencies have been excluded from the tabulation.

The source-code tabulation substantially underestimates mediated contacts, because a precinct captain may call a complaint in to the department's complaint desk, particularly if he or she did not know a contact person in the department. Nevertheless, by tabulating wards by their electoral productivity and their reliance on the various contact channels, we may get a rough picture on differences in citizens' reliance on the party as a service intermediary. Table 6.2 cross-tabulates the source of citizen contacts (ignoring for the present referrals from other government agencies) against ward type, based on the standard measure of party strength and other salient factors about the ward. There it may be seen that there is a dramatic difference among wards in reliance on intermediary organizations to transmit (and presumably follow up) building complaints to city officials. In the machine's best wards 47.2 percent of citizen contacts are mediated, either through party officials, the ward alderman, or community organizations. In all other wards, mediated contacts are below 7 percent. Many of the mediated contacts come from the Eleventh Ward's code survey (and a companion one conducted by a community organization, the Back of the Yards Neighborhood Council, in the Fourteenth Ward). Nevertheless, the differences are impressive.

Also interesting is the almost total lack of reliance on intermediary organizations in black wards. West side black wards, where white party officials have staffed precincts until recently, are served even less well by intermediary structures than south side black wards. While the white politicians who controlled these ward organizations were electorally productive, they seem to have been less adept at maintaining the party organization as a service intermediary operation—which is not surprising, given that most of them did not live in the precincts they worked.

The Mechanics of Regulatory Coproduction

Service coproduction is a "process in which the *combined* efforts of consumers and service personnel determine the quality and quantity of services actually available."[19] Coproduction refers to the impact of services; the level of effort supplied by government is never enough by itself to achieve a desired level of service. If citizens behave in certain ways, they can maximize the impact of the service effort. Part of the party's role as service intermediary involves coproduction. In the case of building regulations, this can involve working with owners, organizing demonstrations against slumlords, and producing witnesses to testify in housing court against owners.

Normally coproduction has been applied to positive government services such as community cleanliness. Here, clearly, the behavior of citizens can contribute to the attaining of public goals. Moreover, community organizations can in some situations mobilize effort in order to coproduce. This would happen, for example, when a neighborhood organization sponsors a "clean up the park day."

Special problems arise when citizens or community organizations try to coproduce regulatory services. Regulatory services are rooted in the police power, and service impact is produced by coercing citizens into behaving in ways consistent with public goals. Community groups and ward organizations are not in legal possession of the police power, although they are often strongly tempted to use that power to coerce recalcitrant neighbors into achieving collective ends. Ward organizations and community groups may, of course, use persuasion to get a landlord to comply with the city's codes, but the line between persuasion and coercion is thin indeed. It is especially tempting for a ward organization to use the codes to achieve political ends. In Chicago a still not uncommon practice is to send the city inspectors down on an unsuspecting small businessman who has not cooperated in achieving the organization's political ends. This can be done even without the complicity of

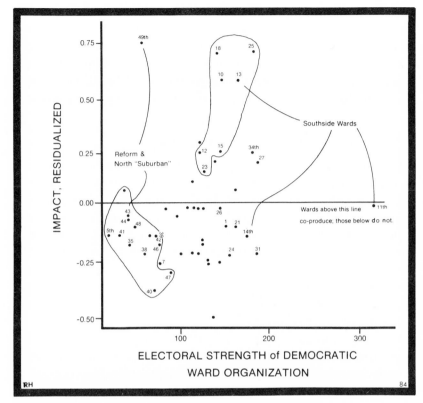

Figure 6.2. Coproduction and Electoral Strength of Ward.

the city inspectors: so long as inspectors come and write up violations, simply making the city's inspectional bureaus aware of possible violations of the city's stringent codes can cause headaches for the small businessman.

Figure 6.2 diagrams the electoral strength of ward organizations against the extent of impact, measured as the extent of compliance with the building department's orders. Impact has been adjusted for the severity of the action taken by the department, since the more severe the measure taken, the more extensive the compliance. Hence figure 6.2 depicts the ability of wards to secure owners' compliance with city codes beyond the impact achieved by the formal actions of the department.

Clearly politically strong wards are able to secure more compliance with codes. The ability to coproduce, however, does not follow the patronage allocation pattern of figure 6.1 completely. The Twenty-fifth

Ward of Vito Marzullo distinguishes itself as an effective coproducer, yet that ward is not overly blessed with jobs. The patronage-rich Eleventh Ward is not an outstanding coproducer, perhaps because that ward organization relies more heavily on formal governmental action than on the informal coproduction process (the organization has invested heavily in the ward survey described above).

The most effective coproducer is not a strong ward at all, but the lakefront Forty-ninth Ward. Indeed, the ward organization does not account for the ward's record of coproduction; rather, it is the active community group in the area, the Rogers Park Community Council, that is responsible. That organization was second most effective on the measure of strength of community organizations described in the previous chapter. Although community organizations do not regularly coproduce in Chicago, they occasionally do so; the Rogers Park Community Council is an outstanding example of what can be achieved. That such spectacular successes are not regularly achieved is a matter that we shall explore later.

Community Organizations and the Party

In the urban neighborhoods of America, few material incentives are available for building citizens' loyalty to community organizations.[20] While it is possible for community organizations to serve as intermediaries in the service-delivery process by initiating demands and acting as conduits for citizen demands, they generally do not perform this function in Chicago. The party apparatus has monopolized the service intermediary function, at least for building-code enforcement. However, as table 6.2 indicates, contacts from community groups are most numerous where ward organizations are strong. These groups have, in recent years, worked cooperatively with ward organizations.

This crowding of community organizations by the political party conditions the role of these groups in Chicago. Open-ended interviews with leaders of neighborhood-based organizations elicited responses indicative of underlying conflict over the urban "turf" between community groups and ward organizations.[21] The conflict seems to have been primarily resolved by a pattern of specialization and cooperation on the part of community groups. Some groups specialize in areas that the ward organizations are not particularly interested in, while others work out a cooperative arrangement with the ward organization. Only a handful engage in protracted conflict with the party.

From interviews with leaders of community organizations, it was clear that neighborhood-based groups in Chicago play four separate roles in the building-regulatory process. While many organizations combine roles, the four polar types are: (1) groups acting to enforce housing codes; (2) groups active in such community-development activities as building repair and rehabilitation; (3) tenant organizing groups; and (4) groups acting to stem "real estate abuses." This latter category included groups primarily interested in stopping unsavory real estate practices associated with racial integration.

Most of the community groups interested in the code-enforcement process in order to force owners to maintain or upgrade their properties could be best described as "conservationist." Several had conservation committees to find violations and lodge complaints with the city or, in the case of cooperative owners, work out solutions without involving government. Few of these groups, as noted above, were particularly successful in this activity.

Table 6.3. Organization Type by Source of Funding

Primary Activity in Housing Field	Primary Source of Funds			
	Local Contributions and Dues	Private Foundations	Public Funds	N
Code violations	11	2	0	(13)
Community development	3	5	3	(11)
Violations and development	3	4	5	(12)
Tenant organizing and violations	5	0	0	(5)
Real estate abuses	4	0	0	(4)
Total				(45)

Groups differed in their sources of funding for their activities. Cross-tabulating the type of organization with source of funding for the activities yields table 6.3. All organizations except those interested in community development or combining a focus on development with rooting out code violations in the neighborhood rely almost totally on local contributions and dues of members and member organizations.

(Several of the community groups were peak associations of the Alinsky model and received dues and contributions from groups and associations within the structure.) The groups oriented toward community development relied heavily on private and public grants to support their projects.

Table 6.4. Organization Type by Perceived Cooperativeness of Ward Organization

Ward Organization Cooperative?

Primary Activity in Housing Field	Yes	Sometimes	No	Don't Know No Answer	N
Code violations	7	2	3	1	(13)
Community development	0	3	4	4	(11)
Violations and development	5	3	0	4	(12)
Tenant organizing and violations	0	3	1	1	(5)
Real estate abuses	2	0	2	0	(4)
Total					(45)

Table 6.4 tabulates the type of organization with response to a question asking whether the ward organizations in the neighborhood cooperated with the community groups. Leaders of community groups specializing in code enforcement reported good cooperation for the most part. "We work hand in hand with them. We have good relations with the committeeman, alderman, and the precinct captains," commented one. A second said "We get 100 percent cooperation." Several noted some variability in response of ward organization. One commented: "We've called on the alderman in the Forty-eighth Ward, and she's been very responsive. They even have a staff person that goes to housing court. This is not true of the Forty-sixth Ward."

Neither organizations specializing in community development nor those interested in tenant organizing reported much cooperation with ward organizations. Indeed, in the case of tenant organizing the response of leaders was uniformly hostile. One commented that times had changed, and the ward organization did give verbal support to the actions of his group. "They don't fight us, which is important. In fact, to have them *not* fight us is an accomplishment." A second complained that "the last time we went to the alderman, he sided with the owner."

On the other hand, groups active in community development profess indifference to the ward organizations. "We don't ask for cooperation," claimed one representative of a redevelopment group. The problems that development organizations have with the building regulatory process, primarily rigidities in the building code and corruption by inspectors, are perhaps less amenable to the influence of political party activists than the traditional code-enforcement concerns of the conservation-minded community groups.

There seems to be an implicit settlement between community groups interested in building regulation as a primary goal and the ward organizations of the party. The groups adopt one of three primary strategies vis-à-vis the party: cooperative, confrontative, or indifferent. Those groups interested primarily in neighborhood conservation and code enforcement for the most part work out cooperative arrangements with the ward organization. Those focusing on tenant organizing have more problems with the party, although several of the more established tenant-oriented groups had suppressed overt distrust and hostility in order to achieve their aims without interference. Finally, groups focusing primarily on community development seem to be able to conduct their affairs without bumping into the activities of the ward organizations very often.

Conclusions

This chapter has focused on the role of the political party at the neighborhood level as it influences the code-enforcement process. The local presence of the party, the ward organization, acts as service intermediary by forwarding citizens' complaints to the city bureaucracy and by initiating complaints itself. The ability to perform these functions is based on the patronage allocation system, which does approximate the pattern of electoral productivity of wards (albeit with variations corresponding to intraparty factionalism).

Ward organizations also coproduce code enforcement by intervening directly with owners and by providing witnesses in housing court. The wards most prominent in the coproduction of these outputs are those electorally productive wards blessed with numerous patronage positions. Some ward committeemen who are particularly interested in code enforcement are able to produce code compliance beyond what one would expect on the basis of political strength alone, however.

Community groups professing an interest in code enforcement are not generally able to coproduce service, although the Rogers Park Community Council seems to be an important exception to this generalization. Generally the actions of community groups are constrained by the interests of ward organizations, and they are forced to work out cooperative arrangements with the ward organizations for avoiding extended "turf" conflict.

Patronage buttresses a complex, decentralized system in which neighborhood-based party organizations link citizen demands to government actions. Community groups, lacking the resources of patronage, cannot perform this intermediary function. Hence, the decline of the availability of patronage not only weakens the ability of the "boss" to centralize power, it also weakens the linkage between citizens and government in the service-delivery process. Demands for service decline where patronage allocations are lower, even controlling for the severity of problems (see chapter 5).

Service demands can be processed according to standard bureaucratic decision-rules, so that more demand will yield more service. But strong wards also receive special attention to their problems. Chapter 7 examines the genesis and maintenance of such attention rules.

7

Decision Rules and Attention Rules: The Political Party inside Government

The Democratic party in Chicago performs two distinct roles inside government. In the first place, it operates to centralize power in the hands of the mayor by offering certain resources in formulating and implementing his or her public policies. The mix of material incentives and partisan loyalty facilitates the smooth functioning of the organization; hence the term *machine*. Mayors and party bosses are not inevitably able to establish such a smoothly functioning organization; much depends on the particular skill of the mayor and his or her relationship with party chieftains. But the levers of power are there, and they are there because of the party organization.

In the second place, the party organization has a profound effect on the delivery of services, at least within certain of the more politicized city service agencies. In this chapter I examine this second role of party and explore the connection between party operations and the attention rules that play such a prominent part in the delivery of building regulatory services in Chicago.

Decision Rules and Attention Rules

Urban service-delivery organizations must regularly make decisions about when to deliver services, how to deliver them, and to whom they are to be delivered. There are three characteristics of these decisions that affect the when, how, and to whom of delivery.

In the first place, the benefits that citizens derive from urban services are highly individualized. Services such as street lights, sidewalks, garbage collection, police patrolling, and building inspections can easily be delivered to one neighborhood and denied to another. These services have limited external effects, or spillovers. If a service is delivered to one household, at most only neighboring households also benefit. While all of these individual service efforts can add up to significant benefits to the entire community (in deterring crime, or maintaining the housing stock, or preventing epidemics), the individual incidents of service delivery benefit only the recipient and his immediate neighbors.[1]

A second characteristic of urban service-delivery decisions is that most are nonunique. No matter how important the individual thinks his service problem is, it is a safe bet that the agency that is responsible for handling his complaint has seen the same problem over and over again. There are, of course, crisis cases: the armored car robbery, the spectacular slum fire, the collapsed highway; but such incidents are not the normal grist for urban service decisions.

Finally, urban service decisions must be made repetitively. Service demands are both nonunique and numerous; hence service agencies must respond continuously to very similar service situations.

These three characteristics of service-delivery decisions invariably lead to a great deal of routinization. Routines, or standard operating procedures, are developed in order to cope with the service task; the only alternative to routinization is organizational overload. Such procedures are, in effect, programmed into the organization in the sense that a particular situation (say, a complaint about a landlord) automatically calls forth a specific organizational response (say, a housing inspection).[2]

Any kind of decision rule can be programmed into an organization. Consider the following decision rules for a building department: (1) act more expeditiously (by, say, taking a landlord straight to court) when the violation is more serious (that is, more threatening to health or safety); (2) act more expeditiously if the building is located in a politically powerful ward. In either case, the decision rule that has been programmed into the service agency will deal with the repetitive, nonunique nature of the service task. Moreover, it does not necessitate individual-level discrimination, which would call for special exceptions to the rule (whether the individual was requesting special treatment on the basis of need or "clout").

In the literature the former kinds of routines have been termed *bureaucratic decision rules,* while the latter have received the label of *attention rules.*[3] Both kinds of procedures are, however, decision rules, because they structure repetitive decisions. They differ in that attention rules bring in characteristics that are irrelevant to the service task: the political connections of the ward organization, the racial and ethnic composition of the neighborhood, and so on. Decision rules presumably do not do so. They, in theory at least, treat every case similarly *except with respect to the severity of the problem.* Moreover, the problem is severe only in relation to the service task. That the individual who is the target of an action by the Building Department is poverty-stricken is not the concern of the agency; this would bring into play individual considerations that are, in the bureaucratic tradition, forbidden.

The existence of preprogrammed decision rules in an urban service organization does not automatically rule out political considerations in administrative decision making. In the first place, decision rules are never perfectly implemented, so that it is almost always possible to gain exceptions. In the second place, administratively established, procedurally neutral decision rules can and do have distinct distributional effects. That is, even if administrators establish decision rules that treat all clients equally except for the severity of their problems, such procedures will nevertheless treat some individuals (or neighborhoods) differently from others. A classic example is the decision rule to respond to citizens' demands. Demand, it would seem, is a good first approximation to the severity of a problem, but the two are imperfectly related. Reliance on demand to trigger agency action leads to a pattern of service benefits that corresponds to service demands rather than service needs, yet such a procedure seems eminently reasonable and fair on the face of it.

Finally, it is possible for attention rules to be programmed into organizations so that some people with some characteristics are favored by the organization, alongside bureaucratic decision rules. These decisions can be quite routine and follow an established procedure. The source of the contact with the agency, not the nature of the objective problem, will then trigger service. This would result in a *dual* decision-rule structure, with both problem severity and contact source serving to trigger agency action. In chapter 5 we found that race and class do not serve as bases for attention rules, but that party does, and that this attention rule coexisted with standard bureaucratic decision rules.

Decision Rules

Ideally, formal bureaucratic decision rules link all situations that an agency faces to standard responses, and are linked together so that any response to a situation will generate further agency action, if necessary.

They have the effect of standardizing the organization's response to the information it receives. As far as the standard routines are followed, they make the exercise of discretion unnecessary. Decision rules may, however, require judgment. Sometimes a situation may be classified in more than one way, and agency responses will differ according to the classification. It can make a big difference to an owner, for example, whether the Building Department classifies his violation as severe enough to be sent straight to court rather than to the internal hearing board, the compliance board, according to usual procedures. The latter action will give the landlord more time to delay and allow him or her to continue collecting rents.

Decision rules in the Building Department differ by bureau and activity. New-construction inspectors follow different rules from those that plan examiners follow. The most formal set of decision rules applies to the inspection of existing buildings, and these rigid decision rules are monitored by the management-information system described in chapter 4.

The Genesis of Decision Rules

Decision rules implement the policies of a service agency so that policy may be applied repetitively and routinely. Because they implement formal agency policy, bureaucratic decision rules are written by agency management and implemented via the organizational hierarchy. They may be modified, replaced, or altered beyond recognition as formal policy clashes with the reality of delivering services. But the formal decision rules that structure the service-delivery process are the policies of the agency. Where decision rules have not been implemented, there is no more than a symbolic agency policy.

One area in which symbolic policies of the Chicago Building Department clashed with operative decision rules is in the area of differential code enforcement.[4] Bureaucrats in the Chicago Building Department were almost unanimous in denying that they ever employed discretion, and most insisted that they had no legal power to engage in such practices. The deputy director responsible for the Conservation Division, after denying that the division ever engaged in differential code-enforcement programs, indicated that departmental policy was to keep the inspectors productive: "We expect them to do eight buildings a day. Of course it is up to the district directors and the chiefs to weigh factors, how far they have to travel, how many multiples, the quality of his work. But we do not want too little work.''

This standard was enforced in all areas of the city. With a standard number of buildings to inspect, however, the inspector in the slums is going to have to ignore some of the more insignificant violations that the inspector in the middle-class neighborhood will not ignore. Differential code enforcement is implemented by promulgating a uniform standard, and bureaucrats retain the ability to deny the use of discretion.

In most cases, however, decision rules do conform to agency policies and are established by agency management. Moreover, they are directly related to the legislatively established task of the organization. These two facts legitimize the rules in the eyes of agency personnel.

Bureaucratic decision rules come into being because of two imperatives. The first is the necessity of handling workflow. The motive for establishing many decision rules is efficiency. In a street-level service-delivery organization the sheer volume of work normally dictates some standard procedures of operation to stave off overload. The complaint-handling procedure described elsewhere is an example of this.

The second motive for establishing standard operating procedures is a desire to limit corruption by limiting discretion. Discretion can be employed for good or ill. Code enforcement can be made more lenient for the widow who is desperately trying to raise the necessary funds to improve her three-flat, but exceptions may also be granted to the electrical contractor who offers the largest bribe. Better, in the eyes of management, to stop all discretion by implementing standard procedures than to allow the possibility of corruption. Because of this desire to impose uniformity, departmental policies are normally implemented through the promulgation of procedurally neutral decision rules.

Nursing Homes. Numerous corruption-controlling decision rules have been implemented in the Building Department during the last decade, with mixed success, as we saw in chapter 3. One example, however, is especially instructive, because it illustrates the limits of such rules.

On January 30, 1976, the Wincrest Nursing Home burned, and twenty-three residents were killed. Within three months the city council had passed an ordinance to require all nursing homes to eliminate dead-end corridors and install sprinkling systems. In November of 1978 the Illinois Court of Appeals upheld the ordinance, disolving a circuit court injunction that had been won by the nursing-home owners. In February of 1979 the Building Department began enforcing the ordinance. How best to implement the ordinance? Commissioner Fitzgerald ordered John Dean, his chief of the Bureau of Institutional Inspections, to refuse to deliver all nursing-home license renewals until owners had complied with the provisions of the ordinance.

This was no trivial sanction. A license renewal would not normally be held up by the Building Department, but by doing so the department could potentially impose severe costs on nursing-home owners. Medicare and Medicaid payments are withheld from homes not in compliance with state and local licensing requirements. This could be especially costly to the marginal homes that relied heavily on Medicaid patients—the very homes most likely to resist the imposition of the costs of sprinkler systems.[5]

Here we have a very simple decision rule, adopted to implement departmental policy in an evenhanded and procedurally equitable manner. License renewals would be keyed to compliance. And such procedures would doubtless have worked, had not the nursing-home business been so politicized in Chicago.

Several politicians have financial interests in nursing homes, and many of the homes they have interests in were not in compliance. In some situations a politician-lawyer will agree to represent a nursing home in return for part interest in the business—an indication of the shaky financial circumstances of the home. Two particularly well-connected politicians became deeply involved in the nursing-home industry—Alderman Edward Burke, ward committeeman of the southwest-side Fourteenth Ward, and Daniel O'Brien, state representative and ward committeeman of the Forty-third Ward. Burke paid a visit to Commissioner Fitzgerald and emerged with his license. This was clearly an affront to the bureaucratic style, so the rules were changed in order to treat all owners equally. All licenses were approved "on affidavit," which required owners to sign an agreement to comply with the ordinance.

By the time 1980 licenses were due, the majority of homes had still not complied, and once again licenses were held. Burke again went to see the commissioner of the department, now William Duggan, a former police inspector who had been brought in by Mayor Byrne with the mandate to control corruption. Duggan was inclined to release Burke's license, but John Dean convinced him that if he did so, all licenses would have to be approved. Duggan denied Burke's request. Soon afterward Duggan received a telephone call from Mayor Byrne, who was supporting Burke in a primary election campaign for state's attorney against Richard M. Daley. "Are you and Burke having problems?" she asked. Duggan answered negatively. The 1980 licenses were approved, again on affidavit—this time if 25 percent of the work was done. In Chicago exceptions are almost always possible. But the bureaucratic mentality is strong enough to generate a new rule based on the exception.

Business Licenses. Not infrequently the exercise of political influence results in the establishing of new bureaucratic procedures where none existed before. In the absence of standard decision rules, it is easier to use city codes for private ends. But the misuse of discretion by city officials often leads to cries for routinization. Today, the city of Chicago institutes a series of inspections when an application for a business license is received. The application acts as a trigger for the inspection; it is a well-entrenched decision rule implemented by a specific process and accompanied by a record flow. License applications are accepted by the Revenue Department, which forwards the application to the inspectional bureaus responsible for building, plumbing, and health inspections. The inspections are conducted, and the results are sent back to the Revenue Department for final approval.

Not so long ago, however, there was no such decision rule. Then an owner of a restaurant with a capacity of about 150 applied for a liquor license. This was not unusual; normally the license would have been granted after a police background check. This restaurant, however, was located across the street from a meatpacking plant. The packinghouse owner, concerned about the quality of the afternoon work of his men after a lunch-hour repast at the restaurant, paid a visit to his ward committeeman. Building Department inspectors were sent out to the restaurant with explicit orders: close it down. It was closed.

After a few more such incidents, a clamor of "selective enforcement" went up, primarily from the affected businessmen. At that point Mayor Daley issued an administrative order that inspections be conducted on receipt of *all* tavern licenses.

This example is not an isolated one. Daley, upset at the increasing number of X-rated movie theaters in the Loop, once put pressure on the Building Department to take action. The solution was to institute team inspections—a team of inspectors would descend on the offending theaters and conduct particularly meticulous inspections. The age of the buildings and the marginal nature of the business meant that any such systematic inspections were bound to turn up legitimate code violations. Invariably, the theater owners raised the defense of selective enforcement. So the teams were sent out for *all* theaters; some of them were closed too. Again, an attempt to achieve an aim unrelated to the intent of city codes resulted in the establishing of a general rule or operating procedure as a defense for the original action.

The Political Style and the Administrative Style

Unlike Athena, bureaucratic decision rules do not leap fully developed from the head of Zeus. Rather, they are made and enforced by actual people facing real demands and having to make real choices.[6] Fully understanding how organizational rules and procedures operate and how they are affected by political forces requires an understanding of the people who staff the organization. Three questions are important: What are the social origins of agency administrators? What job conceptions do they hold, and how are these conceptions shaped by recruitment patterns and organizational experiences? What demands and pressures do they face on a day-to-day basis?

Within the Building Department there exists a severe and unreconciled tension between political and administrative styles of decision making. Today virtually all city bureaucrats pay at least lip service to the routinized task-relevant decision rules that form the bulwark of the administrative style of decision making. This tension is perhaps best exemplified by Gene Wilega. Wilega is a precinct captain of the old style. He lunches regularly with Alderman Vito Marzullo, the politically connected Twenty-fifth Ward committeeman. He works precincts in three different wards. His constituents often search him out in his office on the ninth floor of City Hall for help with their problems. He is, in the words of one City Hall insider, "the consummate precinct captain."

Yet Wilega is the head of the Building Department's Document Control Section, where he manages a sophisticated computerized system for tracing the flow of records. He is experienced in computerized management-information systems, a rare talent both in and out of government. "I could get over 30K right now myself in private enterprise," he said (in 1979). His reasons for staying in government in the face of such lucrative opportunities are rooted in his political work: "I still live in the old neighborhood, and I like to do things for people—like pay their utility bills when they need it."

"Are you ever able to do things for people here in the department?" I asked.

"No way. The [document control] system is foolproof—as it should be."

Wilega is generally right; with the computerized management-information system he operates it is very difficult (but not impossible) to "lose" a case for a politically connected landlord. More important, however, is his acceptance of the ideology of bureaucracy—that decision rules, enforced by sophisticated management-information systems, ought to be in control.

It was not always thus. In the past the department had a richly deserved reputation for catering to the machine. In the 1930s the son of a powerful west-side ward committeeman sat in a law class at Northwestern University. The professor set the hypothetical situation: If you needed a building permit, and speed was the essence, would you go by writ of mandamus or by injunction?

> *Student*: And speed was of the essence?
> *Professor*: Yes.
> *Student*: I'd go by ward committeeman.

And that was the right answer, for Chicago at the time. Attention rules could always overrule decision rules.

By the 1950s things were only marginally better. A severe tension existed between the inspectors holding patronage positions and the newly instituted civil service appointees. Code enforcement was lax; no systematic efforts to update the code took place; inspectors worked at their own pace. One bureau chief, originally hired through civil service procedures, said, "When I came here in 1954, this place was like a country club. Really laissez faire. No one would give you any information." A query about procedure invariably brought the reply, "You passed an exam; you're so smart, you figure it out." Such a system gave inspectors plenty of time for precinct work; it also gave free rein to political influence in the code-enforcement process.

As time went on, procedures in the department were tightened. The code was regularly updated. A management-information system was instituted to keep tabs on the inspectors. And the traditional culture of tolerance for the antics of Chicago public officials declined. Still, examples of exceptions to standard decision rules abound.

Career Patterns

The tension between professional bureaucracy and political responsiveness is reflected in the career patterns of the men and women who staff the Building Department. There are three basic career patterns that are in evidence in the department: the "pooch," the professional, and the political administrator.

The Pooch. "Pooch" is local slang for payroller. The pooch holds his governmental post for one reason: to perform political (ward) business. He is generally assigned some task, almost always one that takes but a fraction of his day to complete, and then left alone. The word is out that the pooch has clout. His immediate supervisor is unlikely to push him to finish assignments. If the work gets done, all the better for the department. If not, well, that's life in Chicago. The pooch spends a great deal of time on the telephone, conducting ward rather than departmental business. He is almost never assigned major responsibility, because it is generally accepted by everyone that he is not going to get the job done.

Departmental managers are in something of a bind when it comes to such payrollers. Many managers are ward officials themselves, yet they know that they face clear budget limitations. If a department has too many pooches, the job of delivering services cannot got done, and city administrators know that they will be evaluated, in the end, on their performance in the job, not on how many pooches they keep.

Keeping a cap on the number of pooches is complicated by the operation of the personnel system. One line official in the department, himself an Eleventh Ward official, described the system this way: "We can't do initial hiring. We get them all from the mayor's office. We don't know who their clout is by the time they get here. We reject some by using a test here, but we still get some political hacks. For this new group of inspectors, we've got several good new guys—only a couple of political hacks."

For all patronage positions, a recommendation from the mayor's office is essential. The mayor will recommend only those who have the sponsorship of a ward committeeman (the jobholder's "clout" or "chinaman"). The recommendation is normally blind, in that the department receiving the application for employment does not know who has sponsored the applicant. This has the effect of protecting the agency head if he rejects an incompetent. In theory, at least, Chicago does have a civil service system. Indeed, many positions are filled according to standard civil service procedures. Many workers, however, hold "temporary" classifications. They have never taken the civil service test for their job category, often because it has never been given. At the time of this study, not a single member of the department's Systems Division, which is responsible for designing and modifying the computerized management-information system, had taken the civil service test for his or her position. All were classified as temporaries because no exam had been scheduled.

The temporary classification allows summary dismissal. This allows the jobholder's ward committeeman to "vise" (fire) the employee for failing to perform political work. During the late Daley–Bilandic years, vising became an increasingly uncommon practice, but it was revived by Mayor Byrne, as the "Monday Massacre" indicated.

One of the interesting things about the Chicago civil service system is that it works backwards. Some positions are filled by standard civil service procedures: a list of eligibles is forwarded from the Department of Personnel to the hiring agency. Eligibles have passed the relevant tests and fulfilled other educational and experience requirements.

In order to be a building inspector, however, an applicant would have to be recommended by the mayor's office, which generally would have a letter of sponsorship from a ward committeeman. The employee would be placed on temporary or provisional status until he or she "has the opportunity" to take the relevant civil service examination. The job comes before the certification. This system of selection forces the Building Department to use its own screening provisions (for housing inspector, the applicant needs to have a high school diploma and pass a departmental test; construction experience is favored).

The department's personnel are thus divided into three groups. Housing inspectors, for example, can be civil service or career employees who have taken the tests and fill a "title," or a position that the department has been authorized to fill permanently. They can be temporary employees (one is tempted to use the term permanent temporaries). These are the employees who fill positions that the department has not been formally authorized to fill on a permanent basis—similar to a visiting assistant professor that the dean does not want to put on the tenure track. Finally, there are some civil service titles that are filled by temporary employees. Presumably one of these days a civil service examination will be given, and some inspectors will pass it. Then the title would be filled "permanently."

Once a civil service examination for a position is scheduled, the Department of Personnel is bound to follow standard procedures. Because anyone can walk in to the examination and score well enough to be ranked among eligibles, civil service procedures are very threatening to patronage systems. In Chicago two methods are used to limit the impact of civil service. First, the examination process is delayed as long as possible. Second, few permanent civil service titles are authorized for service agencies, far fewer than necessary to carry out the tasks assigned to bring the agency up to its budgeted strength. This accounts for the three-fold division of the work force: civil service, civil service left on temporary authority, and temporary authority.

Most managers in the Building Department, even those interested in upgrading the quality of the personnel in the department and the output of the agency, are tolerant and even supportive of this recruitment system. The director of administration commented that he "found that individuals who have been recommended by the mayor's office have a better attitude about their work than do the career people." A line official, after praising the head of the city's Department of Personnel, noted, "Of course, he is close to Donovan [Daley's and Bilandic's aide in charge of personnel] and Bedore [city budget director and confidante of both mayors], but he has to be for this system to work."

The Professional. Professional managers come in two varieties: staff and line. The staff professional possesses some specialized talent or expertise that allows him or her to maintain an independent stance vis-à vis the machine. These are the systems analysts, the planners, the accountants who cannot be recruited through the sponsorship system. Yet they are indispensable to the operation of modern government. Just as important, they are mobile. The skills they possess give them access to positions in private industry or with other governments.

Perhaps best exemplifying this brand of administrator is Richard P. Moran, principal operations research analyst and head of the Systems Division of the Department. Moran, who holds a master's degree in economics from the University of Chicago, had extensive experience in private enterprise before being recruited in 1970 during an extensive reorganization. Mayor Daley had just appointed a new commissioner of buildings, Joseph Fitzgerald; the previous commissioner had left because of one of the scandals that periodically rack the department. One of Fitzgerald's first actions was to begin instituting a management-information system he hoped would allow management to assign responsibility for corruption, and Moran was hired to institute it.

Although from a solidly Irish north Chicago family, Moran's experience and education made him unsympathetic to the machine. "My sympathies lay more with the demonstrators in Grant Park in 1968 than with the police," he said. Over the years, however, Moran has become more sympathetic to the machine, and its role of governing Chicago. He tends to consider independents naive in their criticisms of machine rule and sees a clear connection between party politics and local democracy: "I've come to appreciate the machine more since I have been working for city government. The worst elements of the machine are terrible, just awful. But, as they will tell you, they are there 365 days a year, and they do get services to the people."

Professionals are not necessarily disdainful of politics. Their jobs simply do not depend on their political work, and they know it. Moran, for example, engages in occasional canvassing in his precinct in the Forty-ninth Ward, and he is capable of working up a substantial amount of venom for the independents who have done increasingly well in that ward. He has also served as a contact for his precinct captain: "My precinct captain knows I work in the Building Department, and he sometimes asks me to prod a supervisor about some violation [that the captain wants action on]."

The second variety of professional administrator is the line employee who has worked his way up the civil service route, competently performing each job he has been assigned. Line administrators are protected not by their expertise but by their civil service status. They are not infrequently promoted into policy positions that are exempt from civil service provisions because of their expertise, belying the charge that machines only promote the politically connected.

John Dean, former chief of the Bureau of Institutional Inspections, is a line professional. Originally hired through civil service provisions, he advanced steadily if not spectacularly because of his thoroughness and his intimate knowledge of the code. "Nobody, not even the commissioner, knows the code better than John," said one colleague. Dean had few political connections, never lunched with anyone more important than his chief assistant, and, as one departmental official put it, "Dean wouldn't know how to get to ward headquarters."

The machine tolerates professionals because it has to. A modern service-delivery organization will not work without them. "The machine," commented one professional, "is not the Neanderthal that some think. If you are good at your job, you won't get fired. On the other hand, if you are *not* good at your job, you can be political, and not get fired."

The Political Bureaucrat. The third variety of administrator in Chicago is the bureaucrat who was hired or promoted because of political considerations but quickly realizes that his first concern is his bureau or division, not the ward organization. Art Moisan worked his way up the civil service ladder to become rehabilitation coordinator in the Department of Planning, the highest civil service category there, all the while maintaining his political ties to the Eleventh Ward organization. Then came the summer of 1966, with the black activist Dick Gregory marching in Bridgeport, the white ethnic heart of the Eleventh Ward and home of Mayor Daley. Crowds gathered and became increasingly hostile as the hot summer wore on. The ward organization, fearing the worst, recruited some people to keep the crowds cool. These crowd-control functionaries were not appreciated by their neighbors, and, as time wore on, fewer and fewer volunteers appeared. Finally only Moisan and two others remained.

Shortly afterward, Moisan received a call from the commissioner of buildings, offering him a position with the Building Department as district director of the Conservation Division. Daley had arranged a promotion for his loyal sergeant.

As district director of the southwest side, Moisan ran a tight ship. He was a no-nonsense administrator and well recognized the heavily political character of his district. Commenting on the very active ward organizations and civic groups in his area, Moisan said:

> These are heavily political areas, and there was the feeling [on the part of the organizations] that "I don't have to live by the law: I'm above it." These attitudes were reflected into the organization, and the law was not administered fairly. There was minimal law enforcement in certain areas. Then Commissioner Fitzgerald came in and said, "Enforce the code."
>
> You have to be careful here, be fair. Sometimes the groups or aldermen don't understand that. A place can look terrible but still come under the code. I'm not on a witch hunt. There can be a local fight, and they will try to use us in it. We can't get caught up in it; we can't let ourselves be used.

Yet there is no doubt that Moisan felt cross-pressured in his dual role as enforcer of the code and political officer. What does one do if a ward organization wants to act against an owner whose code violations, in comparison with those in other areas of the city, are quite minor? Does one accommodate the ward organization, or follow standard departmental procedure for dealing with low-priority violations? What if the ward organization has ulterior motives in its complaint and is using the city codes to harass an electoral opponent (the "local fight" Moisan referred to)? Not infrequently the role of responsible administrator conflicts with the role of responsive politician.

The Attention-Rule Override

It is not hard to understand, in a city as politicized as Chicago, how political actors are able to get bureaucrats to make exceptions to standard decision rules. Even if such violations of standard operating principles occur with some regularity, however, they cannot account for the connection between wards' electoral productivity and the service patterns described in chapter 5. The individual acts of service delivery assessed there are simply too numerous to be accounted for by exceptions to decision rules. Only if the organization is maintaining a separate set of rules, attention rules, can overall service patterns be explained.

Attention rules must be there; the data confirm this fact. How do they become established and how are they maintained? The answer is that the attention rules are maintained by the political managers who walk the tightrope between city bureaucrat and ward official, and by continual surveillance by "pooches" located in key posts in the department.

Attention rules thus become part of the standard operating procedures in the department. They are not, however, part of the written record. Rather, they exist as part of the informal ways of doing things that are a part of every formal organization. Managers establish procedures that correspond to the interests of the ward organizations. These procedures generally exist alongside the standard decision rules that structure the organization's tasks and form part of the written record.

Not infrequently attention rules come into conflict with decision rules in specific circumstances. In other cases the decision rule and the attention rule correspond, but pressing the decision rule to its logical conclusion will result in undue harm to a citizen. In such circumstances the political bureaucrat will feel extremely cross-pressured. In the normal course of events, he will probably go with his bureaucratic instincts rather than with his political inclinations, because he has come to internalize the role expectations appropriate to his governmental position. He may be thwarted in this inclination by the existence of a network of "pooches" who spend at least part of their days in making sure the Building Department's officials expeditiously handle matters of interest to their respective ward organizations. They are the enforcers of the attention rules that benefit their political organizations.

Decision rules, then, are enforced by the formal organization. They are generally imposed from the top of the hierarchy, although each bureau chief also has instituted decision rules appropriate to his particular operation. They are enforced by formal means, primarily by a management-information system that records the responsibility for action and holds organizational members accountable for what they do and by personnel policies that punish nonconforming members. Attention rules are also buttressed by enforcement mechanisms, but the enforcement mechanism is not the formal hierarchy but an informal network of political bureaucrats who serve two masters and "pooches" who serve but one.

Attention rules come into play when strategically placed middle managers override standard decision rules and dispense service according to the perceived political clout of an involved organization or actor. This will happen only when powerful organizations express continued interest in a certain class of cases. Without this continual expression of interest, the manager is likely to slide back into the path of least resistance: the organization's formal standard decision rules. Hence attention rules are inherently instable, while decision rules are not.

Keeping the Pressure On

Politicians—ward committeemen, aldermen, and ward secretaries—often contact administrators directly about problems in their wards. The deputy commissioner for the Conservation Division, for example, was in regular contact with the politicians. The politicians exhibit a variety of styles of influence. Some just call in the complaints, while others check with the district directors, tenaciously following up their complaints. "[Matthew] Bieszczat and his alderman [of the Twenty-sixth Ward], for example, are in here on a regular basis," remarked the deputy commissioner.

Most of the politicians come in requesting stringent code enforcement. There are more voters who are offended by dangerous buildings than there are owners of them; hence the incentive structure encourages ward officials to act against violators. As the deputy commissioner put it, "The politicians don't come in too often to ask us not to enforce the code. They normally have a positive program. . . . We are flexible on enforcement. Sometimes they don't want to go to court, for whatever reason. They ask for more time; usually we say yes."

In other words, politicians generally ask for an attention-rule override of standard formal procedures by requesting immediate and severe action. Occasionally they ask for ad hoc exceptions to the department's decision rules—to keep a case from going to court, for example.

Contacts with administrators do not stop at the deputy commissioner level. Indeed, it is very likely that such contact would not be effective, on a continuous basis, in enforcing attention rules (although it would probably be effective in gaining ad hoc exceptions). The more active politicians go farther down the hierarchy, primarily to the district directors who are directly responsible for assigning inspectors and certifying recommendations for action.

One way to handle such demands from politicians would be to simply route the contactor to the complaint desk. (This could even be formalized as departmental policy.) Then standard departmental procedures would be activated, and at some point in the future an inspection would be conducted. That was not the procedure followed by many bureau chiefs and district directors. Instead they immediately sent inspectors out. Then, in order to make sure their actions conformed to departmental decision rules, they telephoned the central complaint desk and filed a complaint. This would have the effect of entering the complaint into the management-information system and generating a form for recording the bureau's action, which was already in progress. Sending out an inspector immediately had the effect of considerably speeding up the process, since the complaint-processing stage had been circumvented.

The Green Flag. This action will not, however, account for the finding that more severe agency actions are initiated in wards with strong ward organizations. In order for this to occur, one of two things would have to happen. First the inspector would have to report findings to his supervisor that would indicate violations with more frequency than in similar situations not occurring in politically active wards. Second, because supervisors rather than inspectors are responsible for recommendations for action, the supervisor would have to recommend more severe actions based on the inspector's report than he would normally recommend. It is entirely possible, of course, that both occur.

The inspectional system for existing buildings ensures that each citizen complaint will stimulate an inspection. The inspection checklists and recommendation-code system limit the discretion of inspectors and supervisors. The management-information system allows the commissioner and his staff to make sure an inspection is conducted for each complaint. These formal procedures do not eliminate attention rules, however.

A source code, which tabulates whether the complaint originated from the general complaint desk, a community group, an alderman, or a referral, is printed right on the form that the inspectional bureau receives. It would seem that this is an ideal place for a middle manager to substitute an attention rule for a decision rule. This is not, however, where it happens. The reason is that the bureau chief knows full well that for most complaints, the alderman, for example, is simply acting as a conduit for an angry citizen and does not feel strongly himself about the situation. The source code alone offers no indication of personal interest of powerful political organizations. A bureau chief is unlikely to override a standard decision rule unless more interest is expressed by the ward organization.

That interest is in evidence when there is direct contact between the organization and the manager. The cue that triggers a replacement of a decision rule by an attention rule is no longer as remote as a computer-printed source code; the cue is sitting in the manager's office.

In order to encourage inspectors to be especially vigilant in conducting inspections, it was common practice in at least one bureau to attach a green slip of paper to inspection forms in which, in the words of the bureau chief, "the heat was on." These could be cases that the commissioner was very interested in, for whatever reason; or cases that the chief suspected internal affairs had set up in order to test the honesty of inspectors; or cases on which politicians had demanded action. Inspectors then knew to conduct especially thorough inspections, writing up all violations and following standard procedures scrupulously. The bureau chief, by attaching the "green flag," raised the probability that a violation notice or court case would be filed. The attention-rule override was made operational by this signal.

When resources are tight bureaucrats may have to choose whether to follow formal decision rules or to override them and use attention rules.

With slack resources attention rules can be followed without serious disruption of the ongoing operating procedures, but very tight resources may force a direct choice. In such situations the ward organizations may have to increase the pressure in order to get department bureaucrats to override the allocation priority set by central management.

Such a situation occurred immediately after Mayor Byrne was inaugurated. Fearful of hidden budget deficits, she froze personnel additions. Many bureau chiefs in the Building Department found themselves extremely short-handed, especially in the Conservation Division, where personnel turnover is a problem. Art Moisan, district director for the southwest side, commented, "I got all these cases from Senator Daley. He has fifty cases he wants inspected right away. I've got the clerks going through my card file, seeing where they are, what I can do. He's my boss on the political side, and of course I'd like to do what he wants, but I don't know when I can. We are just handling the court inspections and the really 'hot' [very dangerous] ones now."

In order to handle the cases from the Eleventh Ward code survey Moisan would have had to jeopardize the court inspection program, running afoul of the judges, or refuse to handle cases threatening life and health. He did neither, getting the inspections done when personnel restrictions were relaxed.

The Surveillance System

The Building Department has three different computer operations. First, the handling of documents is facilitated via computerization. Second, computers provide a management-control system that is used to monitor the behavior of the constituent parts of the department and to allocate resources. Third, an information-retrieval system is provided. This allows management to ascertain immediately the status of cases by using any of several cathode-ray terminals located in the department.

Ironically enough, this third use of computers allows well-placed party activists in the department to monitor cases too. Eleventh Warders in the department used the CRTs to check on the progress of their code program complaints, so that they could check with the responsible bureau chief to see if things could be expedited if necessary. Doubtless other party activists use the modern technology to monitor cases of interest to them as well.

A second irony is that political activists can use formal decision rules in order to get department personnel to conform to the unspoken attention rules. Here is an instructive comment from a departmental official: "My uncle was a conservation [housing] inspector. He gave a 'pass' to a basement apartment. It *was* illegal, strictly speaking, but he said it wasn't unsanitary or unhealthy or dangerous, in his opinion. But Richie Daley had sent in the complaint, and he was supposed to write it up. They backchecked him and tried to say that he took a bribe. But people knew him around here, and it didn't stick."

While the bribe charge did not stick, it is unlikely that the uncle was lenient on a complaint from the Eleventh Ward again. The informal access of the ward organization to the department's records allows "backchecking" or tracing the responsible inspector through the records system. The climate instilled by such activities doubtless has much to do with our finding that the department initiates more severe actions in politically active wards.

The Statistics of Attention Rules

In the previous chapter we saw that the patronage allocations of Chicago's wards correspond to the electoral strength of the wards, but that south side European ethnic wards get more jobs than north side wards that are equally vote-productive. We also know that electorally productive wards get more outputs from the Building Department, even when the condition of the housing stock is controlled. If we adjust the output measure, which assesses the severity of regulatory action taken by the department, and plot the result against the electoral strength measure, we can examine graphically the effects of attention rules. That graph appears in figure 7.1. It plots the outputs distributed to wards that are *not* due to the operation of decision rules and therefore includes the effects of attention rules, the effects of ad hoc exceptions to decision rules, and idiosyncratic factors.[7]

Note first the strong and clear impact of party on outputs. The slope relating electoral success and outputs is quite steep, indicating that even small increases in vote productivity translate into rather dramatic increases in outputs.

In the second place, the output graph does not divide the electorally strong wards into south side–north side groupings in the same manner as the patronage graph did. It would seem that not all patronage resources are translated into increased outputs for the ward. There may be a

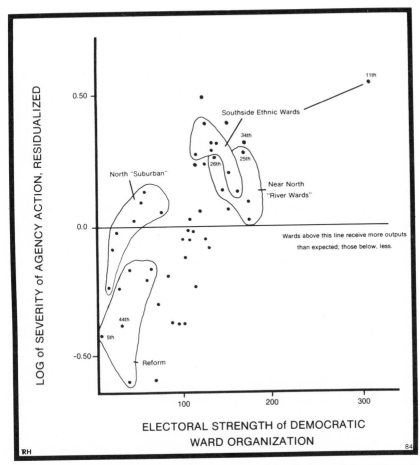

Figure 7.1. Agency Outputs Corrected for Decision Rules and the Electoral Strength of the Ward.

Note. Agency outputs are measured as the logarithm of the frequency of severe actions taken. Actions taken because of decision rules are controlled by using residuals from a regression modeling the decision rules, which used the number of citizen complaints, logged, and the age of buildings as predictors.

saturation point beyond which patronage positions are not really useful in helping to deal with neighborhood problems such as code enforcement.

It is somewhat surprising that the Eleventh Ward organization is not more distinguished in its ability to gain outputs via attention rules. Recall, however, that the organization generates an enormous number of code complaints through its code-enforcement program. Because the program is a "sweep" of the ward, it routinely turns up numerous complaints that are not violations of the city code. Not all ward workers in the code program know the codes, even though the ward organization provides some training. Hence numerous complaints must be dropped; even the Eleventh Ward cannot get nonviolations acted on.

The lakefront wards, which have increasingly voted independently in recent elections, are less able to establish the attention-rule connection than are north-side "suburban" wards, even though the housing stock is in much worse shape in the lakefront wards. This holds despite the fact that lakefront wards have more patronage positions. Perhaps this reflects a general sapping of the strength of the ward organizations along the lake caused by the inroads into the political structure of the wards made by independents. Independents have, for example, captured the aldermanic seats in several of the lakefront wards in recent years. These inroads seem to have affected the ability of these wards to obtain government outputs (at least those not delivered according to formal decision rules).

Also interesting is the success of the Twenty-sixth Ward. Although not one of the favored south-side wards in patronage allocation, the Twenty-sixth does achieve greater-than-expected outputs. Matthew Biezczat, the ward committeeman, is particularly concerned with code enforcement, and regularly contacts Building Department officials. Similarly, Vito Marzullo's Twenty-fifth Ward, not especially blessed in the allocation of patronage but with a reputation for effective operation, receives a disproportionate share of outputs.

Racism and Political Organization

Table 7.1 presents the agency output data controlled for the effects of bureaucratic decision rules in a somewhat different manner. Wards are classified according to electoral blocs.[8] The table also presents the average value of the ward-strength measure by electoral bloc. Not surprisingly, the value of the ward-strength measure varies by electoral bloc. Moreover, as one might expect from figure 7.1, agency outputs vary dramatically by bloc.

The absence of evidence about racial discrimination in these data is intriguing, given the conventional wisdom of the deep racism in the political culture in Chicago and the fact that Chicago ranks as one of the most racially segregated cities in the United States. I have divided the fifteen primarily black wards into two groups in the table: those that

Table 7.1. Building Regulation Outputs, Controlled for Bureaucratic Decision Rules, by Electoral Blocs

Electoral Bloc	Average Ward Strength[a]	Average Value Residualized Output[b]
Machine core (5 wards)	159.22	0.88
South side ethnic (9 wards)	122.65	0.44
North side ethnic (3 wards)	103.95	0.34
Black (15 wards)	119.79	0.19
Electorally strongest (8 wards)	137.12	0.81
Electorally weakest (7 wards)	99.86	−0.52
Northwest "Polish" (10 wards)	62.28	−0.16
Reform (8 wards)	47.25	−1.34

[a](D − R)/%21, where D = number of votes for the Democratic candidate for sheriff, November 1978 general election; R = votes for Republican opponent; %21 = percentage of residents over the age of twenty-one (1970). See chapter 6 for justification.

[b]Outputs are measured as the logarithm of the frequency of severe enforcement actions taken, where severity involved filing a court case or an action before a Building Department hearing officer. Actions taken because of decision rules are controlled by using residuals from a regression modeling the decision rules. The model regressed agency outputs on the number of citizen complaints, logged, and the age of buildings.

electorally supported the party strongly according to the party-strength measure, and those that did not. The electorally strongest black wards rank second only to the machine's core wards in electoral strength, while the electorally weakest rank higher than only the lakefront reform wards and the Polish northwest. These black wards are also divided by the building regulatory services they receive, even controlling for bureaucratic decision rules based on demand and need. Those black wards whose voting behavior indicates mobilization on behalf of machine-supported candidates receive a level of outputs second only to the core machine wards, which is exactly where they should rank on the basis of the ward-strength measure. Those black wards whose voting behavior is not supportive of the machine's electoral aims receive a level of outputs that exceeds only the extremely disfavored reform lakefront wards, somewhat below where they should fall if the ranking of outputs were based solely on the ward's electoral strength.

The only way to interpret these data is to infer that electoral organization overcomes racial discrimination in the provision of outputs. While electorally weak black wards, that is, black wards not supportive of machine candidates, receive somewhat lower level of outputs than could be predicted based on need and citizen demand, black wards that are electorally supportive of the machine receive a far higher level of outputs than could be predicted on the basis of bureaucratic decision rules alone. Moreover, the level of outputs is proportional to the degree of support for machine candidates, at least as measured by the index of ward strength developed here.

The most likely explanation for this finding is not that machine politicians reward black wards or deny them code enforcement because of their electoral activities. Rather, patronage allocation is keyed to vote productivity, and patronage allows ward organizations to produce the agency outputs desired—via, of course, the attention rules that exist in the agency. Electoral productivity translates into policy outputs by providing ward organizations the means with which to interfere in what otherwise would be an entirely bureaucratic process. Not only are black wards no exception to this generalization, but political organization allows them to overcome whatever racial bias exists in the distribution of outputs.

Chapter 6 noted that the intermediary structures for transferring citizens' complaints to the agency were less well articulated than in white wards. Fewer complaints were mediated by the ward organizations or by community groups. Yet this deterioration of the party structure in black wards does not result in a diminution of agency outputs. These seem to be maintained by the attention-rule structure.

The Limits to Politics

In a study of four aspects of urban service delivery in Chicago, Kenneth Mladenka concludes that "distributional decision making is routinized and largely devoid of explicit political content."[9] That is clearly contrary to the results presented here. Is someone wrong?

Not necessarily. It is entirely possible that two agencies in the same political culture will display very different connections between politics and services. There are two reasons for this. First, the outputs of the agencies can differ in their amenability to political allocation. Mladenka notes that he primarily studied the location of service facilities (parks, schools, fire stations), resources that "limit the opportunities for discretionary behavior in distributional decision making."[10] Once a fire station is in place, it is hard to relocate it in response to changing configurations of electoral outcomes.

Second, and more important, agencies themselves differ in their

Table 7.2. Employee Status, January 1, 1974

	Civil Service	Civil Service Leave on Temporary Authority	Temporary Authority	Exempt	Other (Model Cities, EEA, Trainee)	Total
Agency						
Board of Health	1,288	82	743	2	158	2,273
Civil Service Commission	70	31	39	3	245	388
Department of Aviation	496	40	228	1	1	766
Department of Buildings	340	85	185	2	101	713
Department of Finance	129	35	143	3	15	325
Department of Fire	4,498	7	63	3	62	4,633
Department of Human Services	22	2	406	1	42	473
Department of Police	15,442	191	373	70	319	16,395
Department of Public Works	793	139	585	1	34	1,552
Department of Streets & Sanitation	3,320	659	2,380	10	285	6,654
Department of Water and Sewer	1,840	273	1,067	—	50	3,230
Department of Urban Renewal	158	27	111	—	7	303
Public Library	845	53	235	1	500	1,634
Miscellaneous	491	92	1,102	129	107	1,921
Exempt Departments						
Board of Election Commissioners	—	—	—	193	—	193
Chicago Committee on Urban Opportunity	—	—	—	3,289	—	3,289
Department of Law	—	—	—	208	—	208
Total	29,732	1,716	7,660	3,916	1,926	44,950

Source: Compiled by the author from City of Chicago Civil Service Commission, "Employee Figures."

openness to political influence. The single most important key to openness to political influence is political patronage. Only where substantial
patronage positions exist in an agency will there be the political managers and "pooches" to establish and maintain attention rules.

Table 7.2 lists the personnel classification of employees of the city of
Chicago, by agency, as of early 1974 (the only data available). The
entries under "Civil Service" give the number of employees filling civil
service titles. "Civil Service Leave on Temporary Authority" indicates
civil service titles filled by temporary employees, and "Temporary Authority" indicates "temporary" employees hired without long-term ob-
ligations. The latter two categories form the bulk of the patronage
pool.[11]

There is great variation among agencies in the number of patronage
positions. The Police Department and Fire Department, with their own
civil service systems, are almost devoid of patronage. On the other hand,
the Department of Public Works and the Department of Streets and
Sanitation are rich sources of patronage positions. The relatively small
Department of Buildings has a high proportion of its employees on
temporary authority.

Sensitivity to the concerns of the ward organizations is thus likely to
be much higher in the latter departments than in the Police Department
and Fire Department. Reformers, in essence, were able to win the civil
service battle in the Police Department and Fire Department but have
been at least partially thwarted in instituting a vigorous civil service
system in the other departments.

Conclusions

There abounds in the more simplistic literature on machines the idea
that machine politicians simply deny services to wards that are not
regular supporters of the machine, while favoring those wards that turn
out majorities for machine candidates. There are a number of problems
with this quasi-conspiratorial view of machines, including the fact that
most services benefit more than just the immediate recipient. If the
machine does not pick up its opponents' garbage, it may treat its supporters to a plague of rats. If it refuses to pave streets in independent
wards, its supporters may have to use alternate routes to get to work.

There is a more fatal flaw in the conspiratorial view of the machine. It
lacks a convincing mechanism for linking machine support to govern-

mental output. Services are delivered by bureaucracies; hence any explanation of service distribution rooted in machine politics must involve the service bureaucracies.

We have seen in this chapter that the possible mechanisms for linking service output to electoral support of the machine are but two: gaining an exception to the formal decision rules maintained by all modern service bureaucracies or achieving an attention-rule override of those standard operating procedures. There are no further possibilities.

Machines are structurally decentralized operations. The basic political unit is the ward. Hence one expects a great deal of independent, uncoordinated political activity on the part of the ward organizations as they seek to obtain service benefits for their constituents. Moreover, service-delivery decisions are not often made by agency heads, much less by the mayor. They are almost unconsciously handled by bureaucratic decision rules. While it might be possible for a very strong boss to impose a service pattern reflecting electoral statistics, this is a very unlikely occurrence. Such activity simply would not be worth the cost.[12]

Both the decision-rule exception and the attention-rule override require both sympathetic political bureaucrats and sustained pressure from the ward organizations. In the absence of these, a bureaucracy will tend to drift back into the standard formal decision routines established by top management and enforced through the hierarchy. In a modern bureaucracy, this is the path of least resistance.

Civil service systems tend to weaken ward organizations by removing their major source of personnel—patronage positions in government. A rigidly enforced civil service system also tends to remove the incentives for political bureaucrats to replace decision rules with attention rules by decreasing the political pressures on them. As the number of payrollers in the service organization declines the surveillance system decays, removing another enforcement mechanism for attention rules. Fairly soon, political scientists stop decrying political interference into administrative matters and start writing articles about the drones in the "new machines": bureaucrats unaccountable to the public.[13]

Law and Politics
in Housing Court

Housing Court, a division of the First Municipal District Division of Cook County Court, occupies five courtrooms on the eleventh floor and one on the fourteenth floor of the glass-and-steel tower known as the Daley Center. Down below, on the plaza, well-dressed office workers from the adjoining City-County Building or nearby office buildings leisurely eat sack lunches beneath the shadow of the once-controversial Picasso sculpture. Lawyers, carrying their ubiquitous brown briefcases, confer with one another briefly before entering the Daley Center for their court appearances.

Compared to the leisurely pace on Daley Plaza, the activity in the six housing courtrooms is frenetic. Each courtroom is presided over either by a circuit court judge or by an associate judge. Each courtroom is staffed by one or more assistant corporation counsel, who prosecute the housing cases on behalf of the city of Chicago. A clerk keeps records, while in most courtrooms a number of individuals sit on benches facing the judge: owners, lawyers representing owners, building inspectors who will testify for the city, and representatives of the community groups who hope to intervene on behalf of the city.

The courtrooms themselves are specialized. In Room 1111 Richard Jorzak, presiding judge of housing court, hears cases involving dangerous and dilapidated buildings; almost all of his cases have been transferred from other courtrooms. Room 1410 is reserved for cases from the criminal housing management program. Problem cases are assigned to this program so that more time may be devoted to them. The other four courtrooms serve as violation courts; judges there hear cases in which the city has filled the normal run of building-code violation cases. Most cases come from the Conservation Division of the Building

Department, but special calls are reserved for other programs. New-construction violations, for example, are heard every Wednesday in Room 1105; the Electrical Bureau brings its cases to court on Fridays in Room 1109. Some calls in Room 1107 are reserved for overflow cases from the criminal housing management program.

A typical day in a violation courtroom is a hectic affair as judges, corporation counsel, and witnesses try to cope with some eighteen thousand cases a year and about eighty thousand hearings on those cases. In Room 1105 a judge temporarily assigned from another division of circuit court in an attempt to deal with the massive housing-court caseload is hearing cases in an almost-empty courtroom.[1] The corporation counsel has a stack of files in front of him; he is requesting default judgments against owners who have been subpoenaed two or more times and who have still not responded. The clerk reads the case number. The corporation counsel asks for an *ex parte* fine and moves to vacate the case. The judge enters a very large fine and orders an execution to issue, which closes the case and enters the fine. (The average *ex parte* fine was $1,424 in 1978.) The landlord now owes the city a large amount of money, and his title to the property is clouded; but the city has obtained absolutely no compliance. Each case takes approximately fifteen seconds.

After these proceedings have continued for twenty minutes or so, a lawyer rushes into the courtroom and checks with the clerk. His case has been called, and he wants reconsideration. He has evidence that his client has been repairing his property; while not all violations have been corrected, some have. The lawyer wants this judge to continue the case rather than close it. The judge leans over the bench and screams at the lawyer, "The order stands. Motion it back up when all of the violations are complied!" The lawyer, taken aback, walks slowly out of the courtroom.

The judge's attention then focuses on a poorly dressed black man, who has just entered the courtroom. The clerk looks at the crumpled summons held by the man; the case has been called, she says.

"Why are you late?" asks the judge.

"I was in the wrong courtroom. All the violations are complied," answered the owner.

"Either you or the building inspector is a liar," shouts the judge. "Do you want to take a lie detector test?" The judge turns back to the clerk, who calls the next case. The owner, looking puzzled, sits back down, not realizing that the judge has, in effect, denied his motion to reopen his case.

In Room 1107 Judge Mary Whiting is hearing cases from the criminal housing management program. Here the pace is far more deliberate; the frenetic and confusing activity in other violation courtrooms is replaced by more formality, the regular presence of defense lawyers, careful questioning of defendants and witnesses, and the attendance of representatives of community groups.

A typical case involves a hotel with sixty-four units. A previous owner has installed stoves and refrigerators in the units; such a conversion is illegal. The corporation counsel questions the inspector about the state of the building and asks whether any plans or permits have been issued by the Building Department. The inspector testifies that the building is in a deteriorated state and no work is going on.

Judge Whiting asks the defendant to explain. He says that he just bought the building on contract; he did not know about the violations. He is reluctant to spend the twenty-five thousand dollars necessary to convert the building from a hotel to apartments.

> JUDGE WHITING: If he removes the stoves and refrigerators, would that deconvert the building?
> INSPECTOR: Yes, it would.
> DEFENDANT: I have an 80 percent occupancy rate.
> CORPORATION COUNSEL: This building is not that bad, but it continues to deteriorate. No work has been done since July. I request that you issue a mandatory order to vacate. [This is done to threaten the owner with loss of rental income.]
> DEFENDANT: These are minor violations. I have spent thousands fixing the building. Tenants break the building; I don't.
> JUDGE: Are you getting the stoves out?
> DEFENDANT: I am making progress. The tenants will defend me. I can get fifty people to testify that the building is in good condition.

Judge Whiting turns to a well-dressed, middle-aged white woman, a representative from a neighborhood community organization.

> COMMUNITY REPRESENTATIVE: This building is going down. It is dirty, no screens on the building. No grass. There may have been a fire in the building. There is a chance of saving this building, but he's not working on it. It is causing deterioration in neighboring buildings. His tenants are pimps and prostitutes. We got the media in, Channel Nine, then he did a little work. Now he is doing nothing.

DEFENDANT: That is just not so. I worked for Shiller, not Axelrod [in the 1979 Forty-sixth Ward aldermanic race], and that's why she says that. [Axelrod was the incumbent, Shiller the radical challenger.]

Judge Whiting, after lecturing the defendant on the nature of the Chicago building code and his responsibility as a landlord under it, issued a mandatory order to deconvert the building, and continued the case for one month. "I will not," she said, "in the future spend the time talking to you the way I have this time."

The next case is called by the clerk. The same defendant rises. . . .

A third case is called. The inspector testifies that the toilet is blocked and doesn't work. The first floor is vacant; only the second floor is occupied.

The elderly black defendant arises. "I can't get the tenants out. I haven't collected any rent since December 25. The lady there has twenty-five children."

INSPECTOR: I counted seventeen when I was there.

CORPORATION COUNSEL: We have a mandatory order to vacate.

JUDGE: TRB [Tenants Relocation Bureau, a bureau in the Illinois Welfare Department whose duties involve working with housing court] to assist. Can you place them?

TRB REPRESENTATIVE: We're working on it.

JUDGE: Continue MOV [mandatory order to vacate]. Call the tenant to court. TRB to continue to assist.

Next case.

INSPECTOR (responding to the corporation counsel's inquiry): This building is 92 percent complied.

CORPORATION COUNSEL: I recommend that this case be dismissed without court costs, subject to reinspection.

JUDGE: OK.

CORPORATION COUNSEL (aside): I can't believe it. A success.

Next case.

INSPECTOR: There is no compliance. Only two of six units are occupied. There is no gas, no hot water, insufficient cold water.

DEFENDANT: I moved out. They're a gang. They killed a friend of mine. I'm not going back. I called the police, I got nothing. I can't get them out.

COMMUNITY GROUP REPRESENTATIVE: There are gangs in there. We've been working with the police.

INSPECTOR: If you don't get them to vacate it, they are going to burn it.

JUDGE: If the owner can't go there, what good will it do for me to issue a MOV?

COMMUNITY GROUP REPRESENTATIVE: One of the tenants is involved in prostitution. He has three girls on the third floor.

JUDGE: They are just not intimidated, are they?

BUILDING MANAGER: I live where the owner used to live, on the first floor; I manage the building. Can't you do anything? They threatened his [the owner's] life, his children's, so he moved away.

JUDGE: Why don't we just cut off the services; force them out? How about an order to board [secure the building by boarding it up]?

INSPECTOR: They will burn it down as soon as all are forced to leave.

JUDGE: Continue the case until June 21, unless a miracle occurs.

DEFENDANT: What am I supposed to do?

JUDGE: Write to the mayor and the police. I am entering no order.

Urban Civil Courts

Criminal courts, with their power to deprive citizens of liberty, have occupied a central place in the research agenda of social science.[2] Civil courts, courts established to resolve disputes between parties rather than to allocate guilt and punishment, have received scant scholarly attention.[3] This remains true even though the courts established to settle disputes among citizens may tell us as much or more about the urban political process than do criminal courts.

Housing courts operate in limbo between the world of criminal courts and that of civil courts. As in criminal courts, the government is a standard party to the proceedings. As in criminal courts, the defendant is prosecuted by the government; the defendant has violated the law (in this case, the municipal code). In housing court, however, the government is not interested in incarcerating the guilty because of past actions. Rather, prosecutors wish to get defendants to comply with operative parts of the housing and building codes established by local government. Hence the court is in the position of resolving disputes between citizens and government.

The language and procedure of housing court tends to follow civil proceedings. In Chicago the city "brings suit" against a defendant. Housing court is in the civil division of Cook County Circuit Court. Nobody really thinks of a landlord who has failed to comply with the code as a criminal, although there is a criminal housing management program to deal with chronic violators.

Although both lawyers and social scientists have written extensively on the effects of housing codes,[4] there exists only a handful of empirical studies and sound descriptions of housing courts and landlord-tenant courts, the other major judicial institution for dealing with urban housing problems.

In landlord-tenant courts, a landlord is attempting to get the court to grant an eviction notice for nonpayment of rent. This is purely a civil action with two parties locked in a dispute; the court acts as referee. A thorough empirical study of landlord-tenant court in Detroit, however, indicated that the court did not act without bias. It operated primarily as a mechanism by which a landlord could expeditiously recover his premises, regardless of the defenses raised by the tenant.[5] While almost half of the landlords were represented by attorneys, the typical tenant defaulted by not appearing in court. Most who did appear were black, acting without benefit of counsel. Tenants normally did not raise any of the new statutory defenses enacted by the state of Michigan in the late 1960s, and the landlord typically won a judgment. When the tenant did employ a lawyer, court outcomes changed dramatically "in all data categories, from defenses raised, jury demands filed, outcomes, and extra days granted to whether or not a writ of eviction finally [was] issued."[6]

A second serious empirical study focused on Chicago's eviction court, which tries eviction suits filed in Cook County Circuit Court, First Municipal Division (city of Chicago).[7] In 1977, the year of the study, judges sitting in two courtrooms for about three and a half hours a day disposed of almost sixty-five thousand cases per year. The judges spent two minutes per contested eviction. Half of all tenants sued for eviction did not appear; the landlord almost always won a default judgment. Two-thirds of landlords were represented by lawyers; whether lawyers were employed or not, landlords won summary possession of their apartments in over 80 percent of contested cases. When tenants presented substantive defenses, judges ignored the tenants' testimony; when tenants alleged a breach of the implied warranty of habitability by the landlord (that the landlord maintained the premises in substandard condition, violating the building code), judges refused to consider these defenses, even though Illinois law allows them. As in Detroit, the outcomes changed when tenants were represented by counsel.

The authors of the study conclude that, regardless of recent developments in tenant rights, "the eviction court in Chicago serves today, as it has for decades, only as a vehicle by which landlords may summarily and swiftly retake possession unhampered by proper procedure and without regard to the merits of their cases."[8]

It is clear that housing court must play a different role in the urban political system than does landlord-tenant court. Here the state acts against the owner of property; in such a situation the blatant bias in favor of the property owner observed in eviction court is unlikely to be present. Nevertheless, it is not uncommon to hear charges that housing court is prolandlord in many cities, including Chicago.[9] More common complaints, however, are that housing court is a cumbersome way of prosecuting code violations, that legal procedures frustrate code enforcement, and that housing-court judges lack the legal remedies to obtain compliance.[10]

Housing Court: Organization and Procedure

Because of the inherent ambiguities in the role of housing court, the adjudication of code violations is handled by a variety of organizational forms by cities. Historical variations exist as well, with major changes in function and legal remedies assigned to housing court occurring in periods of interest in using regulation to upgrade the urban housing stock.

New York's experiences are more or less typical for large U.S. cities. The basic enforcement mechanism of housing court there and elsewhere is punitive sanctions against landlords. This has been the case since the earliest efforts to enforce New York's tenement-housing acts in the late nineteenth century. (These acts served as models for other cities as they also adopted the remedy of housing regulation.) The first enforcement tools were civil in nature, primarily "the blunderbuss of the vacate order," which required tenants to vacate a building when a judge found the building to be in violation of legal standards.[11]

New York added both civil and criminal penalties in 1901, and from 1901 to 1915 civil fines were the primary enforcement mechanism. In 1915 a statutory change made filing criminal charges easier, and this was the primary tool used by the city's corporation counsel until 1973, when the city put into operation its civil housing court.[12] The new system was a result of widespread dissatisfaction with the criminal housing court—primarily because of small fines and an unwillingness to treat landlords as criminals.

New York's civil housing court was granted broad remedial powers in dealing with property owners. Judges could impose stiff civil fines, issue injunctions, and enforce injunctions through the exercise of the contempt power. Nevertheless, modifications in practice by administrative agencies responsible for filing code-enforcement actions and widespread judicial passivity have made the court into "an institution that is decidedly different from that envisioned by its . . . architects."[13] Few civil fines are imposed, primarily because the penalties quickly get so large as to encourage housing abandonment rather than compliance.

This state of affairs has led the city's attorney to couple proceedings for injunctive orders with civil penalty actions in an attempt to use the large fines as an inducement to obtain compliance with the judicial orders. The focus on injunctions has activated the use of the court's contempt power for recalcitrant owners, a process that has apparently had salutary effects.[14]

In certain critical ways, Chicago's housing-court experience parallels New York's. Dissatisfaction with the existing system of housing referees in municipal court led to the establishment of a separate housing court, staffed with circuit court judges and associate judges, in the 1960s. Housing court judges, like those in New York, have broad remedial powers; they can issue injunctions and set large civil fines.[15] The corporation counsel has joined proceedings for civil penalties and injunctive relief in a manner similar to the practice in New York. Indeed, while it was once common to file for a civil penalty alone in cases involving non-life-threatening situations, dissatisfaction with judicial unwillingness to assess large civil fines has led to a strategy of complete reliance on proceedings for injunctive relief, with the civil action added only as an inducement for compliance to the injunctive order.

Micropolitics and Housing Court

Studies and critiques of housing and eviction courts place these institutions in the context of the public economy of the city. The evidence indicates that landlord-tenant or eviction courts serve primarily the interest of the landlord, providing little substantive or procedural protection for tenants.

The role of housing courts in the city's public economy is more complex. While today's legal reformers stress the inability of housing courts to stem urban housing decay, they differ on the issue of whether the regulation of housing is itself a futile activity or whether housing courts generally lack the legal remedies and the organizational resources to regulate housing. This debate parallels a difference of opinion regarding the effectiveness of housing codes generally.

Whatever the merits of the positions in this debate, there is nevertheless a fascinating micropolitics associated with housing court. Judicial proceedings concerning the regulation of urban housing may not affect the structure of the urban public economy; nevertheless, they activate numerous political actors who at least *believe* the process affects the character of their neighborhoods. It is this micropolitical process, and the associated distribution of benefits to urban neighborhoods, that will preoccupy us for the remainder of this chapter.

Court Politics

Politics runs deep in Chicago; hence there is ample reason to expect political influence to affect outcomes in court. Judges are slated for office by the party, and they owe allegiance to their sponsoring ward organizations. While not as fierce as it was some years ago, before a major court reform in 1964 centralized judicial functions in the Cook County Circuit Court, politics has not been banished from Chicago's halls of justice.[16] In addition, the corporation counsel who try cases in housing court are patronage appointees.

One assistant corporation counsel who worked with the criminal housing management program related the following account. One housing court judge wanted the prosecuting attorneys to dismiss a case. They refused. The judge said, "In that case, you are in contempt of this court. Go over there and stand by the marshal."

When the supervising corporation counsel discovered what was happening, he immediately telephoned the judge's ward committeeman. The committeeman called the judge and said: "You are an embarrassment to this ward organization. Don't you ever do anything like this again. Now, I want you to cancel those contempt citations, and apologize to those boys." The judge did so.

Even though routine housing-court proceedings are a low priority for major Chicago political actors, it is always possible to rouse their attention. That threat may alter the normal routine of judicial proceedings. While anecdotal evidence is not a substitute for more thorough investigation, the following situation is illustrative of the depth to which politics penetrates court life in Chicago.

One prosecuting attorney, the grandson of an important politician of an earlier era, had established a procedure whereby he would not put a witness on the stand unless the witness had been interviewed previously. In the words of the attorney,

> Once Bob Lucas of Kenwood-Oakland [a community organization in a predominantly black neighborhood] called, and said he had some witnesses for a case. I said, "Okay, bring them by before court." He didn't, but he had them in court. He said, "I've got some good witnesses." I said, "You didn't bring them by; I won't put them on the stand." He argued; we went outside the courtroom.
>
> Finally, he said, "I'm going to the mayor [Richard Daley] on this one." I said, "Bob, how do you think I got this job? I'm political. You go to the mayor, I'll go. And I know a lot of influential people; I'll have them contact Daley."
>
> We both knew full well what would have happened; Daley would have killed both of us. Whoever won would have had the most pyrrhic victory possible. After the session, I said, "Bob, you wouldn't have gone to the mayor on this, would you?" He said, "A man can try, can't he?"

There is another reason to expect political influence in these local courts. Housing court is a grinding, bruising process; judges are often unwilling to act harshly against landlords even though they possess the judicial authority to do so. Private property is respected in Chicago, and the judiciary is cautious in demanding that owners do specific things with their property. Many leaders of community groups believe that housing court judges are simply "tools" of landlords. A more likely explanation of the leniency of housing court judges toward landlords is the fear on the part of the judges that by making buildings prohibitively expensive to own they will encourage owners to abandon housing. Moreover, oppressive caseloads cause extensive judicial passivity, with major decisions delayed as long as possible to avoid mistakes.

Even without sympathetic attitudes on the part of judges and the inherent delay caused by large caseloads, landlords can extend court proceedings for years by taking advantage of legal procedures. Lawyers for landlords cannot perhaps alter the final outcome of a case, but they can delay; to an owner delay invariably means money, as rents can be collected.

Both the chief judge of housing court and the corporation counsel in charge of prosecuting housing cases noted in interviews that the entire process moved more speedily where neighborhood groups and ward organizations intervened in the proceedings. The chief prosecutor put it this way:

> Here the squeaky wheel gets the grease. Where community groups are screaming, where the aldermen are active, they get shorter and fewer continuances [delays] and quicker compliance. If someone is on my back, I'll act to get them off. That sets priorities—the most dangerous cases and those that someone is persistent about complaining about—those are the ones I'll give special attention to.

The chief judge of housing court agreed:

> Community pressure—where the community is interested, it can make a difference. The judge might give the owner two weeks [to comply] instead of a month. If a judge sees that the community believes in getting things done, he might require an early status call [inspection of work in progress]. And the community groups have adverse effects on the defendant. They will try to embarrass an owner by showing up in court. Fix it, they'll say again and again, or get rid of it. The owner may decide it's not worth the embarrassment.

According to the two major participants in the process, then, housing-court justice is not blind in Chicago. Those who are able and willing to mobilize politically can affect outcomes.

The Tortuous Proceedings of Housing Court

Except in the most dire of circumstances, the legal requirements of due process are followed in housing cases. The typical case is referred by the Compliance Bureau of the Building Department to the Office of the Assistant Corporation Counsel for Building, Housing, and Urban Conservation. The corporation counsel files a case in the Housing Court Division of Cook County Circuit Court, and a summons is issued. Thirty days is allowed to serve the summons; the return date is typically thirty days after that. So two months often passes before the first hearing in housing court.

At the first hearing the defendant has the opportunity to plead the complaint. He can ask for a continuance in order to plead; the continuance is automatic. At the next hearing the defense attorney can introduce motions—to dismiss, for discovery, and so forth—all before presenting an affirmative defense to the complaint filed against his client. The city must answer each motion, and hearings must be held on each of the motions. According to lawyers familiar with the process, a defendant can delay a case from 90 to 120 days before the first hearing on the merits of the case. The defense attorney can do this without ever requesting a continuance, just by bringing up motions.

In addition to these legitimate ways of delaying a proceeding, there are less savory ways of postponing action. An owner may, for example, fail to respond to a summons. This is particularly effective if the summons server has failed to serve the summons personally. In that case a second (alias) summons is issued; in this case personal service will be required. This will achieve a second sixty-day delay for the owner. Alias summons are issued in more than 9 percent of the cases that come before housing court.[17] A defendant may also delay proceedings by failing to appear in court at appropriate times, forcing the court to issue an order for him to appear. A continuance is granted to see if he is going to show up. If he does not, he leaves himself open to a contempt of court order, so that this cannot be used so often as to anger the presiding judge.

After the procedural motions are disposed of, hearings on the merits of the case begin. If work on the violations is in progress, and the work is what prosecutors and judges call "good faith effort," the case will normally be continued, and the efforts to comply will be monitored through regular hearings. If the owner is not making such a good faith effort, then the prosecuting attorney will ask for an order to comply. There will be a continuance, not infrequently of sixty to ninety days, to see if the defendant will comply with the order. At that time, if there is work, there will be another continuance.

There are, however, a number of cases in which the owner plans to do as little as possible to repair the building. After the order to comply, there is no work. It may take a hearing or two before the prosecutor realizes what is happening. Then the prosecutor has several options. He or she may ask for an order to vacate, on the grounds that the building is dangerous to tenants. Because a vacant building will earn no money for its owner, he may be more willing to comply. The prosecutor may request a transfer to the criminal housing management program, where teams of inspectors and an assistant corporation counsel work together to prosecute particularly difficult landlords. Finally, the prosecutor may petition for a rule demanding that the defendant show cause why he is not in contempt of court. The defendant, of course, is entitled to respond; a hearing is held. If the rule is issued by the court, it must be served on the defendant himself, not on his attorney. Then a hearing on the rule, with the defendant personally in attendance, is held. If there is a contempt finding, the judge could theoretically jail a defendant, but appeals courts have not been sympathetic to such use of scarce prison space. Hence a fine is usually entered.

Normally the situation does not proceed this far. All participants are aware that they have pushed the process beyond what it can bear. Landlords who are familiar with housing court know that judges will be extraordinarily tough if they push too far; judges know that they are limited in the resources that they have to compel landlords to obey their orders. Hence although 1.6 percent of all cases in process in housing court in May of 1979 had contempt proceedings begun against them, almost no contempt citations were issued (0.1 percent).

The Process of Detection

In Chicago, housing-court judges sit at law and chancery. Judgments at law can result in fines or damages only. The only option for a judge sitting at law is to enter a fine against an owner. Because there is no "double jeopardy" in housing-court proceedings, fines can be very large. For each day that a landlord does not repair a violation, a fine can be entered in the maximum amount. Nevertheless, a proceeding at law severely constrains the actions of judges.

When judges sit in chancery court, they are able to issue orders that are mandatory on the defendant. The end result, if there is no compliance, is a contempt of court proceeding. In chancery cases, then, the full range of judicial power is available to judges.

It has been common practice for the city to file severe cases in chancery court and less severe cases in municipal court. The corporation counsel and the Building Department, however, have become dissatisfied with proceedings at law. The judges have been unwilling to enter large fines against owners (except *ex parte*), and will dismiss cases and ask for refiling in chancery court. Hence the city in 1979 made a policy decision to file all cases in chancery court, but to also include a law count when the suit is filed. Hence in the typical housing-court case the city asks both for a fine and an injunction against the defendant.

Just what transpires in a given case depends on the nature of the violations, on the inclinations of the prosecuting attorneys, and on the motives of the defendant. In the regular violation courtrooms, the press of the enormous workload ensures that no case will get a thorough hearing. This is not so in criminal housing management court, but it may be months before a building is transferred from the regular call to the criminal housing management call. In the meantime, legal procedures can be manipulated by the small proportion of owners who do not plan to comply. Key characteristics of such owners are that they do not plan on building equity in a building, because it is in a deteriorating section of the city; they own several slum buildings; they have had experience with housing court before; and they employ lawyers. Many owners of smaller buildings appear *pro se* and really want to repair their buildings but lack the capital to do so.

The ability of unscrupulous owners to manipulate housing court was underscored by John McCaffrey, assistant corporation counsel in charge:

> The worst offenders, those to whom time is money, can get lawyers, evade the system. One game they play is not to let the inspector in. We get a mandatory order of full inspection. They still don't let him in. We petition for a rule [to show cause why the defendant should not be held in contempt]. Then they let him in. The inspector documents the violations, and we get a mandatory order to full compliance. The inspector goes to reinspect, and they don't let him in. They can kill six to eight months playing these games.

All participants in housing court categorize owners into two types, the good and the bad.[18] The first, by far the most numerous, is the individual who, according to McCaffrey, "has his entire life savings tied up in a building, which he bought for retirement income." The neighborhood deteriorates, the owner is unable to rent to reliable tenants, and the building ends up in housing court. The owner, however, lacks the necessary funds to repair.

The second kind of owner is the modern version of the slumlord. He owns several buildings. He employs what George Sternlieb calls cash-flow accounting: amortization is considered an expense, while depreciation charges are not.[19] Owners know that they will not realize capital gains on their buildings, and they behave accordingly. Because the building has no sale value, there is little incentive to undertake repairs or renovation, except to hold tenants or to fend off the building inspector. It is a world of tenement capitalism, a world of owners of questionable character, a world without equity, of short-term profits and long-term losses, of destructive, drug-dependent tenants, of tenement trading among cash-short owners, and of cheap lawyers and housing court.[20]

Detection. Because of this categorization of owners, be it correct or incorrect, housing-court proceedings become a problem in detection. How do the judges and prosecutors know whether they are dealing with a owner who is, in the jargon of housing regulation, "milking the building" or one who is legitimately trying to upgrade his investment but lacks capital and the means to acquire it? Judicial proceedings are used to detect whether an owner belongs in one category or the other, and further actions conform to this categorization. (One of the interesting consequences of this process is that court-wise defendants "dress down" for housing court, trying to appear less affluent than they actually are.)

This role in detection may be pushed onto housing court in Chicago more forcefully than in other cities, for two reasons. The first is that Chicago housing-court judges sit at chancery, which gives them the means to categorize owners. They can order inspections, require plans and permits to check whether work is being scheduled, and demand that an apartment be vacated.

The second reason is that in Chicago the Building Department allows its inspectors, supervisors, and bureau chiefs very little discretion in determining who is a cooperative owner and who is not. Once a violation is found, it becomes difficult to "work with" an owner to get him to comply because of the computerized system used to handle violations. In court this is possible; hence bureau chiefs in the Building Department stress again and again that their role is to "enforce the letter of the code." They add that they are bureaucrats, not judges, and lack the discretion necessary to work with owners. The situation seems to be very different in Boston. According to Nivola, far more discretion is left in the hands of inspectors there than is the case in Chicago.[21]

Because housing-court proceedings are a problem of detection, justice is not blind. The actions of court are keyed to the motives of owners. "Bad" owners are treated differently from "good" ones. It is this characteristic of housing court that disturbs many reformers. The court has assumed a detective role because it wishes to achieve compliance, not determine the presence or absence of a violation, and to act accordingly. It wants to maximize compliance, not determine guilt or innocence. This is exactly why we expect politics to play an important role in housing-court outcomes: political pressures can become more important where courts lose their standard judicial functions and implicitly adopt enforcement as a goal.

The Prosecutor as Detective

In the violation courtrooms, the typical hearing takes but three minutes; the typical courtroom handles fifty to sixty cases a day (court is in session normally from 9:30 to noon). According to one experienced prosecutor, "most defendants move toward compliance when cited. They are scared when called to court; we only want to know how fast they are moving. The typical case keeps moving along; we grant two or three continuances, get full compliance, and everyone is happy. At least one-half of the cases are of this variety."

The problem is the other cases. It is primarily the prosecutor who must decide whether an owner is making a good-faith effort to comply, and he must do so on the spur of the moment. The prosecutor sits at a table with a stack of files in front of him. Inside the file is the city's complaint with a listing of alleged code violations. On the outside of the jacket is a listing, in handwriting, of the violations (by a numbering system employed by the Building Department; the code is not referenced) and the progress made since the last court appearance. The prosecutor almost never opens the file.

The prosecuting attorney will ask the building inspector about the violations and ask the defendant what he is going to do about them. Then normally a continuance is granted.

All major decisions in violation courtrooms are made on the spur of the moment by the prosecuting attorney. Based on what is scrawled on the outside of the file jackets and what the inspector, defendant, and any community-group or ward-organization representatives have said, the prosecutor makes a snap decision: Is this a "good faith" owner or not?

The pressures of time and the nature of housing-court proceedings lead to some interesting violations of normal judicial proceedings. As one prosecuting attorney commented, "In legal theory, you must specify reasons that you are going to ask for a mandatory order in chancery court, and you must send a notice to the defendant beforehand. In housing court this is not normally done. Oftentimes the prosecutor, making a snap decision, being fed up with the lack of cooperation by the defendant, will ask for a mandatory order of full compliance on the spur of the moment, figuring that only one out of a hundred will be appealed."

The same kinds of procedural violations occur when the prosecuting attorney recognizes that a defendant has no intention of complying with a mandatory order of full compliance. Then, in a snap decision, the prosecutor will petition for a rule to show cause why a defendant should not be held in contempt. There is usually no notice to the defendant, because the prosecutor makes up his mind only when he looks at the file jacket.

The prosecutor can then ask for a rule to issue the contempt citation. Now the court is in a legally ludicrous situation. It is about to rule on contempt of court in a situation in which the court has not, strictly speaking, ever ruled on the guilt or innocence of the alleged violator. Nevertheless, the prosecutor can get the rule by the housing-court judge, and it is usually not tested on appeal because of the expense involved.

The prosecutor must prove the rule by detailing the items that are still not in compliance. Full, sworn testimony is taken from individual community groups and, of course, the building inspector. The defendant may raise both technical and substantive defenses, mainly that he is unable to comply with the order because he has no money or because he has destructive tenants in his building. It is possible for the city's attorney to break these defenses by subpoenaing tax records and swearing in tenants, suppliers, and so forth, but the process is extremely time consuming.

At any of several points in a housing-court proceeding, the prosecuting attorney may decide to bring more resources to bear on a defendant to get him to comply. The problem is that each decision to "up the ante" must be made on the spur of the moment and on the basis of very sketchy information. Moreover, each decision to raise the stakes involves a significant encumbrance on the resources available to prosecutors. The two major consequences of operating in such a resource-poor environment are, first, major decisions tend to be delayed; and second, procedural shortcuts are tolerated. A former prosecutor noted that "the rights of individuals are often trampled in the name of expediency. Improper questions are often asked, and the judge will go along with them. Defendants are not given proper notice of requests for orders. Judges do not require a full specification on the petition for a rule to issue [a contempt citation]. In a 'real court,' where the prosecutor has the luxury of time, such proceedings would not be tolerated."

Outcomes

Because housing court serves as a means to achieve compliance, not to determine guilt or innocence, the average number of hearings (and hence the average length of time a case stays in court) is high. The typical case whose last hearing was in May 1979 had been heard over five times previously, according to data kept by observers from the Building Department.[22]

Table 8.1. Housing Court Dispositions

DISPOSITION	Percentage	Average Number of Hearings
Case-Closing Actions		
Dismissed-complied	15.12%	4.84
Nonsuit	0.38	7.99
Execution to issue	1.46	8.07
Finding of contempt	0.12	16.20
Decree of demolition	1.85	7.03[a]
Intermediate Actions		
Alias summons	7.87	4.22
Order permanent injunction	0.43	4.61
Ex parte order and fine	3.30	5.55
Mandatory order full compliance	3.79	6.30
General continuance	46.31	6.40
Mandatory order inspection	2.67	6.71
Order defendant to appear	6.88	6.78
Order to implead party defendant	2.40	6.80
Not on call	0.98	7.12
Judgment on law count	0.52	7.39
Mandatory order to secure	1.21	7.69
Mandatory order plans and permits	0.85	7.83
Order case transferred to another court	1.42	8.17
Order to vacate	0.56	8.27
Petition for rule	1.63	9.14
Petition for receiver	0.27	12.20
All Actions	100.02[b]	5.14

Note: Based on the 16,368 cases in process in the Housing Court Division of Cook County Circuit Court in May 1979.

[a]Issued by demolition court.
[b]Differs from 100.00% due to rounding.

Table 8.1 presents court action at the last hearing of cases in process in May of 1979. The first column of the table gives a percentage distribution of court actions; the second column indicates the average number of hearings held on cases in the category in question.

These data indicate the limitations under which housing-court judges work. Because judges and prosecutors conceive of the function of housing court to be detection and enforcement rather than determination of guilt, they act severely only after a case has been in court for a considerable time. Under the enormous caseloads telling the difference between so-called "good faith" owners and dallying, unscrupulous owners is difficult. Hence it takes numerous hearings before prosecutor and judge become convinced that an owner is behaving irresponsibly.

One can see from the table that by far the most common action taken by housing-court judges was a general continuance. Over 46 percent of cases heard received such a continuance, normally because at least some work was being done on the building. Of course, continuances are also granted when an order is issued, to see if the owner is going to comply. Indeed, the only court actions that result in a case leaving court are dismissed-complied (15.12 percent of all actions); execution to issue (1.46 percent), which closes a case after an *ex parte* fine, thus having the effect of closing a case in the absence of compliance; a finding of contempt (0.12 percent); and a nonsuit (0.98 percent) in which the corporation counsel has decided not to pursue the case and, in effect, administratively kills it. All other actions are intermediate steps in the court process.

Indeed, many buildings never get out of court. An owner will do enough work to satisfy the judges; the city will amend its complaint to include new violations discovered by inspectors on reinspection. The owner may sell the building, in which case the building stays in court, and the defendant changes. If there is a fire, the building may be transferred to demolition court for further action; the case is dismissed only when the owner obeys the decree of demolition.

In general, table 8.1 indicates that the average number of hearings on a case increases as the severity of judicial action increases. That is, judges do not take severe action against owners until numerous hearings have been conducted. Findings of contempt occurred only after sixteen hearings on the typical case; judges entertained petitions for receivership only after twelve hearings. On the other hand, the typical case that was dismissed-complied had experienced less than five hearings.

This category is disproportionately made up of buildings whose violations were relatively minor.

The Distribution of Court Outcomes

The adjudication of housing-code violations involves rapid proceedings, sharp decisions, legal shortcuts, and informal intervention by interested parties. Clearly the distribution of outcomes resulting from such a process cannot be under any central control by political elites, be they party officials or Loop businessmen. The distribution of benefits must emerge from the pattern of interactions within the formal judicial structure.

This does not imply that politics does not affect judicial outcomes. Indeed, we fully expect political considerations to matter. It does mean that any such observable outcomes will result from numerous separate actions on the part of the judges, prosecutors, inspectors, and politicians acting as advocates before the major housing-court participants rather than being set as a matter of policy by the Central Committee of the Democratic Party of Cook County.

Because housing court's actions are ultimately directed at buildings, they affect tenants and nearby residents as well as owners. Indeed, it is the external impacts of court actions, rather than their direct effects on owners, that induce citizens' groups and ward organizations to attempt to influence housing-court proceedings. Hence the geographic incidence of court actions is a critical dimension of judicial outputs.

The question of distribution may be stated as follows: How do the social, economic, and political characteristics of Chicago's neighborhoods affect the housing-court actions taken in those neighborhoods?

Table 8.2 presents the relevant information. The table consists of twenty separate regression equations. Dependent variables are the court outcomes presented earlier in table 8.1. These are the legal actions taken by judges on cases in process; for the most part they are injunctive orders. These orders have been geocoded by using the address of the property against which the order was lodged. A final dependent variable is the average number of hearings conducted per case. Taken together, these variables assess the full range of housing-court outputs. Independent variables are the same for each equation. They assess the characteristics of buildings and residents in wards, and the strength of the major

Table 8.2. Standardized Regression Coefficients, Court Disposition Codes

DISPOSITION	C/D	BLDAGE	OWNER/OCC	BLACK	SEVERITY	PARTY	COMMORG	R^2	F
Execution to issue	−0.500			0.512		−0.295		.218	8.62
Petition for rule	−0.842							.287	16.04
Ex parte		−0.694						.267	8.54
Receiver									
Full compliance						−0.248		.062	3.15
Inspection									
Plans/permits									
Secure	−0.492		0.481	0.284				.081	4.22
Not on call				0.368				.289	6.25
Nonsuit		0.285						.081	4.23
Dismissed	0.420	−0.491		−0.179		−0.315		.790	33.08
Continued		0.368		−0.465	0.288			.243	7.54
Transfer									
Appear				0.343		0.360		.313	10.72
Vacate		0.383						.146	8.26
Demolition						0.369		.136	7.56
Contempt							0.264	.070	3.61
Law count									
Alias									
Party Defendant	−0.449							.202	12.14
Average number of hearings per case		0.612		0.392		−0.189		.614	24.38

Note: Statistically insignificant coefficients (0.05 level) are not included. Disposition categories are percentages of the total number of cases in progress in Cook County Circuit Court, Housing Court Division, May 1979.

urban intermediary groups in Chicago, ward organizations and community associations. The measurement of these variables is described in the appendix to chapter 5.

If politics matters in housing-court outcomes as much as informed respondents indicate, we should observe a link between the strength of intermediary groups—both party and community organization—and court outcomes. The political forces should be able to (1) achieve a favorable distribution of injunctive orders that benefit neighborhood residents; (2) avoid receiving a disproportionate share of court actions that would be detrimental to residents; and (3) achieve a lower number of court hearings on the average case lodged against property in the neighborhood. Since other characteristics of ward properties and residents may also affect the action judges and prosecutors take, these factors must be controlled in the analysis. In particular, we control for the likelihood that owners of property in older neighborhoods characterized by low investment will be less likely to comply with orders promptly, which causes court delays and more severe court action. This is done by including variables measuring age of buildings (BLDAGE) and investment (C/D) into the regressions. We also control for owner occupancy (OWNER-OCC) and racial composition (BLACK). Finally, we control the severity of the problem as judged by the Building Department, as indicated by that agency's decisions about how expeditiously to proceed against an owner. Court actions may be affected by the judgments of bureaucrats, who, after all, testify in court concerning cases they file. In all equations, variables not reaching conventional levels of statistical significance (.05) were dropped from the equation.

While there is much that can be gleaned from this table, from our perspective one fact stands out. While community organizations affect the distribution of court actions in but one incidence (and there only marginally), party organizations regularly do. Strong ward organizations avoid executions to issue (which close cases in the absence of compliance); they avoid dismissals (which are often done without complete compliance); they achieve a higher incidence of orders for defendants to appear; they achieve a higher incidence of demolition decrees; and they bring about a more rapid court action (as measured by the average number of hearings per case). But stronger ward organizations also bring about fewer mandatory orders of full compliance (although the relation is anemic). This could indicate special pleadings on behalf of some politically connected owners.

A number of other findings are worth discussing. First, the racial composition of the neighborhood has strong effects on some outcomes, even when characteristics of structures are controlled. There is no systematic deprivation of benefits, however. Judges issue more orders to secure and orders for defendants to appear in black neighborhoods, for example. Yet they are more likely to dismiss cases uncomplied (execution to issue), and the average time spent in court is higher. Finally, fewer general continuances are granted, indicating that less partial compliance is occurring. (Often general continuances are granted when the judge believes that the owner is making a good-faith effort to comply.) Taken together, these findings do not suggest systematic discrimination on the part of court officers. What they do suggest, however, is that more severe compliance problems exist in black wards than could be predicted from the age of the housing stock, from neighborhood investment patterns and from the extent of renter occupancy in these wards. It may be that owners are keying their decisions about complying with housing-court directives to the color of their tenants' skins rather than to more objective criteria (investment attractiveness, age of housing, and the like).

Two other perhaps surprising points are in evidence. First, the severity of housing problems as judged by Building Department officials has virtually no effect on court actions. Apparently judges and prosecutors make independent judgments after a case gets to court, rather than relying on the Building Department's presuit reports. This probably occurs because prosecutors never read the reports rather than because of any deliberate independence on the part of the judiciary.

Second, court actions are not really much influenced by the ownership characteristics of neighborhoods. Rather they are influenced by the characteristics of structures and investment attractiveness (CD and BLDAGE). What matters is not whether the neighborhood is composed of renters or owners but the conditions of the buildings they inhabit.

The Exceptional Back of the Yards Neighborhood Council

The data presented in table 8.2 clearly show the limited influence of Chicago's community organizations. But every generalization deserves an exception, and the exception here is the Back of the Yards Neighborhood Council.

Back of the Yards operations center in the Fourteenth Ward, and, to a lesser extent, the Eleventh and Thirteenth. It was formed in the late

1930s by Saul Alinsky, who, along with Joseph Meegan, various church leaders, labor-union organizers, and idealistic socialists, wanted an organization that would be able to deal with the problems of the neighborhoods surrounding Chicago's Union Stockyards. The Back of the Yards leadership was instrumental in obtaining national labor-union support and the support of local church leaders for the 1939 strike of packinghouse workers. The owners settled, wages in the packinghouses went from thirty-nine cents to fifty-six cents an hour, and the community organization movement was born.

Saul Alinsky moved from Back of the Yards to national prominence as a "prime mover" behind many community organizations in American cities. He developed a theory of community organizations emphasizing the role of confrontation with entrenched political and bureaucratic interests, as is well known. He also saw community organizations as peak associations for neighborhoods. They would integrate block clubs, local businesses, churches, ethnic organizations, and laborers into a single neighborhood-based force that could affect local politics.

Back of the Yards still maintains its peak associational form, but it has long since shed its radical image. Joseph Meegan, who became executive secretary of the organization after Alinsky's departure, sums his philosophy of community organization in one phrase: "We don't demonstrate; we communicate." Meegan's highest priority is housing. He believes deeply in housing regulation as a force to upgrade urban neighborhoods, and he works very hard at the process. Housing abandonment, in particular, concerns him: "Nothing is worse for a neighborhood than an abandoned building. There are invariably fires. Pretty soon people on either side of it move. The whole block quickly goes downhill."

Meegan backs up his verbal commitment to housing regulation with regular testimony in housing court. The informality of the process and the limited information possessed by prosecutors are tailor-made for Meegan's style. He prowls the halls, stopping to talk to prosecutors, going from one courtroom to another, interrupting the proceedings to interject his comments about owners, buildings, and neighborhood conditions. "Lots of community organizations send representatives to housing court," commented a former prosecutor, "but none of them are like Joe Meegan."

Can dedicated community leadership produce quantifiable benefits for an urban neighborhood? Figure 8.1 indicates that, indeed, it can.

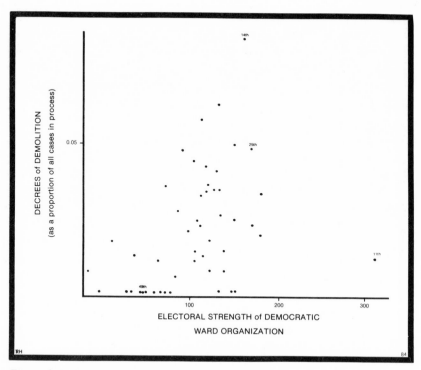

Figure 8.1. Decrees of Demolition Issued by Cook County Circuit Court and Electoral Strength of Democratic Ward Organizations.

There the electoral strength of ward organizations is plotted against decrees of demolition issued by housing court. The figure makes clear that there exists a moderate relationship ($r = .37$) between party strength and demolition decrees. What is remarkable about the figure, however, is the extraordinary performance of the Fourteenth Ward. The demographically and politically similar Eleventh Ward is the locus of far fewer demolition decrees, as are wards with far more severe housing problems than the Fourteenth (although the problems in the Fourteenth are considerable).

Almost certainly the performance of the Fourteenth Ward on this court-output measure is due to the efforts of Joe Meegan and his Back of the Yards Neighborhood Council. Even though community organizations do not generally make a difference in housing-court outcomes in Chicago, in exceptional circumstances they can overcome their inherent weaknesses and make an impact.[23]

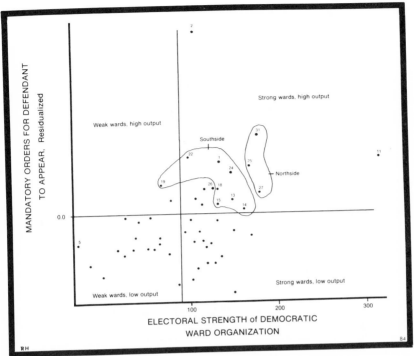

Figure 8.2. Orders for Defendant to Appear Issued by Cook County Circuit Court and Electoral Strength of Democratic Ward Organizations.

A Final Look at the Power of Party

Due process requires that certain orders be served on the defendant personally; moreover, it is often necessary to confront a defendant personally in court to make him aware of his legal responsibilities. Because numerous hearings are held on the typical case, defendants can become casual about attending or rely on legal counsel to represent them. Since the entire housing-court process is geared to achieving compliance rather than determining guilt or innocence, the mandatory order to appear can be a powerful tool in the process of "getting tough" with a recalcitrant owner.

Table 8.2 makes clear that orders to appear are issued more frequently in black neighborhoods and where party organizations are powerful. If we control for the proportion of black residents[24] and plot the proportion of mandatory orders to appear against the strength of ward organizations, figure 8.2 results.

While it is possible for a party organization to be relatively strong and yet not receive a substantial number of orders to appear, it is almost impossible to receive a large number of these orders in the absence of a powerful ward organization. In this case, a powerful ward organization seems to be a necessary but not sufficient condition for gaining orders to appear (above those granted because of the racial composition of the neighborhood).[25]

Conclusions

Housing court is the primary enforcement institution for building codes. It is slow and ineffective, straddling a world of regulatory bureaucrats on the one hand and housing capitalists on the other. Even though judges and corporation counsel are political appointees and theoretically subject to central direction, little coordination with the relevant city agencies exists. These urban civil courts are a separate and distinct policy domain, operating according to a judicial, not bureaucratic, logic, even in the face of huge caseloads and a need for standard operating procedures.

This aspect of implementation is even less coordinated than the bureaucratic process. The party is no unifier or centralizer here. Party is influential in the process, however, as neighborhood interest group and demander of court outputs. Strong ward organizations gain more favorable housing-court actions in their neighborhoods than do weak ones, all other things being equal. The data do not allow us to determine whether this is due to a judicial equivalent to attention rules in the bureaucracy or a stimulation of neighborhood demands. Nevertheless, the influence of party in the micropolitics of housing court is indeed impressive.

9

The Contradiction of Party Government

Americans have simultaneously expected too much from their political parties and limited what they can do by hemming them in with statutes and regulations that diminish the abilities of the parties to perform their democratic functions. Denied the resources required to accumulate the power necessary to coordinate policy making in a formally decentralized governing system, and lacking the ability to mobilize voters as in the past, political parties have, in the eyes of many observers, become hollow shells of the instruments of popular control of public policy making that they ought to be.

Most observers have traced the ambivalent attitudes of Americans about their political parties to contradictory tendencies in the political culture. On the one hand, Americans laud democratic accountability of government. On the other hand, they distrust the accumulation of power in the hands of party leaders that would be necessary to bring policy coordination to the decentralized organs of American government. What they get is nondemocratic policy making without coordination.

Yet I have argued here that there may be an objective basis to the ambivalence Americans feel about their parties. Political parties, at least where they are strong enough to provide both policy coordination and popular control, allow leaders to impose policy settlements and at the same time are corrosive of those policy settlements at the implementation stage.

This study confirms certain conventional axioms concerning political parties, extends others, and strongly challenges a few. In particular, the data support a view of the role of political parties in government that combines elements of the laudatory view of political parties as linkage devices that is common in the political science literature with the perspective from classical public administration that distrusts parties as destructive of rational administration. The political party structure in Chicago, which for all purposes is the Democratic Party Organization of Cook County, allows centralization in policy formation but causes disarray in policy administration, at least in the policy arena that serves as the focus for this study, building regulation. On the other hand, the administrative disarray caused by the party's decentralized structure (based as it is in the city's fifty wards) is accompanied by a large degree of democratic responsiveness to citizens' demands for services. Moreover, the system does not result in direct racial or class discrimination in the service-delivery process.

A Summary of Key Findings

Before continuing this line of argument, I would like to summarize briefly the primary findings from this study, as they relate to the issue of party government and public administration.

The Cement of Corporatism. Public efforts to regulate the built environment of the city invariably affect many private interests, both directly and indirectly. As in any policy system, policy settlements must be forged and enforced. Because of the diversity of interests involved in building regulation, and because this diversity can and often does lead to considerable conflict, the enforcement of policy settlements requires a great deal of power.

In Chicago, building regulations are modified by the Mayor's Advisory Committee on Building Code Amendments. This committee is a highly structured operation, with formal sessions, a subcommittee system, and formal voting on subcommittee proposals. It is composed of representatives from major affected interests—architects, contractors, building-trade unions, engineering firms, and city bureaucrats. The committee is chaired by the commissioner of buildings (now the commissioner of inspectional services). Recommendations of the committee go to the mayor, who incorporates them into the agenda for action by the city council.

The committee's recommendations are conditioned by expectations of what the mayor will accept, but the mayor invariably accepts the committee's recommendations. Generally, architects and contractors want a building code with fewer restrictions, while city bureaucrats want a more stringent code promoting fire safety. The building trades oppose code provisions that might eliminate union construction jobs. The committee prebrokers these diverse interests into a package of proposals that the mayor can accept. Once the mayor accepts the proposals, the policy settlement is made, since it is impossible for an aggrieved interest to gain more than a perfunctory hearing in the city council. The mayor's control of the council assured that, at least until recently.

The source of the mayor's ability to impose this structure on the policy system is his or her position in the local political party. The party itself has no direct interest in the complexities of building regulation, yet it lurks in the background, serving as an important resource for power for the city's chief executive. The party in this arena serves as a kind of hidden hand, forcing the affected interests to forge a policy settlement within the confines of what the mayor will accept.

Excluded from this system, however, were the small architectural firms, contractors, and community groups interested in rehabilitation. The exclusion of these groups, along with the fact that rehabilitation and fire safety are contradictory goals, meant that incremental changes in the rehabilitation provisions of the code were impossible. A change of major proportions, at least in the minds of the participants, came with the rehabilitation code, which was written outside the confines of the existing policy-making system. It represented an important victory for the rehabilitation forces. It is very likely that this breakthrough came because Mayor Byrne, on an insecure base of power, was reaching out to firm her political position. A weakness on the part of the chief executive led to an increase in access to power for these previously excluded interests, although entirely on the mayor's terms. This interpretation is consistent with Crenson's analysis of air-pollution regulation in Gary and East Chicago. Major changes came about during periods when the local machines were undergoing turmoil.[1]

Management Control. Not infrequently the issue of management control reaches the policy agenda of a local political system. Public officials find themselves faced with charges of waste, inefficiency, favoritism, or outright corruption in the service agencies they are supposed to control. Because certain political actors, primarily the media and reform groups, have an interest in raising the issue of management control, a policy system develops around the issue, a policy system for all practical purposes independent of the associated substantive policy system.

The Chicago Building Department has suffered chronic problems of management control. A department bureaucrat characterized it as "perhaps the most corrupt municipal department in the country"; numerous scandals racked the department during the late 1970s and early 1980s. Policy making in the management-control policy system tended to be sporadic, unstable, and nonincremental, yet predictable. A sporadic and unstable policy process results from the unpredictability of corruption scandals; responses must be nonincremental in order to transmit the image of action to an attentive public; predictability stems from the limited response repertoire of the organization. Normally the response involves increases in formal bureaucratic control of the service-delivery process.

In the substantive policy system, the political party acts as a resource for the chief executive, allowing him or her to impose structure on the policy process. When management-control issues, especially corruption, are raised with sufficient force, however, the mayor must fashion a policy response without much aid from the party. While the mayor's position in the party always acts as a potential resource in weathering a crisis of confidence, it is the bureaucracy that serves as the primary instrument of response. To deflect criticism, the mayor bureaucratizes.

Responses to corruption scandals and other lapses in organizational control in the Building Department stressed the institution of formal controls within the agency. Most successful in constraining horizontal discretion was a sophisticated computerized management-information system and the addition of an assistant commissioner over the technical bureaus. In an attempt to limit street-level discretion the department also made changes in procedures—including team inspections and reinspections of inspectors' work by supervisors.

To assume that such formal controls reduce corruption would be to jump to an unwarranted conclusion. They do, however, reduce decision-making discretion at the organization's periphery and strengthen hierarchical control. This both limits the agency's flexibility in dealing with individual circumstances and increases the probability that policies from the mayor and city council, or from the agency head, are reliably implemented. As the "Monday Massacre" suggests, it is formal hierarchy that increases the chief executive's control over the implementation of policies, not the availability of patronage to discipline bureaucrats. Firing bureaucrats for failing to perform their governmental responsibilities is not a well-established norm within a patronage system. Patronage drives the party; it does not drive government—in the sense that it is not a resource for enforcing policy implementation.

Demands. In Chicago those wards that are strong electorally are also effective in stimulating citizen demands for service. Because electorally powerful wards also receive a disproportionate share of patronage allocations, it is clear that the barrage of demands for service from strong wards is caused by the surveillance of the neighborhoods by precinct captains and their assistants. These wards, by virtue of their patronage riches, are able to *coproduce* services by intervening with landlords and testifying in housing court.

Attention Rules and Decision Rules. Decision rules are programmed responses of an agency to stimuli requiring a decision. They are normally related, albeit occasionally indirectly, to the goals of the agency. If the decision rule is programmed so that the organization responds to characteristics of stimuli *not* related to the agency's formal goal, the label "attention rule" applies. In the case of code enforcement, the agency's response would be keyed to the severity of the violation (in terms of safety) if bureaucratic decision rules apply. If, however, the race or class of a violator, or the political power of his ward committeeman, alters the response, attention rules have taken over.

Data presented in chapter 5 show that the distribution of code-enforcement outputs is determined by both bureaucratic decision rules and attention rules based on the strength of ward organizations. The racial composition of wards is *not* connected to the distribution of outputs. Indeed, party strength affected building regulation at each stage of the service-delivery process: at the demand stage, at the output stage, and at the impact stage.

Chapter 7 investigated the organizational structure by which attention rules were maintained. Without consistent pressure from ward committeemen and party activists inside government, attention rules tended to slide into disuse. Bureaucratic rules were justified, if only to get the work processed. Attention rules, however, ran counter to normal bureaucratic tendencies and thus required continuous pressure to sustain, even with the existence of key party operatives in the bureaucracy. The fact that decision rules and attention rules pushed in different directions, the former toward increased hierarchy and the latter toward political favoritism, led to powerful job stress for many bureaucrats. While justifications of machine rule were common, so were complaints of politicians' interference with normal bureaucratic processes.

Housing Court as Enforcer. Housing court serves not as resolver of disputes, but as part and parcel of an enforcement procedure. As a consequence, the court is a target for political action, because political action can affect the distribution of enforcement outputs to neighborhoods. The high proportion of continuances indicates the weakness of housing court as an enforcement mechanism. It also indicates the problems of regulating the built environment in a free market economy. Judges are reluctant to take extreme measures against property owners, and delay is often the major aim of owners and their attorneys.

In this milieu party nevertheless has an impact. The electoral strength of the ward organizations relates to a number of court actions, including demolition orders. The influence holds when other characteristics of the built environment are controlled. Racial composition also predicts court actions in a manner that suggests marked racial discrimination in the real estate market, limiting the court's enforcement effectiveness.

Party and Community Organizations. For the most part, community organizations are ineffective in the code-enforcement process in Chicago. They are not involved in the code-amendment process. They do not stimulate citizen demands. They are unable to enforce attention rules in the bureaucracy. They do not affect housing-court outcomes.

These findings are based on averages, so it is not surprising to find exceptions. A careful look at the data suggests two: The Back of the Yards Community Council active around the old Union Stockyards, and the Rogers Park Community Council on the north lakefront. Even these exceptions appear only on a limited number of measures rather than throughout the regulatory process.

A Contradiction in Party Rule

These findings, taken together, suggest an inherent contradiction in models of party government—or at least in those models centering on American brokerage-style political parties. The contradiction stems from the dual role that material incentives play in building parties and building government. In the absence of sufficient material incentives to construct and maintain broad-gauge political coalitions, long-run coherence in government, and coordination in policy would seem to be impossible—at least in the absence of parties based on political ideologies. Hence the decline of policy coherence and the rise of a politics characterized by disconnected subgovernmental policy making is often blamed, at least in part, on the declining availability of material incentives to political parties, which in effect leaves the field to interest groups and bureaucracies.

The contradiction emerges because strong parties, rooted in patronage, are highly destructive of disciplined implementation. While it is certainly true that strong political parties offer political leaders the resources to centralize policy making at the top, at the bottom the party organization, acting in a decentralized and uncoordinated fashion, makes claims on the implementing bureaucracy that are corrosive of the smooth implementation of programs. In the case of building regulation in Chicago, the party ward organizations resemble geographically based interest groups more than parties. They make claims on agency officials for special treatment for their constituents. They often get a favorable hearing because the officials to whom they make these claims are themselves patronage appointees and ward politicians.

In one very real sense, this is all democratic. Services are, after all, distributable goods, and what is more democratic than the ward organizations acting on behalf of constituents to demand services from a sympathetic government? Here, however, grass-roots party government clashes with the model of overhead democracy with its stress on democratically formulated policies implemented by a neutral, hierarchical bureaucracy.

Many writers have lauded the role of political parties as controllers of interest-group politics. Parties, so the argument goes, are based in popular opinion; they rely on voting majorities. Interest groups, on the other hand, represent specialized publics. It is in the interest of parties to force compromise among interest groups in order to construct a governing coalition. This strain toward compromise would, presumably, limit the operation of single-issue politics and the development of networks of interested citizens who pursue the goals of interest groups to the exclusion of the public interest.

In the case of building regulation in Chicago, certainly the political party served as a resource that contributed to the power of the mayor. This implied power acted to cement an arrangement that might best be described as cozy. Far from breaking the power of subgovernments, the party created one. (To be more precise, the party allowed the creation of one.) What is remarkable about the situation is that the subgovernment was created from interests that were themselves antagonistic and would not have engaged in compromise and conciliation without the imposed structure. Other important interests, less likely to compromise with groups entrenched in the prevailing arrangement, were excluded from the decision-making structure. In other words, the party certainly was important in limiting the unbridled power of interest groups, by a strategy of inclusion for some and denial of access for others, but it is debatable whether this system worked in the public interest.

The party, then, plays a dual role in the governing process. It acts as a resource for centralizing power and imposing structure by simply being there. An adept chief executive can use the power of party in the governing process because he or she is assured of substantial political support for whatever policy proposals he or she supports. Moreover, past policy settlements are enforced by the same system of implied power. Of course the entire notion of the chief executive in a machine city using political resources to govern is somewhat backwards. More frequently a mayor probably uses government to increase his or her political resources. Whether a political leader is using government to gain political advantage or using political advantage to govern at any one time is probably impossible to unravel. Both, of course, occur, oftentimes simultaneously.

The party's second role is as interest group. Political parties as organizations have a limited number of objectives, all of which involve the use of government to gain organizational advantage—just like all interest groups. Some claims on government directly benefit the party—the number of patronage appointments, or favorable election procedures, to cite two very important examples. Other claims might be viewed as investments. It is an investment in the future electoral viability of a ward organization when a precinct captain lodges a complaint about an abandoned building in his territory, or when he helps a small businessman with a problem with an occupancy permit. Whether this investment in good will has an effect at the time is an empirical question; but it is an operating assumption of machine politicians. A second investment is less concerned with good will and more concerned with the maintenance of a stable constituency. Ward organizations are based on geography, not the individual characteristics of residents. If constituents move and are replaced by new constituents with different racial, ethnic, and religious characteristics, the possibility of a challenge to the existing ward committeeman and his minions arises. Good services can help to stabilize an area; hence demanding good services from City Hall is an investment in the future of the existing ward organization.

The party as interest group is usually not concerned with the smooth implementation of policies that the party as resource for the mayor supported at the enactment stage. Each ward organization has interests that differ from another's, from those of the local party structure, and from those of the major governmental officials who are important in party affairs. Milton Rakove has noted that the "political machine today is a highly decentralized structure, based once more [since Daley's death] on autonomous committeemen who run their wards like fiefdoms."[2] As neighborhood-based interest groups, the ward organizations often make demands on government officials that run counter to the bureaucratic decision rules established to implement public policies. In this conflict it is an open question which system of behavior best represents the interest of the public. After all, if the standard procedures of the public bureaucracies always fit the needs of citizens, there would be no need for the party to intervene on behalf of citizens.

The decline of party in America is often attributed to the rise of merit-based bureaucracies with universalistic norms and extensive resources for solving human problems. Wolfinger is doubtless correct in his observation that the number of citizens in need in America's cities suggests that the rise of social programs is not sufficient to account for the decline of the machine.[3] However, the decline of patronage positions in these bureaucracies means a decline in the ability of parties to establish attention rules in those bureaucracies. In the absence of such connections, the party's unique linkage function fails; it is simply an intermediary to an organization whose logic of operation is unaffected by partisan demands.

As good Weberians we are probably more offended by partisan interference in bureaucratic decision rules than the activities of party as intermediary. It is important to remember that the two are intertwined. In the absence of large-scale patronage, both the bothersome attention rules and the neighborhood-intermediary activities of the party disappear, both victims of a lack of personnel. Neither bureaucracy nor neighborhood can be monitored.

Distribution and Collective Benefits

The degree to which we evaluate the machine's performance in the policy process positively depends in part on the degree to which we view urban public policies as distributable. Each urban public service is, in the language of the public economists, an impure public good. On the one hand, services such as refuse collection, police protection, and building regulation make the entire community a better place to live. Because the free market as a mechanism of allocation will underproduce (relative to economic demand) collective goods, the level of such services must be determined through the political process. This view of urban services leads to a preference for the overhead-democracy model, in which the bureaucracy is simply a neutral instrument for implementing whatever levels of service are established by the political branches of government. The party ought not interfere.

On the other hand, urban services may be delivered to some groups and denied others. Most services are specific to a limited geographic area, and income, ethnic, and racial groups are spatially separate in the city. To the extent that this distributable dimension of service delivery is emphasized, it is difficult to deny a role for the party as a neighborhood interest group. Even if the bureaucracy delivers services more effectively (in the sense of making a larger impact on community goals), responding to neighborhood demands for service is more relevant to satisfying citizen preferences than are bureaucratic operating procedures.

Party Competition and Party Responsibility

It is of course very conceivable that the particular disjunction between governing and administration is a consequence of the long rule of the Democratic party in Chicago. V. O. Key, Jr., argued the inadequacies of one-party rule in maintaining honest and responsible government some three decades ago.[4] While most quantitative state-level studies of the effects of partisan competition on the level of policy outputs have suggested a minor role for this variable, there is some evidence that competition does cause a political system to produce policies more closely matching the preferences of the citizenry.[5]

While intraparty factionalism is a pale substitute for vigorous partisan competition, nevertheless the election of Jane Byrne as mayor should suggest possible changes in governing arrangements in a period of elite replacement. There were changes, many of them significant. New interests were brought into the subgovernment centering on building regulation, for example. Yet there was no indication of the demise of the system of attention rules or of the buttressing patronage system. Indeed, Byrne, who was in a weaker position organizationally than Bilandic, was more willing to use patronage as a political weapon. This could result in attention rules benefiting different neighborhoods, but it hardly subverts the system of political interference in bureaucratic processes.

It is also possible that responsible parties[6] rooted in ideological differences among the citizenry could fuse the disjunction between governing and administration. By relying on ideological differences to mobilize support for a chief executive's program, and by relying on ideology as a nonmaterial incentive for party workers, the responsible-party model seems to solve the contradiction that afflicts American "umbrella" parties. And the idea of responsibility is far from dead either among practitioners of the art of politics, some of whom are currently calling for "realignment," or among academics. For example, Stone and Reynolds have argued for the further development of ideologically cohesive parties, on the grounds that administrative accountability ought to be subordinated to partisan accountability.[7]

There are, of course, a number of arguments against the efficacy of the party-responsibility model. Because cohesive parties would polarize the electorate, they intensify social conflict. Because they eliminate insurgency, they limit the number of districts that could be competitive in an umbrella system. In any case, substantial party cohesion already exists.[8]

Whatever the merits of the normative arguments over party responsibility, the empirical reality in America is a party system with appeals to voters based both on material incentives and ideology. The Democratic party is more wed to the material incentive approach to governing; the Republican party tends to be more ideological. Insofar as governing coalitions are built and maintained by material incentives, the coherence of programs will decline as the availability of material incentives declines. Yet as the availability of material incentives grows, the coherence of administration will decline.

The Patronage Connection

Patronage is the lifeblood of the machine; indeed, patronage is a major motivator of human political activity. While chief executives can govern and political parties can exist without extensive patronage, machines cannot. The key to understanding machine governance, and hence strong party rule in America, lies in the operation of the personnel system. Modern municipal government is complex; tasks are specialized and interdependent. The personnel system must be capable of staffing positions with qualified people and managing the demands of ward politicians for the jobs necessary to sustain their ward organizations.

Simply put, patronage and personnel must be coordinated. In Chicago this means a close working relationship between the mayor's patronage chief and the director of the Department of Personnel. A weak civil service system offers opportunities for politicians, yet civil service does play a very important constraining role in Chicago. Politicians must remain cognizant of government's formal commitment to a merit system and must deal with court decisions unfavorable to the operation of the patronage system. Hence politics and bureaucracy are as intertwined in the implementation of personnel policies as they are in service delivery.

While the dominant trend for well over half a century has been toward less patronage, at least one journalist has called for more patronage positions in government. This voice in the wilderness is Charles Peters of the *Washington Monthly,* who believes that patronage positions would attract more risk takers into government and "provide a legitimate reward for political participation." Peters, recognizing the expertise and stability in government promoted by a professional civil service, has called for a mixture of civil service and patronage positions.[9]

Municipal government in Chicago, in modern times, has incorporated such a combination. The results have been mixed. On the one hand, patronage workers do sustain the party-in-the-neighborhood and are sensitive to the demands of citizens in their roles as government officials. On the other hand, a substantial amount of party business is conducted on city time by Chicago's "pooches." Perhaps most important, a conflict between the political ethic and the bureaucratic ethic is incorporated into the agency's style of conducting business, and this tension is reflected in the job stress felt by agency personnel. They have contradictory expectations placed on them, from ward politicians on the one hand and from bureaucratic superiors on the other.

Conclusions

The ideal of overhead democracy, coupled with neutral, disciplined bureaucracies, is so firmly entrenched in the lore of political science that its return as a guiding principle in the discipline has hardly been noticed. Yet its return has pushed aside a model of democratic government that held sway for a quarter of a century: pluralism.

Not so very long ago, pluralism displaced overhead democracy as a normative standard. As modern democracies became more complex, responding to an increasingly differentiated and interconnected economy, many observers rejected the seemingly simplistic overhead-democracy model. Legislatures and chief executives seemed incapable of achieving the statutory formalism and central control necessary for limiting bureaucratic discretion and imposing precise standards of implementation. Indeed, they often seemed uninterested in doing so. Moreover, the overhead-democracy model, with its implied responsiveness to majority preferences, seemed incapable of preserving liberty for minorities.

Pluralism, with its emphasis on transitory governing coalitions, agency discretion, and the weighting of the preferences of organized, interested citizens, seemed capable of providing a rational system of governing. Yet no sooner was pluralism established as the prevailing normative standard than critics began their attacks. Most critics confined themselves to highlighting weaknesses in the model: it mobilized bias on behalf of the well off; it discouraged full democratic participation; it was not self-balancing because of the tendency for group conflict to degenerate into isolated subgovernments; it stymied straightforward implementation of public policies. The one complete presentation of alternatives has been the work of Theodore Lowi. His "juridical democracy" model relies heavily (though without citation) on what earlier students of government termed overhead democracy.[10] Nevertheless, variants of the model clearly serve as a standard for evaluating the policy process. The reliance on this model as a guiding principle is summarized by the term "democratic accountability."[11]

Effective political parties are necessary for the citizen-government linkages of overhead democracy to be realized. In their absence mass democracy is an impossibility. Yet I have argued in this book that parties in America cannot simultaneously serve as "umbrellas" for brokering differences in a diverse society, act as linkages to the mass public, *and* be denied access to the rich patronage of public employment. Umbrella parties require a pragmatic, nonideological approach to politics; hence the party faithful cannot be aroused by programmatic appeals. Government-citizen linkages require parties staffed at all levels, and may even require partisan interference in bureaucratic affairs to satisfy individual citizens' demands on government. Yet both extensive patronage and the violation of bureaucratic procedural fairness would be required to sustain such a system. While such a system worked in Chicago, it does not fit prevailing conceptions of politics in the general American culture. Our dilemma, then, is that our parties are so weakened that they can serve neither as aggregators of diverse interests nor as mechanisms for citizen-government linkages. We cannot strengthen them without weakening the professional civil service so carefully crafted at national, state, and local levels over the years. Politics and administration can, it seems, be separated, but we get both a different politics and a different administration if we do.

Postscript

In the spring of 1983, two events occurred in Chicago that have important implications for the subject of this study. While neither makes any finding presented here any less valid, both suggest the continued decline of the role of the political party in urban governance, even in Chicago.

The first event, mentioned previously, is the election of a reform-minded black mayor in Chicago. The election was both racially and ideologically polarized, with ethnic whites facing blacks and reform-minded lakefront whites. A politics of commitment had replaced, for the time being, the classic urban ethnic skills of conciliation and compromise.[1]

The second, although important for the conduct of government in Chicago, received little media coverage by comparison. On April 4, U.S. District Judge Nicholas J. Bua issued a legal order implementing his 1979 decision that politically based hiring was unconstitutional. The appeals of his order exhausted, Bua imposed by judicial fiat what generations of reformers failed to accomplish through the political process. He mandated merit-based hiring on all but a handful of exempt appointees.

In an April 23 hearing on a Cook County Democratic Party motion to suspend temporarily the order, a lawyer for the challengers of the patronage system claimed that "Mayor Byrne will and has been doing some political hiring."[2] In a true patronage system, of course, that would have been of little consequence. Washington, the incoming mayor, could simply fire them. But under a consent decree entered in 1972, these employees would be protected. The court had already prohibited politically based firing.

Mayor Washington vowed not to use his patronage powers and embraced the Shakman decision against patronage. He acknowledged that this has diminished his authority over the city council but claimed that "it does not mean that there will not be discipline, but it will be of a different form."[3] He did not specify what form that discipline might take.

On December 28, 1983, the city council took a final vote on a budget compromise between the council majority and the mayor. Edward Burke, chairman of the finance committee, in a comment that an earlier Burke perhaps would have found amusing, said, "I must be constrained to admit that it used to be a helluva lot easier in the old days when you got your instructions about what to do."[4] Far more important than the budget compromise, or the increase in council committees that enraged media commentators, was a "job security" provision. The majority bloc won civil service status (after a six-month probationary period) for eight thousand "departmental service" employees. These "permanent temporaries," who were the mainstay of the patronage system, would be granted civil service protection. The irony, of course, is that the majority machine aldermen managed to get civil service protection for their supporters from a reform mayor, who seemed quite willing to hand over resources to his political antagonists.

The limitation on the patronage power has more important implications for the governance of Chicago than does the election of a black, reform-oriented mayor. Slowly the linkages between citizens and government that are mediated by the party will decline. Attention rules will become increasingly difficult to monitor and maintain. Government will become increasingly disjointed, and the office of the mayor will be permanently weakened. Policy settlements will become harder to impose and sustain. Employee unions will gain in power as the party, like its counterpart elsewhere, withers. Groups excluded from the machine's governing coalition will probably find it easier to gain a hearing on matters of concern to them but may well find it no easier to achieve their ends in a more open, but deconcentrated, political system. All of this will likely occur gradually, because the cement of social solidarity and habit die slowly. Eventually, however, Chicago may become as ungovernable as New York and Los Angeles.

I have used a case study of a single agency in a single city during a relatively short period of time to comment on the role of the political party in the process of governance. As such, all conclusions must be strictly qualified. In the absence of such studies, however, our understanding of how the party system affects the governing process is limited.

What is clear from the study is the role of the patronage power in forging policy settlements and in linking citizens to government in the service-delivery process. With the decline of patronage, it will be easier for groups to get issues of concern to them to the community policy agenda. At the same time it will be harder for citizens to gain a hearing on the things that concern them in their neighborhoods. And it will be harder to forge any consensus about governing the city—even if that consensus is exclusive rather than inclusive. Washington is wrong; so long as there exists economic and ethnic diversity in Chicago, the discipline of party is irreplaceable.

Notes

Preface

1. Leon Epstein, "The Scholarly Commitment to Parties," in *Political Science: The State of the Discipline,* ed. Ada Finifter (Washington, D.C.: American Political Science Association, 1983), p. 145.

Chapter 1

1. Lester C. Thurow, *The Zero-Sum Society* (New York: Basic Books, 1980), p. 212.

2. The American Assembly, *The Future of American Political Parties,* Final report of the 62d American Assembly, Columbia University, New York City, April 15–18, 1982, p. 4.

3. A revisionist literature on the "party decline" thesis is beginning to appear. For a review and some new ideas, see Joseph A. Schlesinger, "On the Theory of Party Organization," *Journal of Politics* 46 (May 1984): 367–400.

4. See Bruce A. Ackerman, ed., *Economic Foundations of Property Law* (Boston: Little, Brown, 1975).

5. Kay Lawson, ed., *Political Parties and Linkage* (New Haven, Conn.: Yale University Press, 1980); and Norman Luttbeg, ed., *Public Opinion and Public Policy,* 3d ed. (Itasca, Ill.: Peacock, 1981).

6. American Assembly, *Future of Political Parties,* p. 10.

7. Leon Epstein, *Political Parties in Western Democracies* (New Brunswick, N.J.: Transaction Books, 1980), p. 101.

8. Ibid., p. 103.

9. See Helmut Norpoth and Jerrold G. Rusk, "Partisan Dealignment in the American Electorate: Itemizing the Deductions since 1964," *American Political Science Review* 76 (September 1982): 522–37.

10. Samuel C. Patterson, "The Semi-Sovereign Congress," and Austin

Ranney, "The Political Parties," both in *The New American Political System,* ed. Anthony King (Washington: American Enterprise Institute, 1978). Samuel Eldersveld, however, is more sanguine about the continuing ability of the party system to provide linkage and to increase its ability to do so. See his *Political Parties in American Society* (New York: Basic Books, 1982).

11. Frank Goodnow, *Politics and Administration* (New York: Macmillan, 1900), p. 106.

12. Eldersveld, *Political Parties in American Society.*

13. See Thomas Dye, *Policy Analysis* (University: University of Alabama Press, 1976).

14. Robert Lineberry and Edmund P. Fowler, "Reformism and Public Policies in American Cities," *American Political Science Review* 61 (September 1967): 701–16; William Lyons, "Reform and Response in American Cities: Structure and Policy Reconsidered," *Social Science Quarterly* 59 (June 1978): 118–32.

15. Robert C. Fried, "Party and Policy in West German Cities," *American Political Science Review* 70 (March 1976): 11–24; see also the collection of studies in Kenneth Newton, ed., *Urban Political Economy* (New York: St. Martin's Press, 1981).

16. Thomas Dye, *Politics, Economics, and the Public* (Chicago: Rand McNally, 1966), chap. 9.

17. Robert Erikson, "The Relationship between Party Control and Civil Rights Legislation in American States," *Western Political Quarterly* 24 (March 1971): 178–82.

18. John Fenton, *Midwest Politics* (New York: Holt, 1966).

19. Richard C. Elling, "State Party Platforms and State Legislative Performance: A Comparative Analysis," *American Journal of Political Science* 23 (May 1979): 383–405.

20. Edward Jennings, "Competition, Constituencies, and Welfare Policies in American States," *American Political Science Review* 73 (June 1979): 414–29.

21. David Nice, "Party, Ideology, and Policy Outcomes in the American States," *Social Science Quarterly* 63 (September 1982): 556–65.

22. Robert Lineberry, *Equality and Public Policy: The Distribution of Municipal Public Services* (Beverly Hills, Calif.: Sage, 1977); Bryan D. Jones, with Saadia Greenberg and Joseph Drew, *Service Delivery in the City: Citizen Demand and Bureaucratic Response* (New York: Longmans, 1980); Frank Levy, Arnold J. Meltsner, and Aaron Wildavsky, *Urban Outcomes* (Berkeley and Los Angeles: University of California Press, 1974).

23. Kenneth Mladenka, "The Urban Bureaucracy and the Chicago Political Machine: Who Gets What and the Limits to Political Control," *American Political Science Review* 74 (December 1980): 991–98.

24. David Cingranelli, "Race, Politics, and Elites: Testing Alternative Models of Municipal Service and Distribution," *American Journal of Political Science* 25 (November 1981): 664–92. See also Frederic N. Bolotin and David L. Cingranelli, "Equity and Urban Policy: The Underclass Hypothesis Revisited," *Journal of Politics* 45 (February 1983): 209–19.

25. Kenneth Mladenka, "The Political Machine, the Urban Bureaucracy, and the Distribution of Public Services," in *Chicago Politics Papers* (Evanston, Ill.: Center of Urban Affairs, Northwestern University, 1979).

26. Wallace S. Sayre and Herbert Kaufman, *Governing New York City* (New York: W. W. Norton, 1965), chap. 12.

27. Edward C. Banfield, *Political Influence* (New York: Free Press, 1961).

28. Matthew A. Crenson, *The Un-Politics of Air Pollution* (Baltimore: Johns Hopkins University Press, 1971), chap. 5.

29. J. David Greenstone and Paul E. Peterson, *Race and Authority in Urban Politics* (Chicago: University of Chicago Press, 1976).

30. Paul E. Peterson, *School Politics, Chicago Style* (Chicago: University of Chicago Press, 1976), p. 55.

31. Milton Rakove, *We Don't Want Nobody Nobody Sent* (Bloomington: University of Indiana Press, 1979), p. 12.

32. Raymond Wolfinger, "Why Machines Have Not Withered Away and Other Revisionist Thoughts," *Journal of Politics* 34 (May 1972): 365–98.

33. See George Sternlieb and James W. Hughes, "Back to the Central City: Myths and Realities," in *America's Housing: Prospects and Problems,* ed. George Sternlieb and James W. Hughes (New Brunswick, N.J.: Center for Urban Policy Research, Rutgers University, 1980).

34. *Housing the Chicago Region* (Chicago: Metropolitan Housing and Planning Council, 1981), p. 17.

35. The two best sources on Chicago politics are Milton Rakove, *Don't Make No Waves, Don't Back No Losers* (Bloomington: Indiana University Press, 1975); and Samuel K. Gove and Louis H. Masotti, eds., *After Daley: Chicago Politics in Transition* (Urbana: University of Illinois Press, 1982). On Chicago government, see Chicago Home Rule Commission, *Report and Recommendations* (Chicago: University of Illinois at Chicago Circle, 1972), and League of Women Voters of Cook County, *The Key to Our Local Government,* 4th ed. (Chicago: Citizens' Information Service, 1978).

36. The description relies on Rakove, *Don't Make No Waves,* chap. 4.

37. Ibid., p. 106.

38. See Gove and Masotti, eds., *After Daley,* especially the articles by Kemp and Lineberry, Zikmund, and Grimshaw.

39. Again, see ibid. for the best recent attempts.

40. This argument is made well by Kemp and Lineberry. See Kathleen Kemp and Robert L. Lineberry, "The Last of the Great Urban Machines and the

Last of the Great Urban Mayors? Chicago Politics, 1955–1977," in *After Daley,* ed. Gove and Masotti, pp. 1–26.

41. David Axelrod, "Washington Must Avoid Falling into Byrne Trap," *Chicago Tribune,* February 27, 1983.

42. David Axelrod, "Byrne Puts Bet on 'Fast Eddie,'" *Chicago Tribune,* March 28, 1982.

Chapter 2

1. Floyd Hunter, *Community Power Structure* (Chapel Hill: University of North Carolina Press, 1953), and *Community Power Succession: Atlanta's Policy-Makers Revisited* (Chapel Hill: University of North Carolina Press, 1980); William Domhoff, *Who Really Rules? New Haven and Community Power Reexamined* (New Brunswick, N.J.: Transaction Books, 1978); Michael Parenti, *Power and the Powerless* (New York: St. Martin's Press, 1978); Robert A. Dahl, *Who Governs?* (New Haven, Conn.: Yale University Press, 1961); Nelson Polsby, *Community Power and Political Theory,* 2d ed. (New Haven, Conn.: Yale University Press, 1980); Raymond Wolfinger, *The Politics of Progress* (Englewood Cliffs, N.J.: Prentice-Hall, 1974).

2. Peter Saunders, "The Relevance of Weberian Sociology for Political Analysis," *Geographical Papers,* no. 80, Department of Geography, University of Reading, U.K., January 1982, p. 17.

3. Michael Dear, "A Theory of the Local State," in *Political Studies from Spatial Perspectives,* ed. Alan Burnett and Peter Taylor (Winchester, U.K.: John Wiley, 1981), pp. 183–200.

4. Edward Banfield, *Political Influence* (New York: Free Press, 1961), p. 253.

5. Lawrence Veiller, *Tenement House Legislation in New York, 1852–1900* (Albany, N.Y.: Brandow Printing Co., 1900), p. 11.

6. Edith Abbott, *The Tenements of Chicago, 1908–1935* (Chicago: University of Chicago Press, 1936), p. 37.

7. Veiller, *Tenement House Legislation,* p. 11.

8. Abbott, *Tenements of Chicago,* p. 55.

9. Ernest Ritson Dewsnip, *The Housing Problem in England* (Manchester, U.K.: University of Manchester Press, 1907); C.W. Stewart, *The Housing Question in London, 1855–1900* (London: Jas. Truscott and Sons, 1900).

10. Lawrence Veiller, *A Model Housing Law,* rev. ed. (New York: Russell Sage, 1920), p. 4.

11. Veiller, *Tenement House Legislation;* Roy Lubove, *The Progressives and the Slums: Tenement House Reform in New York City, 1880–1917* (Pittsburgh: University of Pittsburgh Press, 1962).

12. Abbott, *Tenements of Chicago,* pp. 58–61; Warren W. Lehman, "Building Codes, Housing Codes, and the Conservation of Chicago's Housing Supply," *University of Chicago Law Review* 31 (Autumn 1963): 180–203.

13. U.S. Congress. Senate. Committee on Banking, Housing, and Urban Affairs. *Impact of Building Codes on Housing Rehabilitation,* 95th Cong., 2d sess., March 24, 1978, p. 105.

14. Ibid., p. 35.

15. Anthony Downs, "Up and Down with Ecology: The Issue-Attention Cycle," *Public Interest* 28 (June 1972): 37–50; Roger Cobb and Charles D. Elder, *Participation in American Politics: The Dynamics of Agenda Building* (Boston: Allyn and Bacon, 1972); Bryan Jones, *Governing Urban America* (Boston: Little, Brown, 1983), chap. 2.

16. For a description of this process in another jurisdiction, see John E. Stoner, *Building Regulation in Indiana: A Study of Public Rule-Making by Private Specialists* (Bloomington: Bureau of Government Research, Indiana University, 1951).

17. *City of Chicago Building Code,* §21-25.

18. Ray Pahl, *Whose City?* (Harmondsworth, U.K.: Penguin, 1975); and Peter Saunders, *Urban Politics* (London: Hutchinson, 1979), pp. 148–49.

19. Jacob Riis, *How the Other Half Lives* (New York: Hill and Wang, 1957), p. 205.

20. Donald Haider, *When Governments Come to Washington* (New York: Free Press, 1974).

21. Susan E. Clarke, "The Private Use of the Public Interest," Paper presented at the Southwestern Political Science Association, San Antonio, Tex., March 17–20, 1982.

22. Ibid.; Saunders, *Urban Politics,* chap. 4; see also Paul E. Peterson, *City Limits* (Chicago: University of Chicago Press, 1981). While Peterson does not explicitly argue a corporatist position, he does claim that an overriding citywide interest emerges on economic development issues.

23. *City of Chicago Building Code,* §78-8.5, §78-8.2.

24. See the *Metropolitan Housing and Planning Council Reports* 9 (June 1982) for an overview of the rehabilitation code. Changes were also made in the zoning, plumbing, and electrical codes.

25. However, the building trades were able to persuade the city council to remove a provision allowing the use of easily installed plastic pipe.

26. Douglas Yates, *The Ungovernable City* (Cambridge, Mass.: MIT Press, 1977); Frederick M. Wirt, *Power in the City* (Berkeley and Los Angeles: University of California Press, 1974); Donald Haider, "Sayre and Kaufman Revisited: New York City Government since 1965," *Urban Affairs Quarterly* 15 (December 1979).

Chapter 3

1. Robert A. Dahl and Charles E. Lindblom, *Politics, Economics, and Welfare* (New York: Harper and Row, 1953).

2. Thomas C. Schelling, *Micromotives and Macrobehavior* (New York: W. W. Norton, 1978), p. 17.

3. Amitai Etzioni, "Organizational Control Structure," in *Handbook of Organizations,* ed. James G. March (Chicago: Rand McNally, 1965), p. 650.

4. Dahl and Lindblom, *Politics, Economics, and Welfare,* p. 100.

5. Ibid.

6. See Michael Lipsky, *Street-Level Bureaucracy: Dilemmas of the Individual in Public Services* (New York: Russell Sage, 1980).

7. Aaron Wildavsky, *Speaking Truth to Power* (Boston: Little, Brown, 1979), chap. 6.

8. Ibid., p. 49.

9. Michael Lipsky, *Protest in City Politics* (Chicago: Rand McNally, 1970).

10. John J. McGlennon, "The Effects of Corruption Scandals on Police Department Control and Support," paper presented at the Annual Meeting of the American Political Science Association, Washington, D.C., September 1–4, 1977.

11. Ibid., p. 1.

12. James G. March and Johan P. Olsen, *Ambiguity and Choice in Organizations* (Bergen: Universitsforlaget, 1976).

13. Findings reported by Peters and Welch indicate that response is not unwarranted. In a study of corruption allegations in elections for the U.S. House of Representatives, these authors report that candidates who are the subject of such allegations experience definite vote losses. See John G. Peters and Susan Welch, "The Effects of Charges of Corruption on Voting Behavior in Congressional Elections," *American Political Science Review* 74 (September 1980): 697–708.

14. Douglas Yates, *The Ungovernable City* (Cambridge, Mass.: MIT Press, 1977), p. 97.

15. John A. Gardiner and Theodore R. Lyman, *Decisions for Sale* (New York: Praeger, 1978), p. 5.

16. Ibid., pp. 10–11. For other approaches to the issue of political corruption, see Susan Rose-Ackerman, *Corruption: A Study in Political Economy* (New York: Academic Press, 1978); John G. Peters and Susan Welch, "Political Corruption in America: A Search for Definitions and a Theory," *American Political Science Review* 72 (September 1978): 974–84.

17. Edith Abbott, *The Tenements of Chicago, 1908–35* (Chicago: University of Chicago Press, 1936), p. 57.

18. Bruce A. Ackerman, "Regulating Slum Housing Markets on Behalf of the Poor," in *Economic Foundations of Property Law,* ed. Bruce A. Ackerman (Boston: Little, Brown, 1975), pp. 160–214; Chester W. Hartman, Robert P. Kessler, and Richard T. Legates, "Municipal Housing Code Enforcement and Low Income Tenants," *American Institute of Planners Journal* 40 (March 1974): 90–104; Yale Komesar, "Return to Slumville: A Critique of the Ackerman Analysis of Housing Code Enforcement and the Poor," *Yale Law Journal* 83 (1973): 1175–93; Richard S. Markovits, "The Distributive Impact, Allocative Efficiency, and Overall Desirability of Ideal Housing Codes: Some Theoretical Clarifications," *Harvard Law Review* 89 (1976): 1815–46.

19. Daniel R. Mandelker, Julie Gibb, and Annette B. Kolis, "Differential Code Enforcement: The Constitutional Dimension," *Journal of Urban Law* 55 (1978): 516–629.

20. See Zay Smith and Pamela Zeckman, *The Mirage* (New York: Random House, 1979).

21. "Building Code Cases Down 90 Percent," Chicago *Tribune,* December 21, 1980.

22. Apparently the reorganization experience was not unique to Chicago. In a study of twelve comprehensive administrative reorganizations in the U.S. government in the twentieth century, March and Olsen report little impact on cost, efficiency, or control. See James G. March and Johan P. Olsen, "Organizing Political Life: What Administrative Reorganization Tells Us about Government," *American Political Science Review* 77 (June 1983): 281–96.

23. James G. March and Herbert A. Simon, *Organizations* (New York: John Wiley, 1958), p. 38.

24. Pietro Nivola, *The Urban Service Problem* (Lexington, Mass.: Lexington Books, 1979).

Chapter 4

1. Woodrow Wilson, "The Study of Administration," *Political Science Quarterly* 2 (June 1887): 197–220.

2. Frank Goodnow, *Politics and Administration* (New York: Macmillan, 1900).

3. Arthur W. MacMahon, "Policy and Administration," in *Administrative Questions and Political Answers,* ed. Claude E. Hawley and Ruth G. Weintraub (Princeton, N.J.: D. Van Nostrand, 1966), p. 207.

4. Emmette S. Redford, *Ideal and Practice in Public Administration* (University: University of Alabama Press, 1958), p. 89.

5. The model was, of course, once public administration orthodoxy. See Wallace S. Sayre, "Premises of Public Administration: Past and Emerging," in *Administrative Questions,* ed. Hawley and Weintraub, pp. 103–6.

6. Paul Appleby, *Policy and Administration* (University: University of Alabama Press, 1949), p. 170.

7. Norton Long, "Public Policy and Administration: The Goals of Rationality and Responsibility," in *Administrative Questions*, ed. Hawley and Weintraub, p. 55.

8. Jeffrey Pressman and Aaron Wildavsky, *Implementation* (Berkeley and Los Angeles: University of California Press, 1973); Jeffrey Pressman, *Federal Programs and City Politics* (Berkeley and Los Angeles: University of California Press, 1975); Richard Elmore, ed., *Studying Implementation* (Chatham, N.J.: Chatham House, 1982).

9. Michael Lipsky, *Street-Level Bureaucracy: Dilemmas of the Individual in Public Services* (New York: Russell Sage, 1980), chap. 2.

10. Richard Weatherly and Michael Lipsky, "Street-Level Bureaucrats and Institutional Innovation: Implementing Special Education Reform," *Harvard Educational Review* 47 (1977): 121.

11. Chester I. Barnard, *The Functions and the Executive* (Cambridge, Mass.: Harvard University Press, 1938). See also the excellent critique of Barnard's work in Charles Perrow, *Complex Organizations*, 2d ed. (Glenview, Ill.: Scott, Foresman, 1979), pp. 70–86.

12. Richard M. Cyert and James G. March, *A Behavioral Theory of the Firm* (Englewood Cliffs, N.J.: Prentice-Hall, 1963), pp. 104–5.

13. See Theodore Lowi, *The End of Liberalism*, 2d ed. (New York: W. W. Norton, 1979).

14. Richard Elmore, "Backward Mapping: Implementation Research and Policy Decisions," in *Studying Implementation*, ed. Elmore, p. 27.

15. J. Roland Pennock, *Administration and the Rule of Law* (New York: Farrar and Rinehart, 1941), p. 6.

16. E. Pendleton Herring, *Public Administration and the Public Interest* (New York: McGraw-Hill, 1936), pp. 24–25.

17. Aaron Wildavsky, *Speaking Truth to Power* (Boston: Little, Brown, 1979), chap. 1.

18. Anthony Downs, *Inside Bureaucracy* (Boston: Little, Brown, 1967), pp. 146–47.

19. Kenneth L. Kraemer, William H. Dutton, and Alana Northrop, *The Management of Information Systems* (New York: Columbia University Press, 1981).

Chapter 5

1. This chapter is a revised version of Bryan D. Jones, "Party and Bureaucracy: The Influence of Intermediary Groups on Urban Public Service Delivery," *American Political Science Review* 75 (September 1981): 688–700.

2. Frank Levy, Arnold J. Meltsner, and Aaron Wildavsky, *Urban Outcomes* (Berkeley and Los Angeles: University of California Press, 1974); Robert Lineberry, *Equality and Public Policy: The Distribution of Municipal Public Services* (Beverly Hills, Calif.: Sage, 1977); Bryan D. Jones et al. "Service Delivery Rules and the Distribution of Local Government Services: Three Detroit Bureaucracies," *Journal of Politics* 40 (February 1978): 332–68; Kenneth Mladenka, "Rules, Service Equity, and Distributional Decisions," *Social Science Quarterly* 59 (December 1978): 192–202.

3. Lineberry, *Equality and Public Policy,* p. 61.

4. John P. Crecine, *Government Problem-Solving: A Computer Simulation of Municipal Budgeting* (Chicago: Rand McNally, 1969).

5. Herbert Kaufman, "Emerging Conflicts in the Doctrines of Public Administration," *American Political Science Review* 50 (December 1956): 1057–73.

6. Richard C. Rich, "Neglected Issues in the Study of Urban Service Distributions," *Urban Studies* 16 (1979): 143–56, and "The Roles of Neighborhood Organizations in Urban Service Delivery," *NASPAA Urban Affairs Papers,* Fall 1979, pp. 2–20.

7. Kenneth Wald has thoroughly reviewed the existing literature on the electoral support of urban political machines. See his "The Electoral Base of a Political Machine: A Deviant Case Analysis," *Urban Affairs Quarterly* 16 (September 1980): 3–31.

8. Bryan D. Jones et al. "Bureaucratic Response to Citizen-Initiated Contacts: Environmental Enforcement in Detroit," *American Political Science Review* 71 (September 1977): 148–65; and Richard A. Brody, "The Puzzle of Political Participation in America," in *The New American Political System,* ed. Anthony King (Washington, D.C.: American Enterprise Institute for Public Policy Research, 1978), pp. 287–324.

9. Roger Kasperson, "Toward a Geography of Urban Politics," *Economic Geography* 41 (1965): 95–107.

10. Paul Dornan, "Whither Urban Policy Analysis? A Review Essay," *Polity* 9 (1977): 403–27.

11. Kenneth Mladenka, "The Urban Bureaucracy and the Chicago Political Machine: Who Gets What and the Limits to Political Control," *American Political Science Review* 74 (December 1980): 991–98.

12. Michael Lipsky, *Street-Level Bureaucracy: Dilemmas of the Individual in Public Services* (New York: Russell Sage, 1980).

13. Pietro Nivola, *The Urban Service Problem* (Lexington, Mass.: Lexington Books, 1979).

14. The master file contains information on about 800,000 of the 1.5 million dwelling units recorded by the U.S. census in 1970, but these are the dwellings that are most likely to be the targets of agency action.

15. Peter H. Rossi and Phillips Cutright, "The Impact of Party Organization in an Industrial Setting," in *Community Political Systems,* ed. Morris Janowitz (Glencoe, Ill.: Free Press, 1961).

16. Kathleen Kemp and Robert L. Lineberry, "The Last of the Great Urban Machines and the Last of the Great Urban Mayors? Chicago Politics, 1955–1977," in *After Daley: Chicago Politics in Transition,* ed. Samuel K. Gove and Louis H. Masotti (Urbana: University of Illinois Press, 1982), pp. 1–26.

17. *Chicago Community Organization Directory, 1977–78* (Chicago: Community Renewal Society, 1978).

18. This measure probably overestimates the importance of years in existence. The use of it is justified entirely by the absence of feasible alternatives which produce the interval-level measures needed for analysis.

19. Two variables that are intercorrelated may be significant singly but not in combination. The procedure outlined here ensures that both will not be dropped, and the variable with the largest partial correlation with the dependent variable will be retained.

20. The file contained all contacts made with the department except for emergency heat complaints, which were handled immediately in winter and were not read to the computerized processing system. It contained 78,708 records for 1978. The contact variable was adjusted by eliminating certain referrals that were not citizen contacts, and was divided by estimated ward population in 1975 (see the chapter appendix).

21. Forman S. Acton, *Analysis of Straight Line Data* (New York: Dover Publications, 1966), p. 223.

22. The source codes underestimate mediated complaints to some extent, since representatives of mediating organizations may not reveal themselves as such to departmental personnel.

23. The scatterplots between severity and age of buildings and between severity and complaints were substantially curvilinear, suggesting the logarithmic correction. The log transformation adequately corrected the plots, and additionally served to bring "outliers" relatively closer to the main body of the data. The data are from the recommendation file, which contained 47,621 records for 1978. There is no exact match between the complaint file and the recommendation file. Some complaints from 1977 were processed in 1978; some 1978 complaints were processed in 1979. The disparity between the number of complaints and the number of recommended actions is due primarily to the screening process, which eliminates duplicate complaints against buildings recently inspected and complaints against buildings currently in court.

24. Only violations that involve structural repair require permits. Moreover, housing court will often order owners to produce plans and permits for the court to inspect; recalcitrant owners may go through the effort and expense of obtaining a permit and then never complete (or only partially complete) the work.

Most, however, are eventually completed. I have used all the records on the permit file, from 1976 through mid-1979, rather than just those for 1978, because of the relatively small number of permits. The file contained 76,354 records at the time the analysis was performed, but only about 20 percent of these permits were taken out in response to agency action.

25. Mladenka, "Urban Bureaucracy."

26. Brett Hawkins, *Politics and Urban Policies* (Indianapolis: Bobbs-Merrill, 1971); Robert Lineberry and Edmund Fowler, "Reformism and Public Policies in American Cities," *American Political Science Review* 61 (September 1967): 701–16; Albert Karnig, "Private-Regarding Policy, Civil Rights Groups, and the Mediating Impact of Municipal Reforms," *American Journal of Political Science* 19 (February 1975): 91–106.

27. Bryan D. Jones, with Saadia Greenberg and Joseph Drew, *Service Delivery in the City: Citizen Demand and Bureaucratic Response* (New York: Longmans, 1980), chap. 8.

28. Michael Johnston, "Patrons, Clients, Jobs, and Machines: A Case Study of the Uses of Patronage," *American Political Science Review* 73 (June 1979): 385–98.

Chapter 6

1. Harold Gosnell, *Machine Politics, Chicago Model* (Chicago: University of Chicago Press, 1968), p. 74.

2. See Raymond Wolfinger, "Why Machines Have Not Withered Away and Other Revisionist Thoughts," *Journal of Politics* 34 (May 1972): 365–98.

3. Milton Rakove, *Don't Make No Waves, Don't Back No Losers* (Bloomington: Indiana University Press, 1975), p. 123.

4. Recent court decisions have outlawed politically based firing for all but the most sensitive policy positions. See *Elrod* v. *Burns* 427 U.S. 347 (1976); *Branti* v. *Finkel* 445 U.S. 507 (1980); and *Shakman* v. *Democratic Organization of Cook County* 435 F. 2d. 267 (1970). The former two cases are U.S. Supreme Court cases ruling that patronage firings or threats of firing interfere with the First and Fourteenth Amendment rights of employees. The Shakman ruling, decided by the Seventh Circuit U.S. Court of Appeals, found politically based firings to interfere with the rights of candidates and voters, because patronage workers were used to give the regular Democratic organization an unfair advantage in elections. Finally, in a recent decision, currently being appealed, Nicholas Bua, federal district judge for the Northern District of Illinois, prohibited politically based *hirings*. Even if party officials cannot fire precinct workers under current law, it remains possible for them to recruit loyal workers and find them positions in government. Bua's decision prohibits this.

See *Shakman* v. *Democratic Organization of Cook County,* 481 *F. Supp.* 1315 (1979).

5. Len O'Connor, *Clout: Mayor Daley and His City* (New York: Avon, 1975), p. 85. An interesting revisionist literature has recently emerged questioning the role of such material incentives as patronage jobs in sustaining urban machines. These works point to the importance of personal loyalty, partisan affiliation, and group solidarity rather than direct exchange (jobs for political work) in maintaining party organization. See Thomas Guterbock, *Machine Politics in Transition: Party and Community in Chicago* (Chicago: University of Chicago Press, 1980), and John Kinkaid, "Mentoring, Loyalty, and the Persistence of Machine Politics in Jersey City," Paper presented at the Annual Meeting of the Southwest Political Science Association, Dallas, Texas, March 21–23, 1981. While these authors are doubtless correct in emphasizing nonmaterial incentives in motivating party activists, they do not stress sufficiently the mutually reinforcing character of loyalty and exchange in urban party organizations. In the absence of patronage, loyalties decline—not immediately, but gradually over an extended period of time. Quite simply, there exists no strong party organization in America where there is no patronage (although patronage does not ensure strong organization).

6. The higher figure, reported by Milton Rakove, is more believable. See Rakove, *Don't Make No Waves,* p. 112. The lower figure was stipulated by the parties in the court case of *Shakman* v. *Democratic Organization of Cook County,* 481 *F. Supp.* 1315 (1979), at 1325, a case involving a challenge to patronage hiring. Independent estimates to be presented later suggest that even Rakove's more generous estimate may be somewhat low.

7. Rakove, *Don't Make No Waves,* p. 93.

8. Frank J. Sorauf, "State Patronage in a Rural County," *American Political Science Review* 50 (December 1956): 1046–56.

9. Michael Johnston, "Patrons, Clients, Jobs and Machines: A Case Study of the Uses of Patronage," *American Political Science Review* 73 (June 1979): 385–97.

10. See Robert Lineberry, "The Decline and Fall of the Daley Empire," *Arts and Sciences: The Magazine of the College of Arts and Sciences,* Northwestern University, Fall 1979, for a justification of the use of this measure.

11. Specifically, the adjustment was achieved as follows. First, a regression analysis was performed using local government jobs as a percentage of ward population twenty-one years of age and over (to standardize the measure), and with certain demographic variables included as independent variables. The analysis was performed in stepwise fashion, and the final equation included race and income as significant predictors of employment. The final equation was:

Local government employment $= -0.7 + 0.1$ income (thousands) $+ 0.5\%$
                                black
         t: 5.67 9.67   9.22
         $R^2 = .696$; $F = 53.83$; $N = 50$

Regression residuals from this analysis are used for the adjusted employment figures. (All data are from the 1970 census.)

12. Johnston, "Patrons, Clients," p. 397.

13. F. Richard Ciccone, "Bilandic Designs 'Southern Plan,'" *Chicago Tribune,* February 25, 1979.

14. Robert Lineberry and Sharon Watson, "Neighborhoods, Politics, and Public Services: The Case of Chicago," *Urban Interest* 2 (Spring 1980): 17.

15. Paul McGrath, "The Machine's Mystique," *Chicago,* January 1981, pp. 22–24. The poll was conducted the previous September. McGrath also reports that a University of Chicago study in 1975 reported a similar level of calling on political officials for help.

16. National Commission on Civil Disorders, *Supplementary Studies* (Washington, D.C.: U.S. Government Printing Office, 1968), p. 41, reports that some 28 percent of urban dwellers have contacted city officials about services; Joel Aberbach and Jack Walker in "The Attitudes of Blacks and Whites toward City Services: Implications for Public Policy," in *Financing the Metropolis,* ed. John P. Crecine (Beverly Hills, Calif.: Sage, 1970), state that only about a third of Detroiters report complaining to city government. Even lower figures are reported for Milwaukee by Peter Eisinger in *Patterns of Interracial Conflict* (New York: Academic Press, 1976), p. 120.

17. Lineberry and Watson, "Neighborhoods, Politics," p. 15.

18. Ibid., p. 16.

19. Richard C. Rich, "Interaction of the Voluntary and Governmental Sectors: Toward an Understanding of the Co-production of Municipal Services," *Administration and Society* 3 (May 1981): 60. See also Roger Parks et al., "Coproduction of Public Services," in *Analyzing Urban Service Distributions,* ed. Richard C. Rich (Lexington, Mass: Lexington Books, 1982), pp. 185–99; Gordon P. Whittaker, "Co-Production: Citizen Participation in Service Delivery," *Public Administration Review* 40 (1980): 240–46.

20. Richard C. Rich, "A Political Economy Approach to the Study of Neighborhood Organizations," *American Journal of Political Science* 24 (November 1980): pp. 559–92.

21. As noted in chapter 5, these organizations were those active in code enforcement; altogether forty-nine useable interviews were obtained. The basic sampling frame was constructed from a list of registered community organizations maintained by the building department for processing complaints. A "snowballing" technique was employed to ensure that all organizations active in code enforcement were included. A surprisingly large number of organiza-

tions we traced were either no longer active in the housing area or had ceased to exist.

Chapter 7

1. For a fuller discussion of the benefits of urban service efforts, see Bryan D. Jones, "Assessing the Products of Government: What Gets Delivered?" *Policy Studies Journal* 9 (Summer 1981): 963–71.

2. On programmed decision-making in organizations, see James G. March and Herbert Simon, *Organizations* (New York: John Wiley, 1958); Richard M. Cyert and James March, *A Behavioral Theory of the Firm* (Englewood Cliffs, N.J.: Prentice-Hall, 1963); Lawrence C. Pierce, "Organizational Constraints and Public Bureaucracies," in *Political Science Annual*, vol. 5, ed. Cornelius P. Cotter (Indianapolis: Bobbs-Merrill, 1974), pp. 131–76.

3. On decision rules, see Bryan D. Jones, with Saadia Greenberg and Joseph Drew, *Service Delivery in the City: Citizen Demand and Bureaucratic Response* (New York: Longmans, 1980); and Robert Lineberry, *Equality and Public Policy: The Distribution of Municipal Public Services* (Beverly Hills, Calif.: Sage, 1977). The term *attention rule* was coined by John P. Crecine. See his *Government Problem Solving: A Computer Simulation of Municipal Budgeting* (Chicago: Rand McNally, 1969).

4. See Daniel Mandelker, Julie Gibb, and Annette B. Kolis, "Differential Code Enforcement: The Constitutional Dimension," *Journal of Urban Law* 55 (1978): 516–629.

5. Cost estimates (in 1979) were in the $60,000–70,000 range for a medium-sized home, or $400–500 per bed, exclusive of costs for plans and permits.

6. A point made by Michael Johnston with respect to machines. See his "Patrons, Clients, Jobs, and Machines: A Case Study of the Uses of Patronage," *American Political Science Review* 73 (June 1979): 385–98. Political and governmental institutions channel human behavior, but they never dictate it.

7. Outputs are adjusted by regressing the logarithm of the severity of action taken on decision-rule stimulus (state of the housing stock; number of complaints). Residuals from this regression are plotted in figure 7.1.

8. See Joseph Zikmund, "Mayoral Voting and Ethnic Politics in the Daley-Bilandic-Byrne Era," in *After Daley: Chicago Politics in Transition,* edited by Samuel Gove and Louis Masotti (Urbana: University of Illinois Press, 1982), pp. 27–56. The blocs differ only marginally from those presented in chapter 6.

9. Kenneth Mladenka, "The Urban Bureaucracy and the Chicago Political Machine: Who Gets What and the Limits to Political Control," *American Political Science Review* 74 (December 1980): 996.

10. Ibid.

11. I am indebted to Steven Brooks for digging this out. This document indicates that the patronage pool is larger than other estimates, as previous estimates for the city of Chicago were in the 8,000 range. See Milton Rakove, *Don't Make No Waves, Don't Back No Losers* (Bloomington: Indiana University Press, 1975), p. 112. Adding the columns for temporary authority and civil service positions on temporary authority yields over 9,000 positions.

12. Nor would such action conform to available descriptions of modern political bosses. See Edward Banfield, *Political Influence* (New York: Free Press, 1961).

13. Theodore Lowi, "Machine Politics, Old and New," *Public Interest* 9 (Fall 1967): 83–92.

Chapter 8

1. The following events all occurred on July 26, 1979.

2. See, for example, James Eisenstein and Herbert Jacob, *Felony Justice* (Boston: Little, Brown, 1977); Martin A. Levin, *Urban Politics and the Criminal Courts* (Chicago: University of Chicago Press, 1977); Herbert Jacob, ed., *The Potential for Reform in Criminal Justice* (Beverly Hills, Calif.: Sage, 1974).

3. Probably the best study of a civil court by a political scientist is Herbert Jacob, *Debtors in Court* (Chicago: Rand McNally, 1969).

4. See chapter 2 and chapter 3, note 18.

5. Marilyn Miller Mosier and Richard A. Soble, "Modern Legislation, Metropolitan Court, Minuscule Results: A Study of Detroit's Landlord-Tenant Court," *Journal of Law Reform* 7 (Fall 1973): 9–70. The study combined a study of court files for a year (1970–71) and systematic in-court observations. See also the update by Jonathan Rose and Martin Scott, " 'Street Talk' Summonses in Detroit's Landlord-Tenant Court: A Small Step Forward for Urban Tenants," *Journal of Urban Law* 52 (1975): 967–1031.

6. Mosier and Soble, "Modern Legislation," p. 55.

7. Seymour J. Mansfield, ed., *Judgment Landlord: A Study of Eviction Court in Chicago* (Chicago: Legal Assistance Foundation of Chicago, National Lawyers' Guild, and Chicago Council of Lawyers, 1978).

8. Ibid., p. 115.

9. For example, the comments by David Orr, a reform alderman, are fairly typical of housing reformers. He feels that housing court, and the corporation counsel's office in particular, are "in bed with the landlords." Steve Bogira, "Abandoned," *Chicago Reader* 9 (January 25, 1980): 31.

10. See, for example, *Study of Housing Court* (Chicago: Metropolitan Housing and Planning Council, 1970).

11. I focus on New York because of the availability of literature. An excellent summary of New York's past and recent experiences with the adjudication of housing-code violations is Mark C. Ratzick and Richard L. Huffman, "The New York City Housing Court: Trial and Error in Housing Code Enforcement," *New York University Law Review* 50 (October 1975): 738–97; the quotation is from p. 242.

12. Ibid., pp. 743–44.

13. Ibid., p. 758.

14. Ibid., pp. 784–86.

15. See Robert Moses, "The Enforcement Process—Housing Codes," *Urban Lawyer* 3 (1971): 560–63.

16. On the 1964 reform and its effects on the Cook County judiciary, see Wesley G. Skogan, "The Politics of Judicial Reform: Cook County, Illinois," *Judicial System Journal* 1 (September 1975): 11–23.

17. This estimate is based on data from the building department's computer files and from internal reports of the building department's Compliance Bureau.

18. The tendency to stereotype has been noted by other students of urban street-level bureaucracies. See Pietro S. Nivola, *The Urban Service Problem* (Lexington, Mass.: Lexington Books, 1979), p. 75.

19. George Sternlieb, *Tenement Landlord* (New Brunswick, N.J.: Urban Studies Center, Rutgers University, 1966), p. 80. See also George Sternlieb and Robert Burchell, *Residential Abandonment: The Tenement Landlord Revisited* (New Brunswick, N.J.: Center for Urban Policy Research, Rutgers University, 1973).

20. I have fully described this world as it centered on one building in Chicago. See Bryan Jones, "Tenement Capitalism and Building Regulation: The Magnolia Hotel," unpublished MS, 1982.

21. Nivola, *The Urban Service Problem*, pp. 74, 114.

22. These and other data used in this chapter are from computerized court files maintained by the building department. The data are updated at each court hearing. Hence we can determine the last action taken on the case, and how many hearings have been conducted on the case, but we cannot reconstruct the case's history from these data. Moreover, we cannot determine final (exit) characteristics of cases, because of the way the data are accumulated. We can, however, recover characteristics of cases heard at a particular time. This will generally cause no problems so long as the period of time chosen for observation (here, May of 1979) is not atypical. (There is no reason to think that it is.) No other information on court outcomes was kept either by housing court or by any other agency.

23. The Forty-ninth Ward, which fields the second strongest set of community organizations according to our measure, was the locus of virtually no demolition decrees. Here, housing conditions probably made a difference: the Forty-ninth suffers little housing abandonment.

24. Through the use of regression residuals.

25. The divisions on the figure are determined by breaks in the data distributions. I cannot explain the extraordinary performance of the Second Ward on this court-output measure.

Chapter 9

1. Matthew Crenson, *The Un-Politics of Air Pollution* (Baltimore: Johns Hopkins University Press, 1971).

2. Milton Rakove, "Who Controls Chicago?" *Chicago,* July 1979, p. 136.

3. Raymond Wolfinger, "Why Machines Have Not Withered Away and Other Revisionist Thoughts," *Journal of Politics* 34 (May 1972): 365–98.

4. V. O. Key, Jr., *Southern Politics* (New York: Vintage, 1949).

5. R. Kenneth Godwin and W. Bruce Shepard, "Political Process and Public Expenditures: A Re-Examination Based on Theories of Representative Government," *American Political Science Review* 70 (December 1976): 1127–35.

6. In the accepted use of the term in political science. See "Toward a More Responsible Two-Party System," Supplement to *American Political Science Review* 44 (September 1950).

7. Clarence Stone and Kathy Reynolds, "Complexity and Democratic Theory: Administrative Accountability in Post-Industrial Society," Paper presented at the Annual Meeting of the Midwest Political Science Association, Cincinnati, Ohio, April 16–18, 1981.

8. Julius Turner, "Responsible Parties: A Dissent from the Floor," *American Political Science Review* 45 (March 1951): 143–52.

9. Charles Peters, "A Neoliberal's Manifesto," *Washington Monthly,* May 1983, p. 16.

10. Theodore Lowi, *The End of Liberalism,* 2d ed. (New York: W. W. Norton, 1979), chap. 11.

11. "Accountability is the link between bureaucracy and democracy." Michael Lipsky, *Street-Level Bureaucracy: Dilemmas of the Individual in Public Services* (New York: Russell Sage, 1980), p. 160.

Postscript

1. For some insights on this election, see Melvin Holli and Paul Green, eds., *The Making of the Mayor, 1983* (Grand Rapids, Mich.: Eerdmans, 1984).

2. Maurice Possley, "U.S. Judge Refuses to Delay His Ban on Political Hiring," *Chicago Sun-Times,* April 4, 1983.

3. Steve Neal, "Mayor Washington's Own Style Coming Through Now,"

Chicago Tribune, October 2, 1983. See also "The First 100 Days," *Chicago Tribune,* August 7, 1983.

4. Thom Shanker, "City Council Passes $1.88 Billion Budget," *Chicago Tribune,* December 28, 1983.

Bibliography

I. Political Parties and Political Participation

American Assembly, The. *The Future of Political Parties*. Final report of the 62d American Assembly. Columbia University, New York, April 15–18, 1982.

Brody, Richard A. "The Puzzle of Political Participation in America." In *The New American Political System*, edited by Anthony King. Washington, D.C.: American Enterprise Institute for Public Policy Research, 1978.

Crenson, Matthew A. *The Un-Politics of Air Pollution*. Baltimore: Johns Hopkins University Press, 1971.

Dye, Thomas. *Politics, Economics, and the Public*. Chicago: Rand McNally, 1966.

Eldersveld, Samuel. *Political Parties in American Society*. New York: Basic Books, 1982.

Elling, Richard. "State Party Platforms and State Legislative Performance: A Comparative Analysis." *American Journal of Political Science* 23 (May 1979): 414–29.

Epstein, Leon. *Political Parties in Western Democracies*. New Brunswick, N.J.: Transaction Books, 1980.

———. "The Scholarly Commitment to Parties." In *Political Science: The State of the Discipline*, edited by Ada Finifter. Washington, D.C.: American Political Science Association, 1983.

Erikson, Robert. "The Relationship between Party Control and Civil Rights Legislation in the American States." *Western Political Quarterly* 24 (March 1971): 178–82.

Fenton, John. *Midwest Politics*. New York: Holt, 1966.

Fried, Robert C. "Party and Policy in West German Cities." *American Political Science Review* 70 (March 1976): 11–24.

Jennings, Edward. "Competition, Constituencies, and Welfare Policies in the American States." *American Political Science Review* 73 (June 1979): 414–29.

Johnston, Michael. "Patrons, Clients, Jobs, and Machines: A Case Study of the Uses of Patronage." *American Political Science Review* 73 (June 1979): 385–98.

Key, V. O., Jr. *Southern Politics.* New York: Vintage, 1949.

Kinkaid, John. "Mentoring, Loyalty, and the Persistence of Machine Politics in Jersey City." Paper presented at the Annual Meeting of the Southwest Social Science Association, Dallas, Texas, March 21–23, 1981.

Lawson, Kay, ed. *Political Parties and Linkage.* New Haven, Conn.: Yale University Press, 1980.

Lowi, Theodore. "Machine Politics, Old and New." *Public Interest* 9 (Fall 1967): 83–92.

Luttbeg, Norman, ed. *Public Opinion and Public Policy.* 3d ed. Itasca, Ill.: Peacock, 1981.

Newton, Kenneth, ed. *Urban Political Economy.* New York: St. Martins, 1981.

Nice, David. "Party, Ideology, and Policy Outcomes in the American States." *Social Science Quarterly* 63 (September 1982): 556–65.

Norpoth, Helmut, and Jerrold G. Rusk. "Partisan Dealignment in the American Electorate: Itemizing the Deductions since 1964." *American Political Science Review* 76 (September 1982): 522–37.

Patterson, Samuel C. "The Semi-Sovereign Congress." In *The New American Political System,* edited by Anthony King. Washington, D.C.: American Enterprise Institute, 1978.

Peters, Charles. "A Neoliberal's Manifesto." *Washington Monthly,* May 1983.

Ranney, Austin. "The Political Parties." In *The New American Political System,* edited by Anthony King. Washington, D.C.: American Enterprise Institute.

Rossi, Peter, and Phillips Cutright. "The Impact of Party Organization in an Industrial Setting." In *Community Political Systems,* edited by Morris Janowitz. Glencoe, Ill.: Free Press, 1961.

Schlesinger, Joseph A. "On the Theory of Party Organization." *Journal of Politics* (May 1984): 369–400.

Sorauf, Frank J. "State Patronage in a Rural County." *American Political Science Review* 50 (December 1956): 1046–56.

Thurow, Lester. *The Zero-Sum Society.* New York: Basic Books, 1980.

"Toward a More Responsible Two-Party System." Supplement to *American Political Science Review* 44 (September 1950).

Turner, Julius. "Responsible Parties: A Dissent from the Floor." *American Political Science Review* 45 (March 1951): 143–52.

Wald, Kenneth. "The Electoral Base of a Political Machine: A Deviant Case Analysis." *Urban Affairs Quarterly* 16 (September 1980): 3–31.

Wolfinger, Raymond. "Why Machines Have Not Withered Away and Other Revisionist Thoughts." *Journal of Politics* 34 (May 1972): 365–98.

II. Public Policy and Public Administration

Ackerman, Bruce A., ed. *Economic Foundations of Property Law.* Boston: Little, Brown, 1975.

Appleby, Paul. *Policy and Administration.* University: University of Alabama Press, 1949.

Barnard, Chester I. *The Functions of the Executive.* Cambridge, Mass.: Harvard University Press, 1938.

Clarke, Susan. "The Private Use of the Public Interest." Paper presented at the Annual Meeting of the Southwestern Social Science Association, San Antonio, Texas, March 17–20, 1982.

Cobb, Roger, and Charles D. Elder. *Participation in American Politics: The Dynamics of Agenda Building.* Boston: Allyn and Bacon, 1972.

Crecine, John P. *Government Problem-Solving: A Computer Simulation of Municipal Budgeting.* Chicago: Rand McNally, 1969.

Cyert, Richard M., and James G. March. *A Behavioral Theory of the Firm.* Englewood Cliffs, N.J.: Prentice-Hall, 1963.

Dahl, Robert A., and Charles E. Lindblom. *Politics, Economics, and Welfare.* New York: Harper and Row, 1953.

Downs, Anthony. *Inside Bureaucracy.* Boston: Little, Brown, 1967.

———. "Up and Down with Ecology: The Issue-Attention Cycle," *Public Interest* 28 (June 1972): 37–50.

Dye, Thomas. *Policy Analysis.* University: University of Alabama Press, 1976.

Elmore, Richard, ed. *Studying Implementation.* Chatham, N.J.: Chatham House, 1982.

Etzioni, Amitai. "Organizational Control Structure." In *Handbook of Organizations,* edited by James C. March. Chicago: Rand McNally, 1965.

Gardiner, John A., and Theodore R. Lyman. *Decisions for Sale.* New York: Praeger, 1978.

Godwin, R. Kenneth, and W. Bruce Shepard. "Political Process and Public Expenditures: A Re-Examination Based on Theories of Representative Government." *American Political Science Review* 70 (December 1976): 1127–35.

Goodnow, Frank. *Politics and Administration.* New York: Macmillan, 1900.

Hawley, Claude E., and Ruth G. Weintraub, eds. *Administrative Questions and Political Answers.* Princeton, N.J.: D. Van Nostrand, 1966.

Herring, E. Pendleton. *Public Administration and the Public Interest.* New York: McGraw-Hill, 1936.

Kaufman, Herbert. "Emerging Conflicts in the Doctrines of Public Administration." *American Political Science Review* 50 (December 1956): 1057–73.

Kraemer, Kenneth L.; William H. Dutton; and Alana Northrop. *The Management of Information Systems.* New York: Columbia University Press, 1981.

Lipsky, Michael. *Street-Level Bureaucracy: Dilemmas of the Individual in Public Services.* New York: Russell Sage, 1980.

Long, Norton. "Public Policy and Administration: The Goals of Rationality and Responsibility." In *Administrative Questions and Political Answers,* edited by Claude E. Hawley and Ruth Weintraub. Princeton, N.J.: D. Van Nostrand, 1966.

Lowi, Theodore. *The End of Liberalism.* 2d ed. New York: W. W. Norton, 1979.

McGlennon, John J. "The Effects of Corruption Scandals on Police Department Control and Support." Paper presented at the Annual Meeting of the American Political Science Association, Washington, D.C., September 1–4, 1977.

MacMahon, Arthur W. "Policy and Administration." In *Administrative Questions and Political Answers,* edited by Claude E. Hawley and Ruth G. Weintraub. Princeton, N.J.: D. Van Nostrand, 1966.

March, James G., and Johan P. Olsen. *Ambiguity and Choice in Organizations.* Bergen, Norway: Universitsforlaget, 1976.

————. "Organizing Political Life: What Administrative Reorganization Tells Us about Government." *American Political Science Review* 77 (June 1983): 281–96.

March, James G., and Herbert A. Simon. *Organizations.* New York: John Wiley, 1958.

Pennock, J. Roland. *Administration and the Rule of Law.* New York: Farrar and Rinehart, 1941.

Perrow, Charles. *Complex Organizations.* 2d ed. Glenview, Ill.: Scott, Foresman, 1979.

Peters, John G., and Susan Welch. "Political Corruption in America: A Search for Definitions and a Theory." *American Political Science Review* 72 (September 1978): 974–84.

————. "The Effects of Charges of Corruption on Voting Behavior in Congressional Elections." *American Political Science Review* 74 (September 1980): 697–708.

Pierce, Lawrence C. "Organizational Constraints and Public Bureaucracies." In *Political Science Annual,* vol. 5, edited by Cornelius P. Cotter. Indianapolis: Bobbs-Merrill, 1974.

Pressman, Jeffrey. *Federal Programs and City Politics.* Berkeley and Los Angeles: University of California Press, 1975.

————, and Aaron Wildavsky. *Implementation.* Berkeley and Los Angeles: University of California Press, 1973.

Redford, Emmette S. *Ideal and Practice in Public Administration.* University: University of Alabama Press, 1958.

Rose-Ackerman, Susan. *Corruption: A Study in Political Economy*. New York: Academic Press, 1978.

Sayre, Wallace S. "Premises of Public Administration: Past and Emerging." In *Administrative Questions and Political Answers*, edited by Claude E. Hawley and Ruth Weintraub. Princeton, N.J.: D. Van Nostrand, 1966.

Schelling, Thomas C. *Micromotives and Macrobehavior*. New 'York: W. W. Norton, 1978.

Stone, Clarence, and Kathy Reynolds. "Complexity and Democratic Theory: Administrative Accountability and Post-Industrial Society." Paper presented at the Annual Meeting of the Midwest Political Science Association, Cincinnati, Ohio, April 16–18, 1981.

Weatherly, Richard, and Michael Lipsky. "Street-Level Bureaucrats and Institutional Innovation: Implementing Special Education Reform." *Harvard Educational Review* 47 (1977): 120–38.

Wildavsky, Aaron. *Speaking Truth to Power*. Boston: Little, Brown, 1979.

Wilson, Woodrow. "The Study of Administration." *Political Science Quarterly* 2 (June 1887): 197–220.

III. Urban Politics and Public Policy

Aberbach, Joel, and Jack Walker. "The Attitudes of Blacks and Whites toward City Services: Implications for Public Policy." In *Financing the Metropolis*, edited by John P. Crecine. Beverly Hills, Calif.: Sage, 1970.

Ackerman, Bruce A. "Regulating Slum Housing Markets on Behalf of the Poor." In *Economic Foundations of Property Law*, edited by Bruce A. Ackerman. Boston: Little, Brown, 1975.

Banfield, Edward C. *Political Influence*. New York: Free Press, 1961.

Bolotin, Frederic N., and David L. Cingranelli. "Equity and Urban Policy: The Underclass Hypothesis Revisited." *Journal of Politics* 45 (February 1983): 209–19.

Branti v. Finkel 445 *U.S.* 507 (1980).

Cingranelli, David. "Race, Politics, and Elites: Testing Alternative Models of Municipal Service Distribution." *American Journal of Political Science* 25 (November 1981): 664–92.

Dahl, Robert A. *Who Governs?* New Haven, Conn.: Yale University Press, 1961.

Dear, Michael. "A Theory of the Local State." In *Political Studies from Spatial Perspectives*, edited by Alan Burnett and Peter Taylor. Winchester, U.K.: John Wiley, 1981.

Dewsnip, Ernst Ritson. *The Housing Problem in England*. Manchester, U.K.: University of Manchester Press, 1907.

Domhoff, William. *Who Really Rules? New Haven and Community Power Reexamined*. New Brunswick, N.J.: Transaction Books, 1978.

Dornan, Paul. "Whither Urban Policy Analysis? A Review Essay." *Polity* 9 (1977): 403–27.

Eisenger, Peter. *Patterns of Interracial Conflict.* New York: Academic Press, 1976.

Eisenstein, James, and Herbert Jacob. *Felony Justice.* Boston: Little, Brown, 1977.

Greenstone, J. David, and Paul E. Peterson. *Race and Authority in Urban Politics.* Chicago: University of Chicago Press, 1976.

Haider, Donald. "Sayre and Kaufman Revisited: New York City Government since 1965." *Urban Affairs Quarterly* 15 (December 1979).

———. *When Governments Come to Washington.* New York: Free Press, 1974.

Hartman, Chester W.; Robert P. Kessler; and Richard T. Legates. "Municipal Housing Code Enforcement and Low Income Tenants." *American Institute of Planners Journal* 40 (March 1974): 90–104.

Hawkins, Brett. *Politics and Urban Policies.* Indianapolis: Bobbs-Merrill, 1971.

Hunter, Floyd. *Community Power Structure.* Chapel Hill: University of North Carolina Press, 1953.

———. *Community Power Succession: Atlanta's Policy-Makers Revisited.* Chapel Hill: University of North Carolina Press, 1980.

Jacob, Herbert. *Debtors in Court.* Chicago: Rand McNally, 1969.

———, ed. *The Potential for Reform in Criminal Justice.* Beverly Hills, Calif.: Sage, 1974.

Jones, Bryan D. "Assessing the Products of Government: What Gets Delivered?" *Policy Studies Journal* 9 (Summer 1981): 963–71.

———. *Governing Urban America.* Boston: Little, Brown, 1983.

———, et al. "Bureaucratic Response to Citizen-Initiated Contacts: Environmental Enforcement in Detroit." *American Political Science Review* 71 (September 1977): 148–65.

———, et al. "Service Delivery Rules and the Distribution of Local Government Services: Three Detroit Bureaucracies." *Journal of Politics* 40 (February 1978): 332–68.

———, with Saadia Greenberg and Joseph Drew. *Service Delivery in the City: Citizen Demand and Bureaucratic Response.* New York: Longmans, 1980.

Karnig, Albert. "Private-Regarding Policy, Civil Rights Groups, and the Mediating Impact of Municipal Reforms." *American Journal of Political Science* 19 (February 1975): 91–106.

Komesar, Yale. "Return to Slumville: A Critique of the Ackerman Analysis of Housing Code Enforcement and the Poor." *Yale Law Journal* 83 (1983): 1175–93.

Levin, Martin A. *Urban Politics and the Criminal Courts.* Chicago: University of Chicago Press, 1977.

Levy, Frank; Arnold J. Meltsner; and Aaron Wildavsky. *Urban Outcomes.* Berkeley and Los Angeles: University of California Press, 1974.

Lineberry, Robert. *Equality and Public Policy: The Distribution of Municipal Public Services.* Beverly Hills, Calif.: Sage, 1977.

―――, and Edmund P. Fowler. "Reformism and Public Policies in American Cities." *American Political Science Review* 61 (September 1967): 701–16.

Lipsky, Michael. *Protest in City Politics.* Chicago: Rand McNally, 1970.

Lubove, Roy. *The Progressives and the Slums: Tenement House Reform in New York City, 1880–1917.* Pittsburgh: University of Pittsburgh Press, 1962.

Lyons, William. "Reform and Response in American Cities: Structure and Policy Reconsidered." *Social Science Quarterly* 59 (June 1978): 118–32.

Mandelker, Daniel; Julie Gibb; and Annette B. Kolis. "Differential Code Enforcement: The Constitutional Dimension." *Journal of Urban Law* 55 (1978): 516–629.

Markovits, Richard S. "The Distributive Impact, Allocative Efficiency, and Overall Desirability of Ideal Housing Codes: Some Theoretical Clarifications." *Harvard Law Review* 89 (1976): 1815–46.

Mladenka, Kenneth. "Rules, Service Equity, and Distributional Decisions." *Social Science Quarterly* 59 (December 1978): 192–202.

Mosier, Marilyn Miller, and Richard A. Soble. "Modern Legislation, Metropolitan Court, Minuscule Results: A Study of Detroit's Landlord-Tenant Court." *Journal of Law Reform* 7 (Fall 1973): 9–70.

National Commission on Civil Disorders. *Supplementary Studies.* Washington, D.C.: U.S. Government Printing Office, 1968.

Nivola, Pietro. *The Urban Service Problem.* Lexington, Mass.: Lexington Books, 1979.

Pahl, R. E. *Whose City?* Harmondsworth, U.K.: Penguin, 1975.

Parenti, Michael. *Power and the Powerless.* New York: St. Martin's Press, 1978.

Parks, Roger, et al. "Co-production of Public Services." In *Analyzing Urban Service Distributions,* edited by Richard C. Rich. Lexington, Mass.: Lexington Books, 1982.

Peterson, Paul E. *City Limits.* Chicago: University of Chicago Press, 1981.

Polsby, Nelson. *Community Power and Political Theory,* 2d ed. New Haven, Conn.: Yale University Press, 1980.

Ratzick, Mark C., and Richard L. Huffman. "The New York City Housing Court: Trial and Error in Housing Code Enforcement." *New York University Law Review* 50 (October 1975): 738–97.

Rich, Richard C. "Interaction of the Voluntary and Governmental Sectors: Toward an Understanding of the Co-production of Municipal Services." *Administration and Society* 3 (May 1981): 59–76.

―――. "Neglected Issues in the Study of Urban Service Distributions." *Urban Studies* 16 (1979): 143–56.

————. "A Political Economy Approach to the Study of Neighborhood Organizations." *American Journal of Political Science* 24 (November 1980): 559–92.

————. "The Roles of Neighborhood Organizations in Urban Service Delivery." *NASPAA Urban Affairs Papers,* Fall 1979, pp. 2–20.

Riis, Jacob. *How the Other Half Lives.* New York: Hill and Wang, 1957.

Rose, Jonathan, and Martin Scott. "'Street Talk' Summonses in Detroit's Landlord-Tenant Court: A Small Step Forward for Urban Tenants." *Journal of Urban Law* 52 (1975): 967–1031.

Saunders, Peter. "The Relevance of Weberian Sociology for Political Analysis." *Geographical Papers,* no. 80. Department of Geography, University of Reading, U.K., January 1982.

————. *Urban Politics.* London: Hutchinson, 1979.

Sayre, Wallace S., and Herbert Kaufman. *Governing New York City.* New York: W. W. Norton, 1965.

Sternlieb, George. *Tenement Landlord.* New Brunswick, N.J.: Urban Studies Center, Rutgers University, 1966.

————, and Robert Burchell. *Residential Abandonment: The Tenement Landlord Revisited.* New Brunswick, N.J.: Center for Urban Policy Research, Rutgers University, 1973.

————, and James W. Hughes. "Back to the Central City: Myths and Realities." In *America's Housing: Prospects and Problems,* edited by George Sternlieb and James W. Hughes. New Brunswick, N.J.: Center for Urban Policy Research, Rutgers University, 1980.

Stewart, C. W. *The Housing Question in London, 1855–1900.* London: Jas. Truscott and Sons, 1900.

Stoner, John. *Building Regulation in Indiana: A Study of Public Rule-Making by Private Specialists.* Bloomington: Bureau of Government Research, Indiana University, 1951.

U.S. Congress. Senate. Committee on Housing and Urban Affairs. *Impact of Building Codes on Housing Rehabilitation.* 95th Cong., 2d sess., March 24, 1978.

Veiller, Lawrence. *A Model Housing Law,* rev. ed. New York: Russell Sage, 1920.

————. *Tenement House Legislation in New York, 1852–1900.* Albany, N.Y.: Brandow Printing Co., 1900.

Whittaker, Gordon P. "Co-Production: Citizen Participation in Service Delivery." *Public Administration Review* 40 (1980): 240–46.

Wirt, Frederick M. *Power in the City.* Berkeley and Los Angeles: University of California Press, 1974.

Wolfinger, Raymond. *The Politics of Progress.* Englewood Cliffs, N.J.: Prentice-Hall, 1974.

Yates, Douglas. *The Ungovernable City.* Cambridge, Mass.: MIT Press, 1977.

IV. Chicago Politics and Government

Abbott, Edith. *The Tenements of Chicago, 1908–1935*. Chicago: University of Chicago Press, 1936.

Axelrod, David. "Byrne Puts Bet on 'Fast Eddie,'" *Chicago Tribune*, March 28, 1982.

———. "Washington Must Avoid Falling into Byrne Trap." *Chicago Tribune*, February 27, 1983.

Banfield, Edward. *Political Influence*. New York: Free Press, 1961.

Bogira, Steve. "Abandoned." *Chicago Reader* 9 (January 25, 1980).

"Building Code Cases Down 90 Percent." *Chicago Tribune*, December 21, 1980.

Chicago Area Geographic Study. "Population Estimates for the Chicago SMSA by Census Tract Area within the City of Chicago, 1975." Chicago: Department of Geography, University of Illinois at Chicago Circle, n.d.

Chicago Community Organization Directory, 1977–78. Chicago: Community Renewal Society, 1978.

Chicago Home Rule Commission. *Report and Recommendations*. Chicago: University of Illinois at Chicago Circle, 1972.

Chicago Statistical Abstract. Part 4, *1979 Census-Ward Summary Tables*. Chicago: City of Chicago Department of Planning, 1973.

Ciccone, F. Richard. "Bilandic Designs 'Southern Plan,'" *Chicago Tribune*, February 25, 1979.

City of Chicago Building Code. Chicago: Index Publishing Corp., 1979.

"Election Summary Statistics." Chicago: Board of Election Commissioners of Chicago, 1978. Mimeo.

Elrod v. Burns 427 *U.S.* 347 (1976).

"First 100 Days, The." *Chicago Tribune*, August 7, 1983.

Gosnell, Harold. *Machine Politics, Chicago Model*. Chicago: University of Chicago Press, 1968.

Gove, Samuel K., and Louis H. Masotti, eds., *After Daley: Chicago Politics in Transition*. Urbana: University of Illinois Press, 1982.

Guterbock, Thomas. *Machine Politics in Transition: Party and Community in Chicago*. Chicago: University of Chicago Press, 1980.

Holli, Melvin, and Paul Green. *The Making of the Mayor, 1983*. Grand Rapids, Mich.: Eerdmans, 1984.

Housing the Chicago Region. Chicago: Metropolitan Housing and Planning Council, 1981.

Jones, Bryan D. "Party and Bureaucracy: The Influence of Intermediary Groups on Urban Public Service Delivery." *American Political Science Review* 75 (September 1981): 688–700.

———. "Tenement Capitalism and Building Regulation: The Magnolia Hotel." Wayne State University, 1982. Mimeo.

Kasperson, Roger. "Toward a Geography of Urban Politics." *Economic Geography* 41 (1965): 95–107.

Kemp, Kathleen, and Robert L. Lineberry. "The Last of the Great Urban Machines and the Last of the Great Urban Mayors? Chicago Politics, 1955–1977." In *After Daley: Chicago Politics in Transition,* edited by Samuel Gove and Louis Masotti. Urbana: University of Illinois Press, 1982.

League of Women Voters of Cook County. *The Key to Our Local Government.* 4th ed. Chicago: Citizens' Information Service, 1978.

Lehman, Warren W. "Building Codes, Housing Codes, and the Conservation of Chicago's Housing Supply." *University of Chicago Law Review* 31 (Autumn 1963): 180–203.

Lineberry, Robert. "The Decline and Fall of the Daley Empire." *Arts and Sciences: The Magazine of the College of Arts and Sciences,* Northwestern University, Fall 1979.

———, and Sharon Watson. "Neighborhoods, Politics, and Public Services: The Case of Chicago." *Urban Interest* 2 (Spring 1980).

McGrath, Paul. "The Machine's Mystique." *Chicago,* January 1981, pp. 22–24.

Mansfield, Seymour J., ed. *Judgment Landlord: A Study of Eviction Court in Chicago.* Chicago: Legal Assistance Foundation of Chicago, National Lawyers' Guild, and Chicago Council of Lawyers, 1978.

Metropolitan Housing and Planning Council Reports 9 (June 1982).

Mladenka, Kenneth. "The Political Machine, the Urban Bureaucracy, and the Distribution of Public Services." *Chicago Politics Papers.* Evanston, Ill.: Center for Urban Affairs, Northwestern University, 1979.

———. "The Urban Bureaucracy and the Chicago Political Machine: Who Gets What and the Limits to Political Control," *American Political Science Review* 74 (December 1980): 991–98.

Moses, Robert. "The Enforcement Process—Housing Codes." *Urban Lawyer* 3 (1971): 560–63.

Neal, Steve. "Mayor Washington's Own Style Coming Through Now." *Chicago Tribune,* October 2, 1983.

O'Connor, Len. *Clout: Mayor Daley and His City.* New York: Avon, 1975.

Peterson, Paul E. *School Politics, Chicago Style.* Chicago: University of Chicago Press, 1976.

Possley, Maurice S. "Judge Refuses to Delay His Ban on Political Hiring." *Chicago Sun-Times,* April 4, 1983.

Rakove, Milton. *Don't Make No Waves, Don't Back No Losers.* Bloomington: Indiana University Press, 1975.

———. *We Don't Want Nobody Nobody Sent.* Bloomington: University of Indiana Press, 1979.

———. "Who Controls Chicago?" *Chicago,* July 1979, p. 136.

Shakman v. Democratic Organization of Cook County 435 F. 2d. 267 (1970).

Shakman v. *Democratic Organization of Cook County* 481 *F. Supp.* 1315 (1979).

Shanker, Thom. "City Council Passes $1.88 Billion Budget." *Chicago Tribune,* December 28, 1983.

Skogan, Wesley G. "The Politics of Judicial Reform: Cook County, Illinois." *Judicial System Journal* 1 (September 1975): 11–23.

Smith, Zay, and Pamela Zeckman. *The Mirage.* New York: Random House, 1979.

Study of Housing Court. Chicago: Metropolitan Housing and Planning Council, 1970.

Zikmund, Joseph. "Mayoral Voting and Ethnic Politics in the Daley-Bilandic-Byrne Era." In *After Daley: Chicago Politics in Transition,* edited by Samuel Gove and Louis Masotti. Urbana: University of Illinois Press, 1982.

Index

Abbott, Edith, 48
Air pollution: as policy issue, 10, 181
Alinsky, Saul, 122, 175
American Assembly, 1–2, 5
American Institute of Architects, 48
Appleby, Paul, 62–63
Attention rules: hypothesis, 90, 100, 209 (n. 3); intermediary groups and, 86–90; overrides, 133, 141–43; political parties and, 144, 183, 188, 194; as political favoritism, 188; in service delivery, 125–27, 139–40, 145, 183, 194; ward organizations and, 105, 144–46, 183

Back of the Yards Neighborhood Council, 117, 174–76, 184
Banfield, Edward C., 10–11, 22
Barnard, Chester, 64
Bedore, Edward, 113, 136
Better Government Association, 52, 55
Bieszcat, Matthew, 140, 146
Bilandic, Michael, 6, 15–16; corruption and, 52–53; Daley organization and, 17–18; license inspection, 53; Mayor's Committee, 29, 38–39; patronage, 112, 135, 188; policy making, 38; southern strategy, 113
Boston: code enforcement, 59, 90, 166; service distribution in, 9
Bua, Nicholas J., 193, 206 (n. 4)
Building and Zoning Committee, 28–29
Building code: amendments to, 28–29; defined, 22; enforcement, 47–51; fire safety, 32–33; history, 22–24; Mayor's Advisory Committee, 27–31; the Mirage, 51–53, 57, 61, 76; nationalization, 25–26; policy mak-

ing, 25–26, 34; rehabilitation code, 30–31, 35–39, 181; as service distribution, 3
Building code enforcement: attention and decision rules, 88–90, 128–30, 183; in black wards, 146–48, 174, 177, 183; in Boston, 59, 90, 166; citizen demands, 87–88; Code Enforcement Program (Eleventh Ward), 115, 143–46; community groups and, 4, 30–31, 35, 65, 85, 94–98, 101, 120–24, 184, 208 (n. 21); control problems, 47–61; corruption in, 4, 44, 47–55, 69–70, 77, 181–82; differential code enforcement, 49–51, 128; history, 22–24; inspections, 49–61, 69–77; intermediary groups and, 86–87, 96–98, 120; lax enforcement, 51; licensing, 53–61, 130–32; mayor's office, 29–30; nursing homes, 129–30; ward organizations, 2–3, 91, 98–99, 123–24, 140–48, 181–83; regulatory policy, 25–31, 35, 37; regulatory agencies, 25–27, 85–86; as service, 3; discretion in, 37, 88–89, 129. *See also* Department of Buildings, Mayor's Advisory Committee
Building Officials and Code Administrators, International (BOCA), 25
Bureau of Dangerous and Dilapidated Buildings, 70
Bureau of Electrical Inspection, 43; FBI investigations and, 51–52
Bureau of Institutional Inspections, 69, 130, 137
Bureau of Plumbing Inspection, 43
Burke, Edward, 18, 130–31, 194
Business licenses, 131–32
Byrne, Jane: building department reforms, 56,

225

ABOUT THE AUTHOR

Bryan D. Jones is Professor and Chair, Department of Political Science, Wayne State University. He received his bachelor of arts degree from The University of Alabama and his doctorate from The University of Texas. He is also the author of *Governing Urban America* (1983) and *Service Delivery in the City* (1980).